DATE DUE			

ESSAYS IN
EARLY
VIRGINIA LITERATURE

Richard Beale Davis

ESSAYS IN
EARLY
VIRGINIA LITERATURE
HONORING
Richard Beale Davis

EDITED BY

J. A. Leo Lemay

Burt Franklin & Company, Inc.

© 1977 Burt Franklin & Co., Inc.
235 East 44th St.
New York, New York
10017

Library of Congress Cataloging in Publication Data
Main entry under title:

Essays in early Virginia literature honoring
Richard Beale Davis.

"Bibliography of Richard Beale Davis": p.
Includes index.
1. American literature—Virginia—History and
criticism—Addresses, essays, lectures. 2. American
literature—Colonial period, ca. 1600-1775—History
and criticism—Addresses, essays, lectures. 3. Davis,
Richard Beale. I. Davis, Richard Beale. II. Lemay,
Joseph A. Leo, 1935-
PS266.V5E8   810'.99755   76-56260
ISBN 0-89102-067-5

CONTENTS

RICHARD BEALE DAVIS

Richard Beale Davis was born on the Eastern Shore of Virginia on June 3, 1907, graduated from Randolph Macon College in 1927, and took his advanced degrees at the University of Virginia during the Depression, the A. M. in 1933 and the Ph.D. in 1936. He and Lois Camp Bullard were married on August 25, 1936. His early teaching positions were at the McGuire University School, 1927-1930; Randolph Macon Academy, 1930-1932; and the University of Virginia, 1933-1936. From 1936-1940 he taught at Mary Washington College and from 1940-1947 (with time out for service as an officer in the U. S. Navy) at the University of South Carolina. Since 1947, he has been a professor at the University of Tennessee, where, in 1962, he became Alumni Distinguished Service Professor. He has been a Fulbright professor at the University of Oslo in 1953-54 and a lecturer for the U. S. Department of State in India in 1957.

Mr. Davis has served on the Executive Committee of the American Studies Association in 1958-1961, and 1968-1971; on the Executive Committee of the Center for Editions of American Authors, 1963-1969; and on the Fulbright Board's Advisory Committee in American Studies, 1958-1961. From 1966 to 1969, he served on the Editorial Board of *American Literature;* from 1956 to 1972, he was one of the two general editors of the annual

Tennessee Studies in Literature; and he is a member of the editorial board of *The Complete Works of Washington Irving.*

Mr. Davis is a member of Phi Beta Kappa, Blue Key, Phi Kappa Phi, Raven Society, and Sigma Upsilon. He was awarded Huntington Library Fellowships in 1947 and 1950, a Folger Library Fellowship in 1955, a National Endowment for the Humanities Senior Fellowship in 1974; and he has twice been a Guggenheim Fellow. He has also received grants from the Colonial Williamsburg Foundation, the American Philosophical Society, and the American Council of Learned Societies. He has held a variety of offices in the Modern Language Association of America: Chairman of the Literature and Science Group in 1956, Chairman of the Early American Literature Group in 1974, Chairman of the American Literature Section in 1975, and President of the South Atlantic Modern Language Association in 1964-1965. Mr. Davis served as Chairman of the Southern Humanities Conference in 1961 and and as President of the Society for the Study of Southern Literature in 1968-1970. He has been elected an honorary member of the Virginia Historical Society, and elected to the American Antiquarian Society. He is currently, 1975-1978, a member of the Council of the Institute for Early American History and Culture. In 1955, he was awarded a Doctor of Letters degree by Randolph Macon College.

All discriminating scholars of American literature have reasons to know and admire Richard Beale Davis. His first book, *Francis Walker Gilmer: Life and Learning in Jefferson's Virginia* (1939), indicated the major field of scholarship—Southern Literature—and the major approach—a wide-ranging cultural study—that he was to follow in the future. The research for his first book demonstrated to him the necessity for making available the basic documents for the study of Southern literature and culture, and so his second monograph was an edition of the *Correspondence of Thomas Jefferson and Francis Walker Gilmer* (1946). His investigations in the manuscripts of California's Huntington Library led to his careful, annotated editions of Thomas Holley Chivers, *Life of Poe* (1952) and to *Jeffersonian America: The Notes on the United States of America Collected in the Years 1805-6-7 and 1811-12 by Sir Augustus John Foster* (1954).

Mr. Davis's careful studies of literary and cultural history made him increasingly aware of the importance and vast amount of colonial American literature. He therefore began to investigate the writings of the first settlers in the South, and in 1955 published the standard biographical and critical work on *George Sandys, Poet-Adventurer: A Study in Anglo-American Culture in the Seventeenth Century*. In the same year, his researches into another figure of Jeffersonian America came to fruition with *The Abbé Correa in America, 1812-1820: The Contributions of the Diplomat and Natural Philosopher to the Foundations of Our National Life*. Continuing his efforts to make available and to indicate the importance of the basic materials for the literary and cultural study of the early South, Mr. Davis brought out an elaborate edition of the letter-book of William Fitzhugh: *William Fitzhugh and His Chesapeake World, 1676-1701* (1963). The following year marked the capstone of his studies of Early National America: his definitive *Intellectual Life in Jefferson's Virginia, 1790-1830* (1964) appeared, winning the manuscript award of the American Association for State and Local History.

With the publication of this magnum opus, Mr. Davis shifted his major research back to the earlier period of Southern literature, for this rich literature was, he believed, almost invariably ignored or slighted in previous literary and cultural studies. When the American literature section of the Modern Language Association of America decided to sponsor an annual review of the scholarship in American literature, naturally Mr. Davis was asked to write the chapter dealing with the early period, and he performed this task for the annual volume *American Literary Scholarship* for 1963 through 1969. In 1967 he brought out another of his painstaking and elaborate editions of the basic sources for the study of early Southern literature: *The Colonial Virginia Satirist: Mid-Eighteenth Century Commentators on Politics, Religion, and Society*. And in 1969, Mr. Davis gathered together the *Collected Poems of Samuel Davies, 1723-1761*.

The years 1969 and 1970 saw the publication of a series of editions and monographs intended for students. The bibliography *American Literature Through Bryant, 1585-1830* (1969) is the best convenient guide to early American literature and its scholarship. He edited William Wirt's *Letters of the British Spy* (1970) and James Fenimore Cooper's *The Wept of the Wish-Ton-Wish* (1970). And he also edited "Part One Southern Writing: 1585-1800" of an anthology *Southern Writing 1585-1920.* To every specialist in early American literature, this anthology is a revelation, for it contains so many unanthologized pieces by so many heretofore forgotten writers. Most anthologies are repetitive in their choice of writers—and even writings—but this anthology is a basic contribution to knowledge, as well as a direct confrontation and refutation of the previously held ideas of the "standard" canon of early American literature.

In 1973, Mr. Davis published a volume of essays, *Literature and Society in Early Virginia, 1608-1840,* which includes, among a host of good things, the talk originally delivered as the Annual Lecture before the Virginia Historical Society for 1970: "The Intellectual Golden Age in the Colonial Chesapeake Bay Country"— an essay which gives us a taste of the book he has been working on for some years, tentatively entitled "An Intellectual History of the Colonial South, 1607-1763," which we expect to revolutionize the study of early American literature and culture.

It is hard to measure the impact that any scholar has on the studies of his own time and of the future. But even the existence of such a scholar as Richard Beale Davis influences the writings—and the opinions—of other scholars. In reading a book manuscript for a university press, the present writer has seen in the margin of a page, beside a slighting reference to the culture of the early South, the comment of a previous referee, "Dick Davis won't like this!" He, more than any other single figure of our time, has created the field of early Southern Literature as a possible area of specialization. His many students who have written dissertations in early Southern literature are one proof of its value and appeal. We hope that this volume is another.

J. A. Leo Lemay
UCLA

RICHARD BEALE DAVIS
BIBLIOGRAPHY

Books

Francis Walker Gilmer: Life and Learning in Jefferson's Virginia. Richmond, Va.: Dietz Press, 1939.

[ed.] *Correspondence of Thomas Jefferson and Francis Walker Gilmer, 1812-1826.* Columbia: University of South Carolina Press, 1946.

[with Fredson Bowers] *George Sandys: A Bibliographical Catalogue of Printed Editions in England to 1700.* New York: New York Public Library, 1950.

[ed.] *Chivers' Life of Poe.* New York: E. P. Dutton, 1952.

[ed.] *Jeffersonian America: The Notes on the United States of America Collected in the Years 1805-6-7 and 11-12 by Sir Augustus John Foster.* San Marino, Calif.: Henry E. Huntington Library, 1954.

The Abbé Correa in America, 1812-1820: The Contributions of the Diplomat and Natural Philosopher to the Foundations of Our National Life. Philadelphia: American Philosophical Society, *Transactions,* 1955.

George Sandys, Poet-Adventurer: A Study in Anglo-American Culture in the Seventeenth Century. London: The Bodley Head; New York: Columbia University Press, 1955.

[ed. with Ben C. McClary] *American Cultural History, 1607-1829. A facsimile Reproduction of "Lectures on American Literature" 1829 by Samuel L. Knapp.* Gainesville, Fla.: Scholars' Facsimiles and Reprints, 1961.

[ed. with John Leon Lievsay] *Studies in Honor of John C. Hodges and Alwin Thaler.* Knoxville: University of Tennessee Press, 1961.

[ed.] *William Fitzhugh and His Chesapeake World, 1676-1701.* Chapel Hill: University of North Carolina Press, 1963.

Intellectual Life in Jefferson's Virginia, 1790-1830. Chapel Hill: University of North Carolina Press, 1964.

[ed.] *The Colonial Virginia Satirist: Mid-Eighteenth Century Commentaries on Politics, Religion, and Society.* Philadelphia: American Philosophical Society, *Transactions,* 1967.

[ed.] *Collected Poems of Samuel Davies, 1723-1761.* Gainesville, Fla.: Scholars' Facsimiles and Reprints, 1968.

American Literature through Bryant, 1585-1830. New York: Goldentree Bibliographies, Appleton-Century-Crofts, 1969.

[ed.] *Letters of the British Spy by William Wirt.* Chapel Hill: Southern Literary Classics Series, University of North Carolina Press, 1970.

[ed.] *The Wept of Wish-ton-Wish by James Fenimore Cooper.* Columbus, Ohio: Merrill Standard Editions, Charles E. Merrill, 1970.

[ed. with C. Hugh Holman and Louis Rubin, Jr.] *Southern Writing, 1585-1920.* New York: Odyssey Press, 1970.

Literature and Society in Early Virginia, 1608-1840. Baton Rouge: Louisiana State University Press, 1973.

[ed. with Alwin Thaler, I-VIII and Kenneth L. Knickerbocker, IX-XV] *Tennessee Studies in Literature,* Annual Volume. Knoxville: University of Tennessee Press, 1956-1972.

Articles

"Forgotten Scientists in Old Virginia," *Virginia Magazine of History & Biography,* XLVI (1938), 97-111.

"Letter of Advice to a Young Virginia Lawyer in the Days of Thomas Jefferson," *Law Student* (1938), 11-12; Kentucky State Bar Journal (1939).

"Literary Tastes in Virginia before Poe," *William and Mary Quarterly,* 2d ser., XIX (1939), 55-68.

"The First American Edition of Captain John Smith's *True Travels and Generall Historie,*" *Virginia Magazine of History & Biography,* XLVII (1939), 97-108.

"George Sandys, Poet-Adventurer," *Americana,* XXXIII (1939), 180-95.

"Homer in Homespun—A Southern *Iliad,*" *Southern Literary Messenger,* 2d ser., I (1939), 647-51.

"James Ogilvie and Washington Irving," *Americana,* XXXV (1941), 435-58.

"The Early Editions of George Sandys's Ovid: The Circumstances of Production," *Papers of the Bibliographical Society of America,* XXXV (1941), 255-76.

"The Library of Alexander S. Salley," *South Atlantic Bulletin,* VIII (No. 1, 1942), 3-4.

"An Early Virginia Scientist's Botanical Observations in the South," *Virginia Journal of Science,* III (1942), 132-39.

"James Ogilvie, an Early American Teacher of Rhetoric," *Quarterly Journal of Speech*, XXVIII (1942), 289-97.

"Forgotten Scientists in Georgia and South Carolina," *Georgia Historical Quarterly*, XXVII (1943), 271-84.

"Two New Manuscript Items for a George Sandys Bibliography," *Papers of the Bibliographical Society of America*, XXXVIII (1943), 215-22.

"Poe and William Wirt," *American Literature*, XVI (1944), 212-20.

"A Variant of Lowell's 'I Go to the Ridge in the Forest'," *Modern Language Notes*, LXI (1946), 392-95.

"A Postscript On Thomas Jefferson and His University Professors," *Journal of Southern History*, XII (1946), 422-32.

"An Unpublished Poem by Paul Hamilton Hayne, *American Literature*, XVIII (1947), 327-29.

"America in George Sandys's 'Ovid'," *William and Mary Quarterly*, 3d ser., IV (1947), 297-304.

"Paul Hamilton Hayne to Francis Peyre Porcher," *Studies in Philology*, XLIV (1947), 529-48.

[with Milledge B. Seigler.] "Peter Freneau, Carolina Republican," *Journal of Southern History*, XIII (1947), 395-405.

"George Sandys and Two Uncollected Poems," *Huntington Library Quarterly*, XII (1948), 105-11.

"George Sandys *v.* William Stansby: The 1632 Edition of Ovid's *Metamorphosis*," *The Library* [London], 5th ser., III (1948), 193-212.

"The Early American Lawyer and the Profession of Letters," *Huntington Library Quarterly*, XII (1949), 191-205.

"Washington Irving and Joseph C. Cabell," *English Studies in Honor of James Southall Wilson*, University of Virginia *Studies*, IV (1951), 7-22.

"The Southern Dilemma: Two Unpublished Letters of Paul Hamilton Hayne," *Journal of Southern History*, XVII (1951), 64-70.

"An Uncollected Elegy by Paul Hamilton Hayne," *South Carolina Historical and Genealogical Magazine*, LII (1951), 53-54.

"The Abbé Correa and the Jefferson Circle: European Culture in America, 1812-1820," *American Philosophical Society Year Book, 1952* (1953), 229-30.

[with John L. Lievsay.] "A Cavalier Library—1643," *Studies in Bibliography*, VI (1953-4), 141-60.

"Some Observations on American Literature and Other Arts in Northern Europe since 1945," *Bulletin of Randolph-Macon College*, XXVII (1955), 26-29, 38-39.

"Hawthorne, Fanny Kemble, and 'The Artist of the Beautiful'," *Modern Language Notes*, LXX (1955), 589-92.

"*In Re* George Sandys' 'Ovid'," *Studies in Bibliography*, VIII (1956), 266-30.

"American Studies in Norway," *American-Scandinavian Review,* XLIV (1956), 348-53.

"Sandys' *Song of Solomon*: Its Manuscript Versions and Their Circulation," *Papers of the Bibliographical Society of America,* L (1956), 328-41.

"The Devil in Virginia in the Seventeenth Century," *Virginia Magazine of History and Biography,* LXV (1957), 131-49.

"The Gentlest Art in Seventeenth Century Virginia," *Tennessee Studies in Literature,* II (1957), 51-63.

"Volumes from George Sandys's Library Now in America," *Virginia Magazine of History and Biography,* LXV (1957), 450-57.

"Living American Writers of the Nineteenth Century," *Hindustan Times Weekly* [New Delhi, India], Sunday, Oct. 6, 1957, 6.

"The Works of William Faulkner," *American Reporter* [New Delhi, India; Madras; Calcutta; etc.], VII, no. 21 (October 9, 1957), 7.

"Early American Interest in Wharton's Manuscript," Appendix to Laura Stryker-H. Wharton, *The Life of Captain John Smith, English Soldier,* Chapel Hill: University of North Carolina Press, 1957, 93-96.

"Thomas Holley Chivers and the Kentucky Tragedy," *Texas Studies in Literature and Language,* I (1959), 281-88.

"The Americanness of American Literature: Folk and Historical Themes and Materials in Formal Writing," *Literary Criterion* [India], III (1959), 9-22.

"A Sermon, Preached at James City in Virginia the 23d of April 1686 before the Loyal Society of Citizens born in and about London and inhabiting in Virginia, by Deuel Pead," *William and Mary Quarterly,* 3d ser., XVII (1960), 371-94.

"The Library of Congress *Guide*" [an essay review], *American Quarterly,* XII (1960), 237-41.

"William Fitzhugh and His Chesapeake World, 1676-1701," *American Philosophical Society Year Book, 1959* (1960), 354-55.

"Jefferson as Collector of Virginiana," *Studies in Bibliography,* XIV (1961), 117-44.

"Edward Tyreel Channing's 'American Scholar' of 1818," *The [Phi Beta Kappa] Key Reporter,* XXVI, no. 3 (Spring, 1961), 1-4, 8.

"Report of the Chairman," *Southern Humanities Conference, Minutes of the Fourteenth Annual Meeting 1961,* 6-7.

"Chesapeake Pattern and Pole-Star: William Fitzhugh in His Plantation World, 1676-1701," *Proceedings of the American Philosophical Society,* CV (1961), 525-29.

"The Jeffersonian Virginia Expatriate in the Building of the Nation," *Virginia Magazine of History and Biography,* LXX (1962), 49-61.

"The 'Virginia Novel' Before Swallow Barn," *Virginia Magazine of History & Biography,* LXXI (1963), 278-93.

"American Literature in the World Today," *Tennessee Studies in Literature,* VIII (1963), 119-39.

"The Ball Papers: A Pattern of Life in the Low Country," *South Carolina Historical Magazine,* LXV (1964), 1-15.

"MLA Discussion Group Faced with Assimilation," *Humanities in the South,* no. 20 (Spring 1964), 8.

"An Intellectual History of the Colonial South, 1607-1763," *Year Book of the American Philosophical Society 1963,* Philadelphia, 1964, 522-23.

"In Memoriam—Durant da Ponte," *Humanities in the South,* no. 21 (Fall 1964), 3.

"American Literature in the World Today," in Marshall W. Fishwick, ed., *American Studies in Transition,* Philadelphia: University of Pennsylvania Press, 1964, 268-97.

"Moncure D. Conway Looks at Edgar Poe—Through Dr. Griswold," *Mississippi Quarterly,* XVIII (1965), 12-18.

"Literature before 1800," in James Woodress, ed. *American Literary Scholarship / 1963,* Durham, N.C.: Duke University Press, 1965, 95-106.

"John Holt Rice vs. Thomas Jefferson on the Great Deluge," *Virginia Magazine of History and Biography,* LXXIV (1966), 108-109.

"Sandys, George (1578-1644)," *Encyclopedia Britannica,* publ. Wm. Benton, P. 1004.

"A Virginia Colonial Frontier Parish's 'Poor' Petition for a Priest," *Historical Magazine of the Protestant Episcopal Church,*" XXXV (1966), 87-98.

"Spadework, American Literature, and the Southern Mind—Opportunities," *South Atlantic Bulletin,* XXXI (1966), 1-4.

"Literature before 1800," in James Woodress, ed. *American Literary Scholarship / 1964,* Durham, N.C.: Duke University Press, 1966, 91-108.

"The American Dream," *Faculty Studies* Carson-Newman College, Vol. I, no. 2 (1966), 5-11.

"Arthur Blackamore: The Virginia Colony and the Early English Novel," *Virginia Magazine of History and Biography,* LXXV (1967), 22-34.

"A Fitting Representation: Seventy-Five Years of the *Virginia Magazine of History and Biography,*" *Virginia Magazine of History and Biography,* LXXV (1967), 259-79.

"Literature to 1800," in James Woodress, ed., *American Literary Scholarship / 1965,* Durham, N.C.: Duke University Press, 1967, 107-28.

"Mrs. Stowe's Characters-in-Situations and a Southern Literary Tradition," in Clarence Gohdes, ed., *Essays on American Literature in Honor of Jay B. Hubbell,* Durham, N.C.: Duke University Press, 1967, 108-25.

"Literature to 1800," in James Woodress, ed. *American Literary Scholarship / 1966,* Durham, N.C.: Duke University Press, 1968, 97-113.

"Three Poems from Colonial North Carolina," *North Carolina Historical Review*, XLVI (1969), 33-41.

"Literature to 1800," in James Woodress, ed., *American Literary Scholarship / 1967*, Durham, N.C.: Duke University Press, 1968, 115-33.

"Charleston in the Golden Age," [review essay], *Southern Literary Journal*, II (1969), 148-51.

"The Intellectual Golden Age in the Colonial Chesapeake Bay Country," *Virginia Magazine of History & Biography*, LXXVIII (1970), 131-43.

"Poe Criticism: Some Advances Toward Maturity," *Mississippi Quarterly*, XXIII (1969/1970), 67-76.

"Literature to 1800," in J. Albert Robbins, ed., *American Literary Scholarship / 1968*, Durham, N.C.: Duke University Press, 1970, 121-41.

"Samuel Davies," "Francis Walker Gilmer," "Thomas Jefferson," "George Sandys," in Louis D. Rubin, ed., *A Bibliographical Guide to the Study of Southern Literature*, Baton Rouge: Louisiana State University Press, 1969.

"James Reid, Colonial Virginia Poet and Moral and Religious Essayist," *Virginia Magazine of History and Biography*, LXXIX (1971), 3-19.

"Literature to 1800," in J. Albert Robbins, ed., *American Literary Scholarship / 1969*, Durham, N.C.: Duke University Press, 1971.

"The Valley of Virginia in Early American Literature," James Madison Lecture, Founder's Day, March 12, 1971. *Madisonian* (Summer 1971), 10-13. And separate, Harrisonburg, Va., 1971.

"A Tribute," in Richard P. Veler, ed., *Papers in Honor of John Ward Ostrom*, Springfield, Ohio: Chantry Press of Wittenberg University, 1972, 3-6.

"Neglected Literary Materials for Writing an Intellectual History of the Colonial South," in Motley Deakin and Peter Lisca, eds., *From Irving to Steinbeck: Studies in American Literature in Honor of Harry R. Warfel*, Gainesville: University of Florida Press, 1972, 29-41.

"William Byrd: Taste and Tolerance," in Everett Emerson, ed., *Major Writers of Early American Literature*, Madison: University of Wisconsin Press, 1972, 151-77.

INTRODUCTION

In the sixteenth and early seventeenth centuries, "Virginia" meant what is now the United States. Only with the settlement of the Puritans at Plymouth in 1620, in what was then the northern region of Virginia, did "Virginia" begin to break into parts. And the first two permanent settlements—Jamestown in 1607 and Plymouth in 1620—foreshadowed the future split in American society and culture. The earliest Virginians were typically representative of their contemporary English society, but the early Massachusetts settlers were a distinctive religious minority. Perhaps Virginians would never have come to think of themselves as aristocratic Cavaliers if the settlers in New England had not been so indisputably categorized as Puritans. But the Puritanness of New England focused the question of the identity of Virginians, and the English Civil War, 1643-1660, decided the matter. Since the Puritans and the Cavaliers were the opposing parties in English seventeenth-century civilization, the Virginians—not being Puritans—were Cavaliers. Of course, such sweeping generalizations oversimplify the matter, though I believe that this one contains at least a symbolic truth.

By the end of the seventeenth century, Virginians had come to think of themselves as the descendants of Royalists and as Anglicans. Their thinking and writing were subtly and profoundly influenced by these beliefs. Even more important, however, was the success of John Rolfe's efforts to grow tobacco. The man who married Pocahontas also created the distinctive Southern way of life, for tobacco demanded large plantations, with many workers, preferably by the side of rivers for easy transportation to the London and European markets. By the time of Rolfe's death in the Indian massacre of 1622, tobacco had become the staple of the Southern economic system, and was to remain King until replaced by cotton in the nineteenth century. Of course, the basic facts of a suitable climate and geography were necessary in order to allow the growth of tobacco. After tobacco was found to be profitable, the workers necessary for the labor would be imported. Thus, a large number of indentured servants, transported convicts, and black slaves were brought to Virginia.

By the eighteenth century, Virginia culture was distinctive, and the writers, most of whom were from the Virginia aristocracy, reflected their culture. They believed in the pastoral tradition which they learned from the Greek and Roman authors, as well as from such ideal men of the late seventeenth century as Sir William Temple. And the pastoral mode was more suitable for celebration by the plantation South than by the comparatively urban and small-farm North. The Southern writers also commonly reflected the widespread eighteenth-century belief in the Great Chain of Being, a view of reality particularly appropriate for justifying degrees in social order. And Virginians, like other Americans, came to love their own part of America. By 1775, nationalism, plus the social, political, and economic oppression of the English colonial system, united most of the Americans against the English in the American Revolution.

The writers of colonial Virginia reflected their society. The earliest promoters—Richard Hakluyt and Samuel Purchas—and the earliest explorers—Thomas Hariot and Captain John Smith—were all Englishmen celebrating the possibilities of America. Captain John Smith reveals that he has begun to love the land, but the idea of America, as much as the actuality, appeals to him. Henry Norwood too was not an American but an Englishman, a Cavalier, merely visiting America when he (like the earlier William Strachey, whose adventures inspired part of *The Tempest*) underwent a series of appalling ordeals and narrow escapes in 1649-1650. But John Cotton, who wrote in 1677 the fascinating history of Bacon's Rebellion in Virginia, was a Virginian. Although Cotton balanced the question of the rights and wrongs of Bacon's Rebellion, he was evidently an aristocratic, anti-Puritan, plantation owner who loved literature in addition to his adopted land.

By the eighteenth century, the first families of Virginia were well-established and already identified with certain great plantations. Robert Beverley and William Byrd of Westover both celebrated American nature, Virginia traditions, and the pastoral view of American plantation life as a retreat from the cares of urban English society. In these authors, we find the traditions of colonial Virginia in their first literary flourishing. They are among the best writers of a group that included such able penmen as William Fitzhugh, Ralph Wormeley, and Sir John Randolph. Although their primary models were the great landed aristocrats of England and the classical republican-statesmen whose works they read in Greek and Latin, the Virginians' own distinctive society found its most symbolic single representative in the person of Robert "King" Carter (1663-1732). Proud, hard-working, intellectual, land-poor, hospitable, and contemptuous of their "inferiors," the plantation owners viewed themselves as descendants of the Cavaliers (some, like Carter, were), as modern versions of Cato, Cicero, and Marcus Aurelius, and as opposers of the Puritans. Like the English aristocrats, the Virginians scorned the merely commercial success of their puritan neighbors in New England and imitated the traditions of hospitality and entertainment that supposedly had flourished among the landed gentry in a bygone England.

Their writings reflected their classical training and the belief that their way of life was closer to the great flourishing civilizations of Republican Greece and Rome than any intervening age. The generation of mid-eighteenth century Virginians, including Richard Bland, George Washington, Thomas Jefferson, Robert Bolling of Chellow, Arthur Lee, and James Madison, grew up with such men as Beverley, Byrd, Carter, and Randolph as their immediate models, while they too considered the classical writers and some few Englishmen as their literary and philosophic progenitors. In addition to this dominant and elitist culture, there was always the mass of poor people, servants and slaves, and a group of immigrants to Virginia including those from England, Scotland, and the other colonies. Virginia's major revivalistic minister Samuel Davies (later a short-lived President of Princeton College) spent nearly all of his adult life on the Virginia frontier. His writings are more like those of his fellow Presbyterian ministers than like the Beverleys and Byrds of the Virginia oligarchy, but he too loved Virginia and tried to rouse Virginians to defend the back-country settlers from the inroads of the French and Indians. The English-born Anglican minister John Camm represents that group of capable English ministers who were continually emigrating to colonial Virginia and who often found themselves at odds with the plantation aristocracy. Other emigrants, like St. George Tucker from the West Indies, fit into the dominant culture of their adopted land.

Early Virginia literature and culture thus found itself defined in part by such exterior causes as the course of English history, the settlement of New England by Puritans, and the literary and cultural ideals of seventeenth and eighteenth century English literature; and defined in part by the rise of the tobacco economy, the climate and geography of the South, and the genius of those men and those cultures who were born in, emigrated to, or were brought over as slaves to colonial Virginia. The number of competent and even excellent literary men produced by early Virginia is one indication of a flourishing civilization. Two centuries after the American Revolution and more than a century after the American Civil War, we are, I hope, in a position to examine the early Virginia writers and their writings with detached appreciation.

J. A. L. L.

THOMAS HARIOT, JOHN WHITE, AND OULD VIRGINIA

Everett Emerson

In *Paterson,* William Carlos Williams tells of finding his fellow citizens, the inhabitants of Paterson, New Jersey, wandering through their lives dreamily because they do not know their origins, the history of the place where they live. For Williams, knowledge of the history of one's place is necessary for *all* men, not merely gratifying for those whose ancestors created the first local white settlement. If Williams' attractive argument is valid, and many rootless Americans are finding it useful to themselves, a case can be made for our needing to know not merely our immediate region but also our land. Unfortunately, the possessive filiopietistic ideals of New Englanders and Virginians of the sixth, seventh, and eighth generations have tended to keep those who later adopted America outside the house of knowledge of American beginnings. Those who are convinced by Williams, himself a son of immigrants, know that to be fully awake, Americans must know their land and its history.

That knowledge might well begin with one's place or with a consideration of the creation of what is now America and its shaping by geologic forces; it might then continue through the relationship between the land and its first human inhabitants, and on to the coming of the white man and the creation of the United States. In this sequence, an important place might properly be

1

reserved for what Captain John Smith called "Ould Virginia," the part of present-day North Carolina that was settled and explored in the 1580s. This attempt at colonization lives on in some men's memory as the Lost Colony. Imagining what might have happened to the abandoned colonists has proved to be an attractive pastime; however, the historical consequences of the settlement and the continuity of which it is a part are what should concern Americans looking for roots.

Three steps can be identified in the creation of the North Carolina, or better, the Roanoke Colony. First, in 1584 Sir Walter Ralegh obtained a patent to "have holde occupy and enjoye" "remote heathen and barbarous landes Contries and territories not actually possessed of any Christian Prynce and inhabited by Christian people."[1] He planned to create a colony in America north of Florida, occupied by the Spaniards. In the same year, 1584, Ralegh sent Captain Philip Amadas and Captain Arthur Barlowe across the water for a reconnaissance. They visited the Carolina Banks and brought back not only reports but also two Indians, Manteo and Wanchese. They selected the Outer Banks area rather than Chesapeake Bay because of their discovery that the Indians of the more northern area were hostile.

Captain Barlowe was excited by what he found in the Banks: an abundance of grapes, deer, rabbits, and woods "not such as you finde in Bohemia, Muscouia, or Hyrcania, barren and fruitless, but the highest, and reddest Cedars of the world, farre bettering the Cedars of the Acores, of the Indias, or of Lybanus, Pynes, Cypres, Sassaphras, the Lentisk [gum?], or the tree that beareth the rinde of blacke Sinamon. . . ."[2] The soil he reported to be "the most plentifull, sweete, fruitfull, and wholsome of all the world" (p. 106), and he found "the goodliest and best fishe in the world, and in greatest aboundance" (p. 115). The voyage was so successful that Ralegh was authorized by the Queen to call the American territories that he now claimed for England, Virginia, in her honor. Though Ralegh seems to imply that he derived the idea from the native inhabitants' name, "Wingandacon," the name "Virginia" had already been used by Richard Hakluyt in his "Particular Discourse of Western Planting," written before Ralegh's men returned from America.[3]

Amadas and Barlowe had an exceptionally fortunate voyage, for they did not learn much about the treacherousness of the Banks. The inlets through which they had passed, to the sounds beyond, are really outlets made by the force of fresh water from the rivers emptying into the sounds, and much turbulence is created at the rather narrow openings by the collision of the fresh water with the tidal salt water. The area is especially dangerous during the hurricane season. Another danger is created by the mixing of the warm Gulf Stream with the cold Labrador Current near Cape Hatteras. The whole area is properly named the Grave-yard of the Atlantic.[4]

The sequel to this preliminary visit began with a carefully plan-ned major undertaking in 1585. Now Ralegh sent out seven ships, and though all did not arrive and the supplies carried by others were damaged, some ships did reach the North Carolina coast by late June. During the summer men from the ships explored Pam-lico Sound (near Cape Hatteras), the mainland west of the Sound, and Albemarle Sound to the north. They began a headquarters, with a fort, at Roanoke Island, in a central area between the two sounds. By late August or early September all of the ships, except some small ones, returned to England. The fact that at least one of the ships returning attacked and captured a Spanish ship suggests that, in addition to whatever else he had in mind, Ralegh intended his colony to serve as a base for privateering.

A group of 107 men under Captain Ralph Lane remained be-hind in America. They included soldiers, gentlemen, merchants, and three specialists: Thomas Hariot, a mathematician, cartog-rapher, and ethnologist who had been resident scientist in Ralegh's household; John White, an artist; and Joachim Ganz, a metallur-gist. Hariot, who probably had tried to learn the language of the Indians Manteo and Wanchese, worked with White in making maps and observations on the Indians, plants, and animals. During the winter some of the Englishmen, probably including White and perhaps also Hariot, explored to the north and west. They entered Chesapeake Bay and also pushed inland, as a map prepared by White shows. But after spending a year in America the colonists were running short of needed supplies and the Indians had become hostile. The settlers took advantage of a visit from Sir Francis

Drake to return to England, but their departure was complicated by stormy weather, including a June hurricane, and as a result valuable papers and materials collected were lost. The abandonment of the settlement was unnecessary since supply ships arrived soon after the hasty leave-taking. But a notable achievement had been made, an important step towards the creation of a permanent colony.

The following year Ralegh sent out a group of men and women who were to create a permanent colony, "the cittie of Ralegh in Virginia." Ralegh had decided that since the Carolina Banks did not yield precious metals, the new settlement should be on Chesapeake Bay. But for reasons that are not wholly clear, the colonists ended up on the more familiar ground of Roanoke Island. John White, who headed the settlement, explained that the captain of the flagship considered it too late in the year to go north to Chesapeake (they did not reach the North Carolina coast until late July) and insisted on landing the colonists at the point they had reached, Roanoke. But the flagship's captain may have still feared the Chesapeake Indians, whom he had encountered in 1584.[5]

White returned to England in late August to insure that adequate supplies would be sent across the Atlantic in the following spring. In the meanwhile Thomas Hariot was at work preparing a pamphlet intended to attract additional colonists and investors to "Virginia" and to counteract unfavorable publicity that had resulted from the return of the 1585-1586 colonists. Hariot's *Briefe and True Report of the New Found Land of Virginia* (1588) did not lead to support for the misplaced colonists of 1587 that White had left behind, for 1588 was the year of the Spanish Armada, when ships were needed for the Queen's service. Two small vessels with some fifteen additional colonists did manage to set out, but one was captured and its supplies taken, and neither reached its destination. Why no attempt was made in 1589 is less certain. Nearly three years after he left, John White finally returned to Roanoke, in August 1590. The settlers were gone, apparently moved to not-very-distant Croatan. Then, as White later explained, "the season was so unfit, & weather so foule, that we were constrained of force to forsake that coast. . . ."[6]

There the story would appear to end. So read many historians.

There was no formal continuity between the Roanoke Colony and Jamestown, for Ralegh lost his rights in America as a result of his trial for treason in 1603.[7] But the new colony was established where White had been instructed to plant his colony in 1587, and the risk being taken by the Jamestown colonists seemed much less great than it would have without the previous effort. Moreover, the planning and knowledge of Ralegh, Hakluyt, and Hariot made the task much easier.[8] For example, Captain John Smith seems to have made use of Hariot's list of Indian words so that he was able to communicate effectively with the Indians.[9]

And there are Hariot's book and White's drawings. Two versions of Hariot's book exist: the 1588 quarto and a folio version that appeared two years later. The latter was published in French, German, Latin, and English versions, with engravings by the publisher, Theodore de Bry. The engravings were based on original drawings by John White. To this folio edition, Hariot contributed captions, which he wrote in Latin; in the English version these appear as translated by Richard Hakluyt. Both the quarto and the folio have been reprinted in facsimile.[10]

All that John White and Thomas Hariot could hope to have published in their time was a book with engravings, but twenty-nine of White's original drawings, in color, have survived, as well as forty-three copies of White's originals—the latter made in the early seventeenth century. With the twenty-four engravings, including de Bry's title page with Indian figures, a total of seventy-eight works are extant. The great book—I make the claim deliberately—that should exist to celebrate the Roanoke Colony unfortunately does not. As David B. Quinn rightly says, "there is no substitute for reading the texts and notes alongside the drawings and engravings themselves."[11] No single book satisfactorily provides the opportunity. One can assemble the materials, but to see the best reproductions of White's work, with the good notes that modern scholarship provides, and to read Hariot's text "alongside" requires assembling *three* books (two very large), an arrangement that is more than awkward.

From one point of view the most important contributions made by the collaborators of 1588-1590 are three maps: an engraving by de Bry of the North Carolina coast and southeastern Virginia as far as the mouth of Chesapeake Bay; an earlier drawing of the same (presumably) by White, called by Quinn "the most careful detailed piece of cartography for any part of North America to be made in the sixteenth century"[12]; and another map by White, less accurate and valuable, of the entire southeastern part of North America, including Florida and the Caribbean. The first of these is of importance because of its wide influence. It was used, for example, by Hondius in the preparation of a map for Mercator's atlas.[13]

The great achievement of the Hariot-White collaboration was that they saw what they looked at. They reported. Hariot, it is true, had his perceptions shaped to a certain extent by an earlier work of a European, Nicholas Monardes' *Joyful Newes Out of the New World* (English translation, 1577), to which he refers; he used it chiefly to identify some medicinal plants.[14] Some of White's drawings also show some Europeanizing. But on the whole both Hariot and White reported with remarkable fidelity. Their work is the first English contribution to knowledge of the people, plants, and animals of the New World. Hariot was by temperament a scientist open to new truths, willing to probe and to question.[15] And Samuel Eliot Morison justly observes that White's "beautiful and accurate paintings" include "the best portraits of American Indians prior to Catlin, the best flora prior to John Bartram, and the best birds and beasts prior to Audubon."[16]

One must be grateful to de Bry for making available White's drawings—as engravings—during the years between 1590 and 1964, when White's original drawings were at last adequately reproduced. But it is White's drawings that should be seen with Hariot's captions, insofar as possible, rather than the engravings with their modifications. (For a few of the engravings, no corresponding colored drawing is extant.) Thus if one compares de Bry's eighth plate, "A chieff Ladye of Pomeiooc," with White's drawing, one sees that the adapter has carefully balanced the woman's pose against the energetic posturing of her daughter, who is portrayed as significantly larger than in the drawing. Hariot's caption applies equally well to drawing and engraving. On the other hand, de Bry provides in his engraving of a religious man (plate V) a second view of the figure, from the rear. (With what authority de Bry undertook this doubling—here and elsewhere—is not known.)

De Bry also Europeanized this face somewhat. In both the fifth
and eighth engravings de Bry added an interesting landscape. A
comparative study of the drawings and the engravings, an agreeable and profitable undertaking, reveals two fundamental kinds of
differences: differences resulting from the character of the two
media, and differences in intention.

White's subjects include plants, birds, fish, and land animals,
but the Indian pictures are of greatest interest. We see men, wom-
en, children; a chieftain, a conjuror, a priest; we see Indians building a boat, fishing, cooking, eating, sitting about a fire, dancing; we
see Indian villages with corn growing in the fields, and even a
house of the dead. The series is remarkably comprehensive.
(There is no picture of Indians going to war.) Hariot's text and his
captions complement the drawings, particularly in their comments
on the Indians. While the first part of Hariot's *Report* describes
the commodities that might draw men to America (commodities
merchantable) and the second part explains what commodities
are available to sustain life, it is the third part, "Of the nature and
manners of the people," which provides the most interesting reading. (The methodical cataloging of the first two parts does not
always sustain interest.) Hariot deals mostly with what White
could not picture: the Indians' religion and their attitude towards
the white intruders.

Repeatedly Hariot emphasizes the Indians' humanity. They are
inferior to Europeans because they lack crafts and science and
especially true religion, but they show "excellencie of wit" (p.
317). Much of his survey of Indian concepts of the creation, the
gods, and immortality is presented objectively, without comment,
although Hariot makes it perfectly clear that his interests in the
new land include leading the Indians to embrace Christianity. For
him, conversion is a not unlikely consequence of English missionary effort, for the Indians' "traditions and stories" "were not sure
grounded," and "through conversing with us they were brought
into great doubts of their owne [religion] and no small admiration of ours, with earnest desire in many, to learne more than we
made means" to communicate, because of imperfect knowledge of
the Indians' language (p. 375). Throughout his report on the Indians, Hariot maintains a respectful attitude. He refers to them as

"our friends" (p. 378), and he never resorts to caricature.

But the report of the Indians is somewhat tangential to Hariot's guiding purpose in the preparation of his pamphlet, the publication of propaganda. In this regard the most surprising feature of the piece is its caution. The *Report* offers remarkably little to entice investors or colonists. (At times Hariot resembles an old-time Ralph Nader writing commercials for General Motors.) Governor Ralph Lane commented in his discourse, published in Hakluyt's *Principall Navigations* (1589), that "the discovery of a good mine . . . or a passage to the Southsea, or someway to it, and nothing else can bring this country in request to be inhabited by our nation." [17] Hariot could promise neither and not much else. He reports that iron was found, but he is not enthusiastic about its value: "I knowe nothing to the contrarie, but that it maie be allowed for a good merchantable commoditie . . ." (p. 332). Indians away from the coast owned "small plates of copper, that had been made as we understood, by the inhabitants that dwell farther into the country, where as they say are mountaines and Rivers that yeelde also whyte graynes of Mettall, which is to be deemed Silver (pp. 332-33). Hariot was given not to imaginative speculation, but to scholarly qualification.

Compared with such later writers on America as Captain John Smith (the comparison is inevitable), Hariot provides his readers with little sense of the possibilities of life in America. He would have his readers "generally know & learne what the countrey is; & therevpon consider how your dealing therein, if it proceede, may returne you profit and gaine; be it either by inhabiting & planting or otherwise in furthering thereof" (p. 322). Hariot is seldom positive: he cannot say that the iron found is of great value, but he knows nothing to the contrary; he recommends that would-be investors consider how they might profit from the colony. The nearest he gets to a grand peroration is this back-handed invitation to his readers to become colonists: "the dealing of Sir Walter Raleigh [is] so liberall in large giving and graunting lande there, as is alreadie knowen, with many helpes and furtherances els: (The least that hee hath graunted hath been fiue hundred acres to a man onely for the aduenture of his person) I hope there remain no cause wherby the action should be misliked" (p. 385).

However much one may admire Hariot's contribution to knowledge, one cannot be astonished that Hariot's *Report* did not cause the docks to be stampeded with volunteers for America.

Hariot's caution is seen more clearly if one puts the passage just quoted against what Captain John Smith held out in his *Generall Historie* (1624):

> Who can desire more content that hath small meanes, or but onely his merit to aduance his fortunes, then to tread and plant that ground he hath purchased by the hazard of his life; if hee haue but the taste of vertue and magnanimity, what to such a minde can bee more pleasant then planting and building a foundation for his posterity, got from the rude earth by Gods blessing and his owne industry without preiudice to any; if hee haue any grain of faithe or zeale in Religion, what can he doe lesse hurtfull to any, or more agreeable to God, then to seek to conuert those poor Saluages to know Christ and humanity, whose labours with discretion will triple requite thy charge and paine. . . .[18]

If Hariot was an unenthusiastic and unsuccessful propagandist, perhaps it is just as well, for Roanoke Island was far from an ideal location for a permanent colony or even as a hideout for English privateering vessels. The capes of the banks, Fear, Hatteras, and Lookout, are infamously dangerous, and the English ships that ventured in the 1580s into the shallow waters of Pamlico and Albermarle sounds frequently ran aground. Just inland are swamps with a large snake population. The Chesapeake Bay area had much more in its favor, though Jamestown itself is not a choice location. Nearly four hundred years after its first settlement, Roanoke Island—which never was the site of another town after the "Cittie of Ralegh in Virginia" of 1587—is chiefly an historical landmark. But Roanoke, Thomas Hariot's pamphlet, and John White's still too-little-known drawings are to be cherished by Americans who would know their origins, for each commemorates the beginnings of the English colonization of America—the beginnings of the America that we know. And White and Hariot show us, tell us, what America was like upon the arrival of the white man.

NOTES

1. David B. Quinn, ed., *The Roanoke Voyages, 1585-1590,* 2 vols. (London: Hakluyt Society, 1955), 82. My account is derived from this splendid edition and the account in David B. Quinn and Paul Hulton, eds., *The American Drawings of John White, 1577-1590,* 2 vols. (London: British Museum; Chapel Hill: University of North Carolina Press, 1964).

2. Barlowe's discourse, published by Richard Hakluyt in *Principall Navigations* (1588) and reprinted in Quinn, *Roanoke Voyages,* 91-116. I quote from 96-97.

3. Ralegh, *History of the World* (1616) excerpted in Quinn, *Roanoke Voyages,* 117.

4. See David Stick, *The Outer Banks of North Carolina, 1584-1958* (Chapel Hill: University of North Carolina Press, 1958), 1-10.

5. See White's narrative in Quinn, *Roanoke Voyages,* 523, and Quinn, *Simão Fernadez, A Portuguese Pilot in the English Service, circa 1573-1588* (Lisbon, 1961), 11-12.

6. Quinn, *Roanoke Voyages,* 715. Probably some of the colonists survived till 1607, when—shortly before the founders of Jamestown arrived—Powhatan had most of them killed. See the instruction to Thomas Gates of about 1609 printed in Philip L. Barbour, ed., *The Jamestown Voyages Under the First Charter, 1606-1609,* 2 vols. (Cambridge, England: Hakluyt Society, 1969), p. 265. There Gates is advised to travel southward from Jamestown for four days to a place "where you shall finde foure of the english alive, left by Sir Walter Rawley which escaped from the slaughter of Powhatan. . . ." No such survivors were found. See also Louis B. Wright in *The American Drawings of John White,* I, 60, and the full analysis in Clifford M. Lewis and Albert J. Loomie, *The Spanish Jesuit Mission in Virginia, 1570-1572* (Chapel Hill: University of North Carolina Press, 1953), 274-77.

It is frequently forgotten that there was a second Lost Colony at Roanoke. Soon after Lane, Hariot, White and the other colonists returned to England in 1586 with Drake, a supply ship arrived, whose commander futilely searched for the colonists. Then, to retain possession of the area, he left a group of some fifteen men with supplies. These men were not to be found by the colonists of 1587. See Quinn, *Roanoke Voyages,* 468-69, 479-80.

7. Ralegh later argued that his voyage to the Caribbean and South America in 1595 was "for the relife of those english, which I had planted in Virginia." See Ralegh's *Discoverie of the Large and Bewtiful Land of Guiana,* ed. V. T. Harlow (London: Argonaut Press, 1928), p. 13; and D. B. Quinn, *Raleigh and the British Empire* (London: Hodder and Stoughton, 1947), 209-10. Ralegh is not persuasive.

8. See D. B. Quinn, *The New Found Land: The English Contribution to the Discovery of America* (Providence: Associates of John Carter Brown Library, 1965), 15, 19-20; and Quinn, "Thomas Hariot and the Virginia Voyages of 1602," *William and Mary Quarterly,* 3rd ser., 27 (1970), 268-81.

9. Philip L. Barbour, *The Three Worlds of Captain John Smith* (Boston: Houghton Mifflin, 1964), 98-99.

10. The quarto has been several times reprinted, most recently by the Da Capo Press, New York, 1971; the folio was reprinted, with a new introduction by Paul Hulton, by Dover Publications, New York, 1972, a very valuable and handsome reprint.

11. Quinn, *Roanoke Voyages*, 314.

12. Quinn, *Roanoke Voyages*, 847-48.

13. William P. Cumming, *The Southeast in Early Maps* (Chapel Hill: University of North Carolina Press, 1962), 123.

14. See Hariot, *Report*, in Quinn, *Roanoke Voyages*, 329, and Quinn's note.

15. These qualities were later to raise questions about Hariot's orthodoxy. See Jean Jacquot, "Thomas Hariot's reputation for Impiety," *Notes and Records of the Royal Society of London*, 9 (1952), 164-87, and D. B. Quinn and John W. Shirley, "A Contemporary List of Hariot References," *Renaissance Quarterly*, 22 (1969), 9-25. I am indebted to Professor Shirley, of the University of Delaware, for some useful leads. (He is actively engaged in Hariot research.)

16. Samuel Eliot Morison, *The European Discovery of America: The Northern Voyages, A.D. 500-1600* (New York: Oxford University Press, 1971), 652.

17. Lane in Quinn, *Roanoke Voyages*, 273.

18. Smith, *Travels and Works*, ed. Edward Arber and A. G. Bradley, 2 vols. (reprint edition, New York: Burt Franklin, n.d.), 722.

THE ADVENTURES OF CAPTAIN JOHN SMITH AS HEROIC LEGEND

Lewis Leary

I

To say, as Howard Mumford Jones does in *The Literature of Virginia in the Seventeenth Century,* that Captain John Smith's celebrity "is due in greater degree to his deeds and his personality than to his achievement in literature," [1] is to overlook one important consideration. It is certainly true that the Pocahontas incident, variously told, quite overshadows much besides in Captain Smith's career, to become part of native folklore with implications of profound psychological importance. But how does one know the story of Captain Smith's rescue by Pocahontas except from Captain Smith's testimony? And how does one know of Captain Smith's tempestuous adventure-filled career, or of his personality, except as he recorded it? Because of his writings, he is remembered. Perhaps, as Thomas Fuller said three hundred years ago, it "soundeth much to the diminution of his deeds that he alone is the herald to proclaim them." [2] But proclaim them he did, and with such vigor that his life has become legend.

Perhaps A. L. Rowse is more correct in suggesting the paradox "that this professed soldier was more of a writer than a man of action," [3] and that it is "the very assertion of personality" which identifies Captain Smith as "a writer by nature," with "an acute sense of others' personalities as well as his own," who "is racy and humorous, at times funny, often indignant, but always alive, with

a naive poetry that is endearing." ⁴ My intention is to demonstrate
that Captain Smith is a writer conscious of craft and of the power
of words, whose deeds fit close to traditional patterns of heroic
legend, and whose vaunting of personality places him at the head
of a line which includes Benjamin Franklin, Walt Whitman, and
Ernest Hemingway, writers who have created personae which
thrust through to illuminate almost everything that they wrote.
Celebrating himself, Captain Smith created assumptions, about
himself and about the new world, which certify him

> one of the first Americans we know,
> And we can claim him, though not by bond of birth,
> For we have always bred chimeras.
>
> And he was one,
> This bushy-bearded, high-foreheaded, trusting man
> Who could turn his hand to anything at a pinch,
> Bragging, canny, impatient, durable,
> And fallen in love with the country at first sight. ⁵

Chimera or not, his story has become history. For what do
we ask of writers but that they be true? To fact, as if the fact or
the appearance of fact was really immutable? Captain Smith was
concerned finally with matters quite beyond fact. However self-
serving and opinionated, he wrote doggedly of an ideal, and he was
at the center of it. "Time dissipates to shining ether the solid angularity of facts," explained Emerson in his essay on history. "Who
cares what the fact was, when we have made a shining constellation to hang in heaven as an immortal sign?" John Smith may
hang somewhere other than in heaven, but his legend, and the
persona which created it, lives on uncorrupted by solid angularity.
In the manner of Melville or Whitman, Goethe or Joyce, he is a
fabulist, concerned, even without knowing it, for self-conscious-
ness of that kind would be self-defeating, with what Chandler
Brossard has recently identified as "that magical-mythical-vision-
ary exercise" which creates living story. If it is true that the "great
western tradition of the fabulist, that artist who . . . dreamed for
all of us, so to speak, who created Ulysses, Roland, the Hunchback
of Notre Dame, Red Riding Hood, Alice in Wonderland, Ishmael,
Bloom, and the Baron Charlus—that apocalyptic light has died in
America," ⁶ it did once live, and Captain Smith may be thought the

first to have measured its dimensions against the promises of the new world.

II

The barbaric yawp of Captain Smith differs in tone and tenor from the yawp of Walt Whitman, yet it combines, like Whitman's, the celebration of self with concern for the welfare of others, for "the fatherless children . . . or young married people that have small wealth to live on"[7] who would find opportunity in the new world. Our concern need not be with whether John Smith was writing only as a self-serving propagandist or whether he is a trust-worthy and dedicated witness, but with the persona he presents and the ideal toward which it reaches. Whitman's disdain for the simpering, over-dressed beaux of New York as expressed in *Democratic Vistas* can be put beside Captain Smith's contempt for the gentlemen adventurers in Virginia who "would rather starve and rot in idleness than be persuaded to do anything for their relief" (p. 9) or his scornful questions to the man who resisted venturing in the new world. Would he rather, Smith asked,

> live at home idly (or think himself worthy to live) only to eat, drink, and sleep, and so to die? Or by consuming that carelessly, his friend got worthily? Or by using that miserably that maintained virtue honestly? Or for being descended nobly, pine with the vain vaunt of great kin-dred, in penury? Or (to maintain a silly show of bravery) toil out thy heart, soul, and time by shifts, tricks, cards, and dice? Or by relating news of other's actions, shark here or there for a dinner or supper; deceive thy friends with fair promises and dissimulation, in borrowing where thou never indendest to pay, offend the law, surfeit with excess, burden thy country, and wish thy parents' death (I will not say damna-tion) to have their estate (pp. 209-10).

That is not to say that Captain John Smith is a seventeenth-century Walt Whitman, though the point might be labored. He was a man of different disposition, different times, and different per-suasions. But a voice emerges from a passage such as that quoted above, and with an accent which becomes unmistakable. "I would be sorry to offend, or that any should mistake my honest mean-ing," he goes on, "for I wish good to all, hurt to none. But rich men for the most part are grown to that dotage through their pride in their wealth, as though there were no accident could end it, or their life" (p. 210). His dedication to purpose is set forth in plain words:

> I have not been so ill bred but I have tasted plenty and pleasure as well as want misery, nor doth necessity yet, or occasion of discontent, force me to these endeavors; nor am I ignorant what small thanks I shall have for my pains, or that many would have the world imagine them to be of great judgment that can but blemish these my designs by their witty objections and detractions. Yet I hope my reasons, with my deeds, will prevail with some, that I shall not want employment in these affairs. . . . I wish all sorts of worthy, honest, and industrious spirits would understand, and if they desire any further satisfaction, I will do my best to give it, not to persuade them to go only, but go with them, not leave them there, but live with them there (pp. 211-12).

He would stand by what he said: "if I abuse you with my tongue, take my head for satisfaction" (p. 212). The new world which he described offered bucolic promise. He chided "fathers that are so foolishly fond or so miserably covetous or so willfully careless" that they would rather "maintain . . . children in idle wantoness" than allow them to adventure abroad (p. 211). Smith's enthusiasm is not tawdry when he challenges: "What exercise should more delight . . . than ranging daily those unknown parts, using fowling and fishing for hunting and hawking?" (p. 213). There was sport in plenty, for fun and profit, not only delight in "that kind of toil or pleasure," but remuneration also, for game in the new world "besides the delicacy of their bodies for food, their skins are so rich as may well recompense thy daily labor with a captain's pay" (p. 214). Anticipations of Crèvecoeur and Isaac Walton rub shoulders in such passages as:

> Here nature and liberty affords us freely, what in England we want, or it costeth us dearly. What pleasure can be more than (being tired with any occasion ashore, in planting vines, fruits, or herbs in contriving their own grounds to the pleasure of their minds, their fields, garden, orchards, buildings, ships, or other works) to recreate themselves before their own doors, in their own boats upon the sea, where man, woman, and child with a small hook and line by angling may take diverse sorts of excellent fish at their pleasure? And is it not a pretty sport to pull up

two pence, six pence, and twelve pence as fast as you can haul and veer a line? He is a very bad fisher [that] cannot kill in one day with his hook and line one, two three hundred cods. . . . If a man work but three days in seven, he may get more than he spend, unless he be excessive. . . . And what sport doth yield more pleasing content, less hurt or charge, than angling with a hook, and crossing the sweet air from isle to isle over the silent streams of a calm sea? (pp. 213-14).

Captain Smith's love affair with the new world is as feverently expressed as his bitterness toward those who would delay or destroy benefits of its bounty. He praised its "sandy cliffs and cliffs of rock," its fertile gardens and fields of corn (p. 708), all the "sweet brooks and crystal springs" of this most "fruitful and delightsome land, the salubriousness of its air, the richness of its soil, the variety of its vegetation, all "so propitious to the nature and use of man" that there is "no place more convenient" for pleasure or profit (pp. 46-49):

here is a place, a nurse for soldiers, a practice for mariners, a trade for merchants, a reward for the good, and that which is most of all, a business (most acceptable to God) to bring . . . poor infidels to the knowledge of God and his holy Gospel (pp. 63-64).

Examples could be multiplied of Captain Smith's conscious literary craftsmanship. It could only have been he who wrote so charmingly of the antic bacchanal masque of Indian maidens prepared for him by Pocahontas. Seated on a mat in a fair, plain field before a fire, he watched as

thirty young women came naked from the woods, only covered behind and before with a few green leaves, their bodies all painted, some one colour, some another, but all differing. Their leader had a fair pair of buck's horns on her head and an other's skin at her girdle, and another at her arm, a quiver of arrows at her back, a bow and arrows in her hand. The next had in her hand a sword, another a club, another a pot-stick: all horned alike; the rest, every one with their several devices. These fiends with most hellish shouts and cries, rushing from the trees, cast themselves in a ring about the fire, singing and dancing with most excellent ill variety, often falling into their informal passions, and solemnly again to sing and dance. Having spent near an hour in this mascarado, as they entered, in like manner they departed. Having reaccom-

modated themselves, they solemnly invited him to their lodgings, where
he was no sooner within the house, but all these nymphs more torment-
ed him than ever with crowding and pressing and hanging about him,
most tediously crying, "Love not you me? Love not you me?" (p. 436).

Denied opportunity for further adventuring, during the last
years of his life Captain Smith became a professional writer. His
Accidence for the Sea, or Pathway to Experience of 1626, his *Sea
Grammar* a year later, and his condescendingly avuncular *Adver-
tisement for the Unexperienced Planters of New England* of 1631
contain spirited dramatic and often patently "literary" passages.
The controlled pathos of his valedictory poem "The Sea Mark"
has been rightfully admired, and newly discovered poems reveal
him "a craftsman with considerable skill."[8] But these are over-
shadowed by the commanding massive presence in Captain Smith's
reports of personal adventure of a man who looms to heroic proportions. Self-proclaimed, he stands in the dawn of our literature
crowing like Chanticleer, and the echo of his voice in song and
story has survived for more than three hundred years.

III

What is the persona which he so vauntingly presented? Captain
Smith, who gives lip-service to religion, is self-confessedly a soldier, bluff and plain; he is a man of persistent single vision, with a
talent for persuasion, who has lifted himself by his own bootstraps
from the simplest of all beginnings to a position of prominence
among men of his time. He had a talent for friendship, but for
quarreling also. There seems to have been something sly about
him, something of swagger or ambition, which has caused men of
his and succeeding generations to suspect him of subterfuge.
Plain-spoken, his candor made enemies. "The style of the soldier,"
he explains, "is not eloquent, but honest and justifiable" (p. 279).

John Smith, so simply named, is a man of confidence bred from
having been places and having seen things, and who does his dog-
ged best to explain them: "This history . . . might and ought to
have been cut in better robes than my rude military hand can cut
out paper ornaments," he confessed in a dedicatory note to his

General History in 1624: "I am no compiler by hearsay," but "take myself to have a property" in the events narrated, "and therefore have been bold to challenge them to come under the reach of my own rough pen" (p. 274). He is a man of action, better trained to wield the sword than the pen: "it were more proper for me to be doing what I say than writing what I know" (p. 179).

Conscious of the limitations of the "observations of a plain soldier" (p. 252), he hopes, however, that his "soldier's plainness" will not cause a reader "to refuse to accept" what he has written (p. 235), for he was an honest man who meant well, confident that each reader's "goodness will pardon my rudeness and ponder errors in the balance of good will" (p. 178). He was sure of himself, and with reason: "Though I be no scholar, I am past schoolboy, and I desire but to [report what] I have learned to tell you by the continual hazard of my life" (p. 442). As a plain man, he had a plain man's virtues, including loyalty to those who had been "companions," he wrote, "with me in my dangers": "I cannot make a monument for myself and leave them unburied whose lives begot me the title of soldier" (p. 809). Quick to anger, opposition could "passionate" him, he said, "beyond the bounds of modesty" (p. 265). He wrote with confidence within an established literary tradition: "Many of the most eminent warriors," he explained, perhaps with Caesar as well as Sir Walter Raleigh in mind, "what their swords did, their pens writ. I hold it to be no great error to follow good examples" (p. 809).

A forthright man, "torn between the spur of desire and the bridle of passion" and often "ridden to death by despair" (p. 260), Captain Smith could carve out a vigorously cutting phrase: "Oh incredulity, that art of fools who slovenly do spit on all things fair" (p. 772). But he had also a sly, usually ironic, comic touch. Walter Blair, like Henry Adams, has supposed·it an unconscious humor, presumably like that of a winsome child whose experiments in language come topsy-turvy, or a zestful primitive whose boasts beguile without persuading. "When that blustering mustachioed Elizabethan soldier-of-fortune," Blair said, "retold his tale of captivity, the number and ferocity of his Indian captors provide comedy of exaggerration not unlike that in Falstaff's famous yarn to Prince Hal." [9]

Perhaps there is a Munchausen-like hyperbole, but perhaps also only an innocent bent toward marveling at the marvelous, not allowing a stupendous wonder to seem less wonderful (as in Diedrich Knickerbocker's description of the height and girth of Wouter van Twiller), in the Captain's description of the Susquehanna warrior, "the calf of whose leg was three-quarters of a yard around" and "whose tobacco pipe was three-quarters of a yard long." There is macabre grotesquerie in his description of one of Powhatan's braves who wore as an earring "a small green and yellow snake near a yard in length which, crawling and lapping about his neck, oftentimes familiarly would kiss his lips," or of others among the Indian band who wore through holes in their ears dead rats tied by the tail (p. 67).

Slapstick mockery is suggested in his account of two venturesome explorers who, with a mastiff bitch and a spaniel as hunting dogs, roamed too far on the track of an evasive deer, until night overtook them, leaving them "no other bed than the earth, nor coverture than the skies." But then "they heard, as they thought, two lions roaring a long time together very nigh them, so not knowing what to do, they resolved to climb up into a tree, . . . an intolerable cold lodging" (p. 753). Comic derision may be found in his account of voyagers to New England who, "pestered nine weeks" in a "leaking, unwholesome ship," soon "grew weary of the sea" (p. 260). He had great fun with Pilgrims at Plymouth "whose humorous ignorances caused them . . . to endure a wonderful deal of misery with infinite patience" (p. 892). Succinct and dour understatement seemed to come natural to him. When foraging for food in the Tappahannock area, he came upon an Indian village which was deserted except for women and children, and he grumbled: "truck they durst not, corn they had plenty, and to spoil I had no commission" (p. 10). He looked on subsequent adventurers in the new world as "but pigs from my sow" (p. 770). His pleas for support at home were received "in such a parsimonious and miserable manner, as if I had gone begging to build universities" (p. 771).

He could fling a fancy and whimsical phrase in comparing himself to "the little ant and the silly bee," asking that "if the endeavors of these vermin be acceptable, I hope mine may be excuseable," and confidently asserting that "Little honey hath that hive where there are more drones than bees, and miserable is the land where more are idle than well employed" (p. 179). He could even venture an occasional pun, as when speaking of too much doting on tobacco as a single export from Virginia where "the rust of covetness doth grow too fast" (p. 932), he remarks that such a "fumous foundation" offers "small stability" (p. 958). In proclaiming his affection for the colonies of the new world, he could rise to rhapsodic fancy: "I call them my children, for they have been my wife, my hawks, my hounds, my cards, my dice, and in total my best content" (p. 265). How effective is the "rude pen" of this astute and witty man. He knew indeed "a ring of gold from a grain of barley" (p. 180).

IV

The dedicatory verses prefixed to *A Description of New England* in 1816, the *General History* in 1624, and the *True Travels* in 1630, though fulsome and perhaps purchased by fee or friendship, further expand his image. To John Davies of Hereford, he is a "dear friend" who is beset by envious traducers "Who by their vice improve (when they reprove)/Thy virtue; so in late procure thee love" (p. 181). George Wither also greets Captain Smith as his "friend" and as an adventurer whose explorations will "make more happy our prosperities" (p. 183). Raleigh Crashaw, who had known him in Virginia, writes in "deserved honor of my honest and worthy captain" who battles not for wealth or "empty praise," but his "country's fame to raise" (p. 184). Other fellow soldiers testify further to his valor (p. 185). "A gentleman desirous to be unknown," inevitably punning on the name Smith, attests that "He Vulcan-like did forge a true plantation," subjecting savages and saving a starving colony (p. 280).

Thomas Macarnesse speaks of the *General History* as having been twice written, once in blood and once on paper, each time at great pains and not for profit (p. 284). Samuel Purchas celebrates his friend and collaborator as "Achilles-like with best arts charged," who "can teach sword grammar,/Can pens to pikes, arms to arts, to scholar soldier hammer" (p. 282). Edward Worse-

ley compares him to Caesar as conquerer and author (p. 285).
John Donne calls him "brave Smith," a man of wit and valor
whose writing, "stored/With strange discovery of God's strangest
creatures,/Gives us full view, how he hath sail'd and oar'd" (p.
285). Robert Norton hails him as "noble Smith," whose "anvil
was experience," but who as a writer "wrought well," with "temper true" (p. 286).

There is sameness in all this praise. Captain Smith is a generous
man, "by true virtue ennobled" (p. 287); he is a "valiant and
deserving friend," learned and wise (p. 815), cherished as well for
wit and valor (p. 825); he is that rarity, a "truly virtuous soldier"
(p. 819) of whom one of his companions in arms could say, "I
never knew a warrior yet, but thee,/From wine, tobacco, debts,
dice, oaths so free" (p. 692). His was a "loyal, loving heart" (p.
284), a "matchless spirit" (p. 817) whose "worth shall stand/A
pattern to succeeding ages," and "ever shall add grace" unto his
native country and his race (p. 814). But not for valor only, for
Captain Smith was also a modest man who

> to pass the world's four parts dost deem
> No more than 'twere to go to bed, or drink,
> And all thou yet hast done, thou dost esteem
> As nothing (p. 691).

One need not ask whether encomium such as this is in every, or
any, respect true. Though these are complimentary verses written
in a fulsome age, they contribute to the inherited image and the
legend of Captain John Smith who becomes "a folk hero,
with . . . attributes like those of a Ulysses, a King Arthur," and a
writer so compelling that his biographers, like those of Benjamin
Franklin, have often been satisfied to accept "his own story, furnish it with rhetoric, fancy, or local color, and send it forth
again." [10] A. L. Rowse reads him from his portrait: "there we see
him beaming at us as if he hadn't a cause or a grievance in the
world, broad-faced, broad-browed, solid, smiling, euphoric," but
with "perhaps . . . a tinge of irascibility in his eyes." [11] The epitaph
beneath the portrait reports him "brass without, but gold within."

V

Second only to his own testimony in establishing the image of Captain John Smith is that provided by his friends and companions in "The Proceedings of the English Colony in Virginia" which in 1612 made up the second, and larger, part of Smith's *Map of Virginia*. Put together by people who wished him, or the colony in Virginia (or their own stake in it), well, and put together, perhaps under his supervision, certainly for his benefit, it certifies him again as a man of valor, intrepid and versatile, who has been traduced by envious enemies.[12] But more than that, the twelve books of the "Proceedings" assume the form of classic story, "like a prose Aeneid," says Howard Mumford Jones, in which Powhatan speaks "like an antique Roman or Greek," in "the spirit of Calgacus in the *Agricola*."

> In this narrative, Aeneas-Smith transplants to unknown shores a divinely guided people and is opposed by Powhatan, like Turnus, a hero of equal eminence. Each is surrounded by lesser heroes and weaker men, each nation appeals to its own dieties, each side utters appropriate orations on friendship, political power, the nature of greatness, authority, and ethics, and speeches of defiance and "pollicie" are virtually classical essays. Aeneas-Smith is wily in diplomacy, skilled in utterance, a ruler, a warrior, a lawgiver, a man above ordinary passions. . . . Almost single-handed he defeats hundreds of warriors, he receives a mysterious wound in the hour of his triumph, and he is removed from the scene. The narrative is single and whole. Some eighteen set speeches are placed in the mouths of the chief contenders, ten being alloted to Smith, five to Powhatan, and three to lesser Indians.[13]

But Captain Smith's story, as he tells it, can seem more disorderly. His genius for repetitive hair-raising adventure and hairbreadth escape may be found to resemble the serial bravery of Natty Bumppo or Marshall Dillon. Evidence has been reported that Captain Smith "was steeped in Amandis of Gaul, Palmerin of Constantinople, and other courtly romances which Anthony Munday was rendering into English."[14] No wonder then that his account of himself reads "like a play for the Elizabethan stage— stormy, crowded with action, without much regard for classic unities, full of zest for danger, prizing life highly so long as it can

be lived intensely," a "wonderful story. But is it true?"[15] William
Gilmore Simms was not the first to find Smith's account of his
adventures "one of those romances which mock the incidents of
ordinary fiction."[16] Nor was Henry Adams the first to suspect
fiction amid what Captain Smith presented as fact.[17] Alexis de
Tocqueville recognized his style as "simple and clear," his narrative exhibiting "the seal of truth": "That which is most remarkable in Captain Smith is that he mingles with the virtues of his
contemporaries qualities which are rare in most of them."[18] Often
overlooked is J. A. Chandler's fine summation of qualities which
characterize the popular conception of this "rugged soldier" who
wrote in haste, but "whose sentences are clear and true," producing
no "dry chronicle of facts, but racy productions of a man of
action, . . . filled with an appreciation of the beauties of nature
and a keen insight into human life," and altogether unsmudged by
the "coarse and vulgar language . . . so common to his time."[19]
Marshall Fishwick has identified Captain Smith as "the last great
knight errant," the first of "Virginians on Olympus."[20]

How close to the lineaments of the persona set forth by the
doughty Captain and his friends is the description by Moses Coit
Tyler of John Smith as a writer whose pages glow with "delightful
strokes of imagery, quaint humor, shrewdness, and . . . rough unconscious grace."[21] He leaves, Carl Halliday has said, "to all succeeding writers in America a most virile and happy example of
vigorously expressed thought."[22] For Captain Smith, explained
Tyler, belonged to

> that noble type of which the Elizabethan period produced so many
> examples—the man of action who was also a man of letters, the man of
> letters who was also a man of action: the wholesomest type of man-
> hood anywhere to be found; body and brain both active, both culti-
> vated; the mind not made fastidious and morbid by too much bookish-
> ness, nor coarse and dull by too little; not a doer who is dumb, not a
> speech-maker who cannot do; the knowledge that comes from books
> widened and freshened by the knowledge that comes from experience;
> the literary sense fortified by common sense; . . . at once bookman,
> penman, swordsman, diplomat, sailor, courtier, orator. Of this type of
> manhood, spacious strong, refined and sane, were the best men of the
> Elizabethan time, George Gascoigne, Sir Philip Sydney, Sir Walter Ra-
> leigh. . . . To this type of manhood Captain John Smith aspired to be-
> long.[23]

VI

And this aspiration has been fulfilled. "He is our Odysseus, our Siegfried, our Aeneas," declared Bradford Smith. He joins within himself "many of the qualities we notice in Odysseus—prowess in battle, guile, the ability to stand hard knocks, a love of wandering and attractiveness to women." But Captain Smith "outdid Odysseus by being his own Homer. He wrote his own Odyssey in the *True Travels,* his own Iliad in the *General History,* and his own Aeneid in the *Description of New England.* Here is a feat none of the ancient heroes can match." And one of "the signs of the folk hero is that a certain mystery surrounds him. Smith gives us even that," for "after we have said all that can be said of his Hungarian exploits, his affair with Pocahontas or the pirates, a touch of mystery remains." Fact never quite catches up with legend: "The size of the person seems to exceed the ability of documents to prove," and that is a "pure sign of a hero."[24] What though he was, in John Fisk's words, a gallant but garrulous hero,[25] or, as Everett Emerson has found him, "a story book hero . . . both charming and infuriating."[26] Walt Whitman reminds us in *November Boughs* that the "best literature is always the result of something greater than itself—not the hero but the portrait of the hero."

That portrait can be placed beside the twenty-two typical incidents in the career of the mythic hero discovered by Lord Raglan: (1) the hero's mother is a royal virgin; (2) his father is a king, and (3) often a near relative of his mother, but (4) the circumstances of his conception are unusual, and (5) he is also reputed to be the son of a god; (6) at birth an attempt is made, usually by his father or his maternal grandfather to kill him, but (7) he is spirited away, and (8) reared by foster-parents in a far country; (9) we are told nothing of his childhood, but (10) on reaching manhood he returns or goes to his future kingdom; (11) after a victory over a king and/or a giant, dragon, or wild beast, (12) he marries a princess, often the daughter of his predecessor, and (13) becomes king; (14) for a time he reigns uneventfully, and (15) prescribes laws, but (16) later he loses favor with the gods and/or his subjects, and (17) is driven from the throne and city, after which (18) he meets with a mysterious death, (19) often at the top of a hill: (20) his children, if any, do not succeed him; (21) his body is not buried, but nevertheless (22) he has one or more holy sepulchres.

Matching incidents in the stories of twenty heroes as handed down through generations against the typical incidents above, Lord Raglan found that only Oedipus scores all twenty-two points; that is, the incidents in his life story match point by point with the twenty-two typical incidents. Theseus and Moses each score 20 points; King Arthur and Dionysos, 19 points; Romulus, Perseus, and Javanese Wutu Gunung, 18 points; Heracles and the Welsh Llew Llawgyffes, 17; Bellerophon 16; Jason and Zeus, 15; the Egyptian Nyikang, 14; Pelops and Robin Hood, 13; Asclepios and Joseph (son of Jacob), 12; Apollo and Siegfried, 11; and Elijah, 9.[27] In John Smith's life story, it is possible, with what Huckleberry Finn would have called a "stretcher" here and there, to count nine, perhaps ten, even eleven.

His birth seems to have been regular enough, his mother not a royal virgin nor his father a king, only a simple freeman yeoman in Lincolnshire.[28] His mother, however, is said to have been "of slightly higher social standing than her husband," with connections by marriage with a knight and a "tie with an Archbishop" (p. 4). But John Smith speaks in the *True Travels* of descent from "the ancient Smiths of Creedley in Lancashire" (p. 821), suggesting something, if not of royal, of rightfully respectworthy origin. Stretching a very great deal, he might therefore be given a single shakey point, perhaps half of a point, on the basis of the combined first and second of Lord Raglan's qualifications. It is not known that his father was a near relation of his mother, or that the circumstances of his conception were in any way unusual, or that he was the son of a god—except as admiring writers of complimentary verses found his achievements to parallel those of Vulcan. No attempt seems to have been made by anyone to kill him at birth, though the state of prenatal and post-natal care in the sixteenth century may have made his advent perilous, and his father may be thought to have metaphorically buried him at birth under the most anonymous of English names. Taking them all together, he may be given a single protestworthy point on the basis of Lord Raglan's first six requirements.

With the seventh, John Smith's life begins to fit more securely to the heroic pattern. Though not spirited away, he was orphaned at thirteen (he said, though actually it was three years later) and tried then secretly to run away to sea, "his mind being even then set on brave adventures" (pp. 821-22). He did leave home at fifteen, apprenticed to Thomas Swendall of King's Lynn, sixty long miles away (p. 9), and at sixteen, being orphaned in truth by his father's death, he came under the guardianship of George Mersham, a distant relative of Lord Willoughby de Eresby (pp. 7, 10). Not long after (the chronology is confused), he accompanied Master Peregrin Berties, Lord Willoughby's second son, on a tour of France, and apparently after that, fought under the command of Captain John Duxbury in the Netherlands (p. 10, p. 828). These combined personae—his master, his guardian, his aristocratic young companion, and his captain—may be considered a cumulative kind of foster parent. France and Holland may not have seemed far away countries, but Hungary and Turkey—to where young John Smith would soon be off for brave adventuring—certainly were. He may therefore, with fewer stretchers, be given three points in meeting Lord Raglan's qualifications, numbers seven, eight, and nine.

After heroic adventures in far lands, at twenty-six (or was it twenty-seven?) John Smith set out for the new world, his future kingdom, satisfying qualification number ten. His victory—actual or psychological—over Powhatan (or, if this is to be argued aside, over the ravaging wild beast of starvation in Jamestown) qualifies him for Lord Raglan's number eleven. But there are leitmotifs in John Smith's tumultuous career. His victories in single combat, "to delight the ladies, who did long to see some court-like pastime" (pp. 838-40), over three (the mystic three) loud-vaunting Turks, and his bludgeoning of the Bashaw of Nalbrits in Cambia (p. 866) were actual anticipations of his later, and perhaps more symbolic—certainly more certifiable—victories.

The marriage with a princess (required by qualification number twelve), may also be symbolic in Captain Smith's relationship—in Virginia and in England—with the Princess Pocahontas, daughter of the King who ruled in the strange new world before Captain Smith and his fellows arrived. And this relationship is anticipated also by those with the other "honorable and virtuous ladies" who offered him "rescue and protection": the "beautious Lady Tragabiganza," who, said Captain Smith, "when I was a slave to the Turks did all she could to secure me," and the "charitable Lady Callamata" who in Tartary "supplied my necessities," and is duplicated later when, escaping the cruelty of pirates in a small boat at sea, he is driven ashore in France, where the "good Lady Madam Chanoyes," he said "assisted me." (pp. 276-77). Again a trio, and one which cumulatively seems certainly to allow Captain Smith another point. The total, so far, is six.

When he was finally elected President of the colony at Jamestown, Smith, as required by qualification number thirteen, became ruler of his kingdom. Then, as required by qualification number fourteen, it can be said that he ruled, if not altogether uneventfully, then with greater poise and calm and efficiency than the colony had known before he took it over. He prescribed new regulations, but later lost favor with his subjects (and perhaps the gods also) and, himself a wounded god (p. *280*), was deposed. Thus he picks up three more points, to a total of nine, doing as well as Elijah did, and close on the heels of Apollo and Siegfried.

Adding points thereafter becomes difficult. Because the circumstances surrounding his death are not known (p. *393*), he may pick up another. No evidence testifies to his death having occurred on top of a hill, though it is supposed that he spent at least part of his final year as a guest of Sir Humphrey Mildmay at his estate called Danbury Place in Essex (p. *387*), not far from the East Anglian Heights. No children are known to have succeeded him—this certainly entitles him to one more point. His body was buried in St. Sepulchre's in London, but the Great Fire of 1666 destroyed the memorial tablet which covered his tomb, so that these circumstances rule out claims for qualifications numbers twenty-one and twenty-two. But his epitaph had been recorded in John Stow's *A Survey of London* thirty-three years earlier, certifying that John Smith had

> done things
> Which to the world impossible would seem,
> But that the truth is held in more esteem (p. 489).

What is your count? Mine is nine fairly certain, with maybe

two more if I may be allowed to fractionize, admitting some reasonably far-stretched possibilities. Either way, the counting demonstrates that analytical criticism, even when constructed from the
quicksilver of myth, can be beguiling good fun, second only to the
better fun of recognizing the revelatory new myths which an adventurer's accounts of his adventures beguilingly create. More than
that, it may suggest more than fact can reveal.

VII

Small wonder then that Captain Smith's story remains so irresistably, so indelibly with us. It is not only his legend. It is legend
certified by heroic adventure the world over, since legend began.
Fact and fable nudge his recorded adventures toward the "one
shape-shifting yet marvelously constant story" of which legends
are made.²⁹ And other elements of traditional lore move in and out
of the *True Travels,* skirting close to the boundaries of ancient
fable. In preparation for his brave adventures, John Smith retires,
he does not say for how many days, to a woodland wilderness
where "by a fair brook he built a pavillion of boughs" where (Oh,
Walden Pond and locusts and wild honey!) he read Machiavelli on
war and Marcus Aurelius on courtesy, and practiced horsemanship,
tourney-bound with "lance and ring," while people all the country
round wondered at such a hermit as he (p. 823). His studies in
warfare bore fruit when, as a soldier in Hungary, and like Jove, he
flung flaming thunderbolts among the enemy, and with Olympian
serenity reported that "the lamentable noise of the miserable
slaughtered Turks was most wonderful to hear" (p. 832).

The Jonah story, so often reenacted, appears, though truncated,
in Captain Smith's autobiography. Taking ship at Marseilles,
bound for Italy with "inhumane provincials" and "a rabble of
pilgrims of various nations going to Rome," he was cursed hourly,
"not only for being a Huguenot, but his nation they swore were all
pirates, and . . . wildly railed on his dread sovereign Queen Elizabeth." Finally, "their disputations grew to that passion, that they
threw him overboard." No kindly whale appeared, "yet God
brought him to that little isle where there was no inhabitants but a

few kine and goats," where like a briefly sojourning Robinson Crusoe, he remained until the next morning when he was picked up by a passing vessel (p. 826).

Captain Smith in Europe and Asia, on the Mediterranean and the Atlantic, in Virginia and New England, survived a succession of trials, miraculous tests, and ordeals: "The ultimate adventure," explains Joseph Campbell, "when all the barriers and ogres have been overcome is commonly represented by a mystical marriage . . . of the triumphant hero-soul with the Queen Goddess of the World."[30] Little stretching is required to find Pocahontas as that mystical bride: she who is the heroine of so much subsequent story; "the mother of us all"[31]; a "mythical nature-symbol," Hart Crane called her[32]; our earth mother, who, with Captain Smith, has "gone hand in hand to immortality."[33]

Having accomplished his quest, the hero-adventurer returns with a "life-transmuting trophy," a Golden Fleece or magic chalice (John Smith's writings) or his sleeping princess (Pocahontas in England), "back into the kingdom of humanity, where the boon may redound to the renewing of the community, the nation." In traditional formula, a "hero ventures forth from the world of common day (the countryside of sixteenth-century England) into a realm of supernatural wonder (Europe and Asia) and a decisive victory is won (over three adversaries in single combat). The hero comes back from this mysterious (unbelieved by many of his contemporaries and ours) adventure with the power (the experience, the knowledge of warfare and tactics of survival in an alien land) to bestow boons on his fellow men (invitations to and fervent descriptions of the promise of the new world)."[34] His story fits to a pattern found over and again among the Greeks, the Incas, African tribes, and North American Indians as "this most common and best known myths of the world," which "also appears in our dreams," recounts "a hero's miraculous but humble birth, his rapid rise to prominence or power, his triumphant struggle with the forces of evil, his fallibility to the sin of pride (hybrus), and his fall through betrayal or a 'heroic' sacrifice which ends in death."[35]

It need not be supposed that John Smith was conscious of the parallels between his story and that of traditional heroic adventure. Otto Rank and Carl Jung and Sigmund Freud have each explained, from one vantage or another, how dream and imagination and fiction—and fact which may be even stranger than these—cluster about and boldly enter the domain of archetypal story. From John Smith to William Faulkner, ancient patterns have emerged.[36] And the outlines of heroic story discernible in the adventures of Captain John Smith help explain why those adventures continue at the head of native legend. Attempts to prove Captain Smith or what he reported untrue have been of little avail. His deeds and personality and his achievement in literature merge to a single remembrance, coalesced to legend.

Captain Smith's autobiography is as representative of the bold colonial adventurer of the seventeenth century as Benjamin Franklin's autobiography is representative of the self-reliant American of the eighteenth century or as Henry Adam's autobiography is representative of the self-suspecting retreat of that American in the nineteenth century. No more than these others does it submit utterly to the solid angularity of candor or completeness, but like them provides a constellation of experience and purpose which remains undimmed.

NOTES

1. (Charlottesville: University Press of Virginia, 1968), 36.

2. *The Worthies of England* (London: Allen & Unwin, 1952), 75-76.

3. Introduction to the *Generall Historie of Virginia, New England and the Summer Isles, By Captain John Smith, 1624* (Cleveland, n.d.), 3.

4. *The Elizabethans and America* (New York: Harper, 1959), 208.

5. Stephen Vincent Benet, *Western Star* (New York: Farrar & Rinehart, 1943), 72.

6. "Commentary (Vituperative)," *Harper's*, 244:106 (1972).

7. *A Description of New England*; this and all subsequent quotations from John Smith are taken from *Travels and Works of Captain John Smith, President of Virginia and Admiral of New England, 1580-1631*, 2 vols., edited by Edward Arber. A new edition, with biographical and critical introduction by A. G. Bradley (Edinburgh, 1910), in this instance from page 214. Hereinafter page numbers in parenthesis following a quotation will identify the place in these volumes from which the quotation is taken. The volumes are paged consecutively.

I have modernized the spelling, and sometimes the punctuation, of all quotations, it being my conviction that John Smith is important for what he said, not for an ancient "quaintness" in his ways of spelling, nor for idiosyncracies of his own or his printers in pointing. It is my hope that students of sixteenth-century or seventeenth-century writings in or about America will profit in this respect by adopting the sensible and uncondescending practice observed over many years by students of English literature who have quoted from or edited the writings of, among others, Shakespeare and Milton. A modernized edition of the writings of Captain Smith is greatly to be desired.

8. Everett Emerson, *Captain John Smith* (New York: Twayne, 1971), 91-92; see also Philip L. Barbour, "Two 'Unknown' Poems by Captain Smith," *Virginia Magazine of History and Biography*, 75: 156-57 (1967).

9. *Native American Humor* (San Francisco: Chandler Publishing Co., 1960), 7; see also Henry Adams, *Historical Essays* (New York, 1891), 53-54.

10. Bradford Smith, *Captain John Smith, His Life and Legend* (Philadelphia: Lippincott, 1953), 13.

11. Introduction to *The Generall Historie*, 12.

12. For a sensibly cautious estimate of Smith's part in preparation of the "Proceedings," see Philip L. Barbour, *The Three Worlds of Captain John Smith* (Boston: Houghton Mifflin, 1964), 300-302; see also Ben McCary, *John Smith's Map of Virginia* (Williamsburg: Virginia 350th Anniversary Celebration Corporation, 1957).

13. *O Strange New World: American Culture in the Formative Years* (New York: Viking Press, 1964), 117.

14. Dixon Wecter, *The Hero in America: A Chronicle of Hero-Worship* (Ann Arbor: University of Michigan Press, 1963), 18.

15. Bradford Smith, *Captain John Smith*, 13.

16. *The Life of Captain John Smith, the Founder of Virginia* (New York, 1846), 10-11.

17. "Captain John Smith," *North American Review*, 104:1-30 (1867).

18. *Democracy in America*, ed. Phillips Bradley (New York: Vintage Books, 1945), II, 361.

19. *Library of Southern Literature* (Atlanta, 1907-1923), XI, 4929-32.

20. "Virginians on Olympus," *Virginia Magazine of History and Biography*, 58:40-57 (1950).

21. *A History of American Literature during the Colonial Times* (New York and London, 1897), I, 30.

22. *The Literature of Colonial Virginia* (New York, 1909), 17.

23. *A History*, I, 19-20.

24. *Captain John Smith*, 305.

25. *Old Virginia and Her Neighbors* (Boston, 1897), I, 80-81; see also his *The Beginnings of New England* (Boston, 1889), 77.

26. *Captain John Smith* [5].

27. Fitzroy Richard Somerset Raglan, *The Hero* (London: Methuen & Co., 1936), 178-89.

28. I recreate John Smith's heroic life from his own writings, but have Philip L. Barbour's meticulous *The Three Worlds of Captain John Smith* by my side for guidance; information derived from it will be identified in the text by page numbers in parentheses.

29. Joseph Campbell, *The Hero with a Thousand Faces* (New York and Cleveland: World Publishing Co., 1956), 3. Smith's career, with only a little ingenuity, can be made to fit the successive stages of the heroic quest as set forth in John Alexander Allen's *Hero's Way: Contemporary Poetry in the Mythic Tradition* (Englewood Cliffs, N.J.: Prentice-Hall, 1971): The Call, The Journey (The Road of Trials), The Lady, The Father, The Return.

30. *The Hero with a Thousand Faces*, 109.

31. Philip Young, "The Mother of Us All: Pocahontas Reconsidered," *Kenyon Review*, 24: 391-515 (1962). For a survey of Pocahontas in historical criticism, fiction, poetry, and drama, see Jay B. Hubbell, "The Smith-Pocahontas Legend in Literature," *Virginia Magazine of History and Biography*, 65: 275-300 (1952), slightly expanded in *South and Southeast: Literary Essays and Reminiscences* (Durham, N.C.: Duke University Press, 1965), 175-204.

32. Brom Weber, ed., *The Letters of Hart Crane* (Berkeley and Los Angeles: University of California Press, 1965), 305.

33. Wecter, *The Hero in America*, 19.

34. Campbell, *The Hero with a Thousand Faces*, 109, 30. The parenthetical interpolations are mine.

35. Joseph L. Henderson, "Ancient Myths and Modern Man" in *Man and His Symbols*, ed. Carl G. Jung (New York: Dell Publishing Co., 1964), 110.

36. See William Gilman, "The Hero and Heroic in American Literature" in *Patterns of Commitment*, ed. Marston La France (Toronto: University of Toronto Press, 1967), Theodore L. Gross, *The Heroic Ideal in American Literature* (New York and London: Free Press, 1971), and Kay S. House, *Reality and Myth in American Literature* (Greenwich, Conn.: Fawcett Publications, 1966), none of which, however, considers Captain Smith as one among us.

SAMUEL PURCHAS:
THE INDEFATIGABLE ENCYCLOPEDIST
WHO LACKED GOOD JUDGMENT

Philip L. Barbour

To explore Samuel Purchas' writings in an article of reasonable length is like trying to investigate the Mammoth Dome in Mammoth Cave by the light of a single *ignis fatuus.* We could not see the great waterfall, but we could briefly glimpse bits of stalactitic tracery adorning the walls and know that we were contemplating immensity.

Satistics are questionable aids to comprehension, but an object lesson may be of some help to those who are unacquainted with the *Pilgrimes,*[1] Purchas' *magnum opus.* A moderately rapid and attentive reader hurrying along at the rate of one octavo page of the usual size of type would require four weeks of steady application, eight hours a day and five days a week, to read the *Pilgrimes,* and still have two hours and twenty minutes' worth yet to go on Monday morning of the fifth week. Let us therefore limit this study of Purchas' work to a brief survey of the man, and a handful of details concerning the Virginia and New England voyages.

It has long been an article of faith among historians, particularly those specializing in Elizabetho-Jacobean times, to compare Purchas with his fellow-preacher (neither of them acquired fame by the profession), Richard Hakluyt, on an effect-and-cause basis, largely to the detriment of the former. Indeed, the *Pilgrimes* is an exasperating work for what it includes as well as what it omits.

Yet, without Purchas at all it is hard to envision how modern scholars would reconstruct, among other things, the early history of Virginia.

Samuel Purchas was born in Thaxted, Essex, forty-odd miles north-northeast of London, and baptized there on November 20, 1577. Thus he was a quarter of a century younger than Richard Hakluyt. The son of a yeoman, he was educated at St. John's College, Cambridge, where he proceeded to the degree of B.D. In 1601 he was appointed curate of Purleigh, a few miles south of Maldon, Essex, where he married Jane Lease before the year was out, and where the couple acted as servants in the household of the parson. Then, on August 24, 1604, Purchas was instituted to the vicarage of Eastwood, ten miles to the south.[2]

Eastwood bordered on Leigh-on-Sea, an active seaport, and it was obviously there that Purchas began to assemble sailors' yarns for a book. His literary inspiration clearly was Hakluyt's *The Principal Navigations, Voiages, Traffiques and Discoueries of the English Nation, . . .*[3] which had been published in London in three folio volumes during the years from 1598 to 1600. Purchas' original aim, however, was different from Hakluyt's. Without the vision of empire that animated Hakluyt, Purchas labored piously in a religious and proto-ethnological vein, presenting to a somewhat surprised public in 1613, a thick folio called *Purchas His Pilgrimage, or Relations of the World and the Religions Observed in All Ages and Places Discovered from the Creation unto this Present.*[4]

Tactfully, or perhaps ambitiously, dedicated to George Abbot, Archbishop of Canterbury, whose own *A Briefe Description of the Whole Worlde*[5] had appeared in its third edition in 1608, Purchas' vastly larger gazetteer, as it has been described,[6] quickly became an educational bestseller. Even more important, it led to an appointment as chaplain to His Grace of Canterbury, and his induction in 1614 as rector of St. Martin's, Ludgate, by patronage of the Bishop of London, George King.

So popular was the *Pilgrimage* that Purchas published an expanded edition the following year, and a third, still more elaborate, in 1617.[7] Richard Hakluyt had died in 1616 without evincing any urge to publish a new edition of the *Principal Navigations* despite the mass of documents which had been accumulating since

1600. Other hands would now have to prepare it. Purchas, whose egoism seems to have been out of proportion to his abilities, seized Hakluyt's torch. Where Hakluyt's hand had failed, Purchas' fingers would carry on. It would be relatively simple. Hakluyt had left box upon box of manuscript and printed material. Since his heirs set little store by such things, all soon passed over to the rector of St. Martin's, Ludgate—at an unknown price.[8]

At this point, the mere abundance of grist for his mill seems to have lured Purchas into devising "a grandiose work, which should embrace all the chief voyages that had ever been made and should supersede not only Hakluyt but all other writers on the subject."[9] He would entitle it *Hakluytus Posthumus, or Purchas His Pilgrimes, Contayning a History of the World, in Sea voyages, & lande-Trauells, by Englishmen & others...* , with the self-centered inclusion of his surname that was to be characteristic of his printed works. And he set to work with a will, only to find that the *Pilgrimes* proved more than a match for his ingenuity. In his own words, he could not establish any firm plan,

> first because I had such a confused Chaos of written and printed Bookes, which could not easily be ordered: partly because this Method by way of voyages often repeats the same countries . . . and partly because in this long space of imprinting (from August 1621.) many things have come to my hand by diligent enquiry, which were not enrolled, nor in [my] possession to be mustered in their due file and ranks. . .[10]

In spite of all, however, the huge work was completed, and Purchas was able to present a copy of his four volumes to the East India Company on January 10, 1625[11] (a definite date for completion, although that was the year 1624 according to the English legal calendar). There were a few minor problems on the way, including separate pagination for Book I of Volume I because it was printed after the bulk of the work, but these were passed over or corrected. The East India Company gratified Purchas with a gift of £100 (£40 a year was a reasonable specialist's fee), and King James intimated that he should add a new edition of the *Pilgrimage* to the whole, as Volume V.[12] This was accomplished by reprinting the edition of 1617, but the effort seems to have been too great for the author. On September 30 of that year the parson of

St. Martin's, Ludgate, was laid to rest, presumably in that same church.[13] He was not yet forty-nine.

Purchas' *Pilgrimes* is in all truth an exasperating book, as much for the superfluities it includes as for the unique source material known to have been thrown away, not to mention its size. The fault lay with the unrealistic all-inclusiveness of the plan, for which "The World and the Religions" was not a tenable theme, as Hakluyt's "empire" had been. No longer a gazetteer like the *Pilgrimage,* the *Pilgrimes* might even have slipped into mere journalistic excess but for the example set by Hakluyt and Purchas' own innate fear of being "tedious"—a word often introduced to excuse an abrupt abridgement of a source. Lacking a sound editorial sense, or a bent for thematic anthologizing, Purchas reprints books already on the market only to suppress "intriguing" manuscripts with a bare hint of what they contained; he lops off the beginning or the end of many an invaluable account because somebody else has written on the same subject, and he inserts editorial comments where they are truly superfluous; in some instances he discards dates and other logbook details from vital accounts, and in others perpetuates original blunders without questioning their accuracy, and so on; and through all this he gives no clue to what prompts his course of action.

To illustrate at least some of these points, then, out of the vast mass of the *Pilgrimage* in its three ever-expanding editions and the independent though similar *Pilgrimes,* the passages dealing with Virginia and New England have been chosen for analysis. While Purchas fitted these in with Hakluyt's pattern (particularly in the *Pilgrimes*), they have the advantage of showing us Purchas' mixture of manuscript and printed material obtained on his own, with a minimum of indebtedness to his predecessor. In addition, they show the development of Purchas' handling of such material from 1613 to 1625.

I. First edition: The *Pilgrimage* of 1613.

Chapter V, "Of Virginia," pp. 631-36.

After an unctuous editorial in praise of Virginia and a brief summary of Ralegh's Roanoke Colony and later voyages to New England, largely taken from Hakluyt, Purchas introduces the Jamestown voyages:

> After this followed the plantation by the present Aduenturers, in the yeare one thousand six hundred and six, at which time a hundreth of our men were left there for the foundation of a *New Britanian* Common-wealth: and the East and West parts of England ioyned in one purpose of a two-fold plantation, in the North and South parts of Virginia.[14]

Here a marginal note states that this information came from *"Relat. Cap. Smith. M.S. & W.S. M.S."* Since the *Pilgrimage* was dedicated on November 5, 1612, it would appear that Smith's *Map of Virginia,* as prepared for publication by the Rev. William Symonds ["W.S."], was still in manuscript at that time, and that Purchas possessed, or had seen, a copy of it. In any case, he continued:

> True it is, that some emulations did euen then becloude that morning Starre, and some disastrous Comets did arise in that Hemisphære, in place of better Starres, shining rather with combustion in ciuill broiles, and bralls, then comfortable illumination and influence to the common good: these disorders were attended with idlenesse of the most, sicknesse of many, and some dyed. A cleare skie did afterwards appeare in their agreement on the choise of Captaine *Smith* for their President, who hauing before fallen into the hands of the Virginians, had beene presented Prisoner to *Powhatan,* where he tooke aduantage by that disaduantage, to acquaint himselfe with the State and condition of the Countrie and inhabitants.[15]

This is "pure Purchas," based on Smith. It is next followed by an account of the colony summarized from Robert Johnson's *New Life of Virginia,*[16] which had been entered for publication as recently as May 1, 1612, and which contains not one word about Captain John Smith. Purchas somewhat capriciously then returns to *"Man Script. W.S. ex lit[teris] multorum,"* which refers to the second part of Smith's *Map* called the *Proceedings,*[17] which is attributed to "a number of diligent observers," presumably by "W.S." All in all, however, Purchas relies mostly on Johnson's *New Life* and Lord De La Warr's *Relation*[18] until he gets around to "the description of the Countrie," concerning which

Captaine *John Smith,* partly by word of mouth, partly by his Mappe thereof in print, and more fully by a Manuscript which hee courteously communicated to mee, hath acquainted me with that whereof himselfe with great perill and paine, had beene the discouerer, being in his dis- coueries taken Prisoner, and escaping their furie, yea receiuing much honour and admiration amongst them, by reason of his discourses to them of the motion of the Sunne, of the parts of the Worlde, of the Sea, &c. which was occasioned by a Dyall then found about him. They carryed him prisoner to *Powhatan,* and there beganne the English ac- quaintance with that Sauage Emperour.[19]

For one folio page Purchas' summary then agrees well with Smith's *Map* as it was printed, but this part of the description he closes abruptly:

To speake of *Powtuxunt, Bolus,* and other Ruiers . . .: likewise, of diuers places . . .: or to mention the numbers which euery people can make, would exceede our scope, and the Readers patience. Captaine *Smiths* Mappe may somewhat satisfie the desirous, and his booke when it shall be printed, further. This Captaine saith, that hee hath beene in many places of Asia and Europe, in some of Africa and America, but of all holds Virginia . . . the fittest place for an earthly Paradise.[20]

"Asia and Europe . . . Africa . . . "—here is one of the earliest ref- erences to Smith's youth as it was to be described in the *True Travels.* Then, after a brief bit based on Hakluyt and Theodore de Bry, Purchas returns to Smith for a few details, and closes Chapter V with a little more from Hakluyt.[21]

Chapter VI, "Of the Religion and Rites of the Virginians," pp. 636-41.

This, without regard to chronological sequence, brings Purchas back to his general subject, "the Worlde and the Religions." Al- though the first third of the chapter is based on Hakluyt and de Bry, the remainder comes, often literally, from Smith. An incon- spicuous marginal note announcing the change of Purchas' source all but hides a significant hint: "Newes from Virginia and a *M.S.* of Cap. *Smith.* "[22]

"Newes from Virginia" is the runninghead on every page of Smith's *True Relation.*[23] Printed in 1608 while Smith was in Virginia, this small book was first attributed to Thomas Watson, Gent., and then to "a Gentleman of the said Collony." Only with a third title page did John Smith get the credit due him as author. This confusion about who wrote the book takes on added importance when it is known that a copy now in the British Museum (shelfmark C.33.c.5), which gives Watson as the author, contains a number of marginal notes in an early seventeenth-century hand which bears a remarkable resemblance to that of Samuel Purchas.[24] If Purchas did write these notes he would have thought that the book was Watson's, and therefore would logically have cited "Newes from Virginia" as his source, along with "a *M.S.* of Cap. *Smith.*"

Whatever the facts, Purchas was reasonably faithful to the *True Relation* in his quotes. One somewhat humorous exception may be noted: Smith wrote that in a religious ceremony the priests counted the little sticks they placed between grains of corn "as an old woman her Pater noster." Purchas, a pious Anglican pastor, changed this to read, "as the Papists their Orisons by Beades." For him, the "papists" were also "savages."[25]

II. Second edition: The *Pilgrimage* of 1614.

Chapter V, "Of Virginia," pp. 754 [misprinted 748] -762.

After reprinting the high-flown introduction of 1613 and the bit about the New England voyage of Bartholomew Gosnold and his cousin-by-marriage Bartholomew Gilbert, Purchas here adds considerable new material on that general region, including hair-raising stories of cannibals with teeth three inches long, along with one of the first descriptions of snowshoes—a typical mixture of tall tales and hard facts. These notes seem to have come from material assembled by Hakluyt after 1600, but we cannot know. "In winter," Purchas writes, the Indians "are poore and weake, and do not then company with their wiues, but in summer when they are fat & lusty." Then, without so much transition as a new paragraph, he continues:

> But your eyes[,] wearied with this Northerne view, which in that winter [1607-1608] communicated with vs in extremity of cold, looke

now for greater hopes in the Southerne Plantation, as the right arme of
this Virginian body, with greater costs and numbers furnished from
hence.[26]

And straight off he begins borrowing from the *Proceedings*,
with a marginal reference to "*Richard Pots*, Tho. Studley, &c."
The mention of Pots as well as Studley (to whom the passage is
attributed in the *Proceedings*) lends support to the surmise that
Potts was one of the leading co-authors of the book, and perhaps
co-compiler with Smith. The main point of interest, however, lies
in the text and marginal note on p. 760 concerning the Jamestown
voyage, that

> Captain *Iohn Smith*, partly by word of mouth, partly by his map there-
> of in print, & more fully by a Manuscript, which he courteously com-
> municated to me, hath acquainted me with that whereof himselfe with
> perill and paine, had beene the discouerer, being in his discoueries
> taken Prisoner, as is before said, and escaping their furie. . . .[27]

Though this passage reprints the 1613 version, with minor
alterations, Purchas, rather than alter the reference to Smith's
"Manuscript," merely inserted a marginal note reading, "Since
printed at Oxford." Yet Purchas' careless way of revising his text
is in itself of value to the historian. We have learned here that
Smith's engraved map (categorically attributed by Purchas to
Smith, *pace* Alexander Brown and other hard-bitten skeptics) was
in print before the text of the book, *A Map of Virginia*, and that
the book itself was published too late in 1612 to be available to
Purchas before November 5.

Immediately below, Purchas repeats Smith's error in the geographical situation of Virginia ("between 34. and 44. degrees"—
lege 45), thereby showing that the slip was in the manuscript and
not due to the typesetter. A little farther on Purchas adds a marginal note from the correspondence of Alexander Whitaker, who
arrived a year and a half after Smith's departure, and who disagreed with Smith about Virginia's climate.[28] Well, Smith's whole
approach to Virginia was realistic. Others were collateral ancestors
of Pippa, who passed, singing, "All's right with the World!"[29]

The following page contains an additional communication from

Whitaker, and below that a manuscript note form Smith, in itself of little importance, which shows that Smith made notes which were not used in his *Map*.[30]Finally, at the end of the chapter, there is a first communication from George Percy, brother of the earl of Northumberland, who was one of the original colonists and who returned to England late in July, 1612. The brief passage is from Percy's "Discourse," more extensively quoted in the *Pilgrimes* (see below).[31]

Chapter VI, "Of the Religion and Rites of the Virginians," pp. 762-69.

This chapter is but little expanded from 1613. The marginal note about the "Newes from Virginia" and Smith's manuscript remains untouched, probably out of sheer neglect.[32] But a few additions were made, beginning on p. 766. William White, listed among the original colonists as a laborer, had apparently returned to England, perhaps on the same ship with Percy (according to whom White had lived with the Indians), and Purchas seized on him promptly for whatever information might be available. The result is a fairly long section on a ceremony White had witnessed at "Rapahannock" (properly, "Quiyoughcohannock," across the river from Jamestown), followed by a mock sacrifice of adolescents as an initiation into manhood. This account Purchas nominally attributes to Smith, but internal evidence suggests that Smith got it from White in the first place. In any event, Purchas gives White credit for the rest of the account in the next paragraph, while gratuitously inserting a bit of misinformation supplied by himself.[33]

On p. 767, after a long passage from Smith, Purchas adds further comments by White, followed by brief extracts both from the Virginia Company's apologia, *A True Declaration of the Estate of the Colonie in Virginia*,[34] and from further letters from Whitaker. The next page has descriptive passages from George Percy and Edward Maria Wingfield, the first president of the council at Jamestown whose social status proved no guaranty of any executive ability. Wingfield's contribution is worth reprinting, for it illustrates Purchas' occasional value as a unique source.

Master Wingfield saith, [the Virginians] would be of good complexion, if they would leaue painting (which they vse on their face and shoulders). He neuer saw any of them grosse, or bald: they would haue beards, but that they plucke away from haires: they haue one wife, many loues, and are also Sodomites.

Their elder women are Cookes, Barbers, and for seruice, the yonger for daliance. The women hang their children at their backes, in Summer naked, in Winter vnder a Deere-skin. They are of modest behauior. They seldom or neuer brall: in entertaining a stranger, they spread a mat for him to sit downe, and dance before him. They weare their nailes long to flea their Deere: they put bow and arrowes into their childrens hand beforre they are six yeares old. [35]

III. Third edition: the *Pilgrimage* of 1617.

Chapter V, "Of Virginia," pp. 937-48. (The 1626 *Pilgrimage*, pp. 828-38, is virtually identical.) Note that the chapters are now divided into sections, due to the increased mass of material available to Purchas.

Section I is titled "*The Preface, Sir* Walter Raleighs *Plantation, and the Northerne Colony.*" The principal addition summarizes Smith's *Description of New England,*[36] which is introduced with informality and inaccuracy: "But first let me tell you that by some lately these Northerne Parts are stiled by the Name of *New-England,* as being supposed in the same Latitude with Noua Albion on the South Sea, discouered by Sir *Francis Drake,* hauing New France on the North, and the Southerne Plantation of Virginia on the South. . . ."[37]

Section II, "*Of the Southerne Plantation and Colonies; and many causes alledged of the ill successe thereof at the first,*" is little more than a reprint of the 1614 material; the same applies to Section III, "*Of the Soyle, People, Beasts, Commodities and other Obseruations of Virginia.*"

Section IV, "*Of the present estate of Virginia, and the English there residing,*" is composed of completely new material, abstracted from John Rolfe's "True Relation of the state of Virginia. . . ."[38] with the pious interjection of a few editorial comments. Purchas' pastorly piety was as profound in its persistence as it was superficial in its scope—to ape Purchas' own alliterative syndrome.

Chapter VI, "Of the Religion and Rites of the Virginians," pp. 948-57. (The 1626 *Pilgrimage,* pp. 838-45, is again virtually identical.)

Outside a major addition in Section III, mentioned below, there are only a few points that should be made. For some reason Purchas continued, at the beginning of Section II, to refer to the "Newes from Virginia, and a *M.S.* of Captaine *Smith,*" and repeated it in the *Pilgrimage* of 1626.[39] Then, in the passage about the "sacrifice of Children," he takes advantage of a comment by John Rolfe to digress. "Yea," he writes, "the Virginians themselues, by false reports might delude our Men" especially in regard to their "diuellish mysteries."[40]

The most interesting passage in the chapter is inserted in Section III. Here we have, remarkably, a report of Purchas' personal interview with an Indian from Virginia, Tomocomo, Powhatan's son-in-law and "councillor." With uncharacteristic modesty, Purchas neither elaborated on this in his *Pilgrimes* in 1625, nor even gave it more than a passing marginal note, though one passage in the *Pilgrimes* is quite obscure without reference to the *Pilgrimage* (1617 and 1626). Tomocomo, it reads, was

> but a blasphemer of what he knew not, and preferring his God to ours, because he [their God] taught them (by his owne so appearing) to wear their Devill-lock at the left ear; he acquainted mee with the manner of that his appearance.[41]

In the *Pilgrimage* Tomocomo's God, "Okeeus," appeared

> in forme of a personable Virginian, with a long blacke locke on the left side, hanging downe neere to the foot. This is the cause why the Virginians weare these sinister lockes: which some thinke (I haue heard Sir *Thomas Dale* and Master *Rolph* of that opinion) was first by our Men in the first Plantation, little aboue thirty yeeres since, borrowed from these Sauages: (a faire vnlouely generation of the Louelocke, Christians imitating Sauages, and they the Deuill). . . .[42]

Some lines below, Purchas seems to have taken off on his own again, and by his misunderstanding brought about a mistake in Smith's reprint of his own original. In the *Map,* Smith had told about the "sacrifices of children." Purchas had retold the story, with addition, also already referred to. Now, in relating his personal interview with Tomocomo, Purchas bethinks himself once more of such a sin as the sacrifice of children described in Smith's *Map*: "Fifteene of the properest youngest boyes . . . they painted white. . . ."[43]

But apparently Smith recounted the ceremony to Purchas in person, and in so doing used the northern dialect word "blake" for white—a word that meant "dead white." Either Purchas misheard the word or his typesetter misprinted it, and "blake" became "black": "They use to make Blacke Boyes once in fourteene or fifteene yeeres generally [more confusion, for "of fourteene or fifteene yeeres"!], for all the Country. . . ."[44]

Though Purchas' blunder is only too obvious, Smith took the "correction" to heart, and in his *Generall Historie* we read again, "Fifteene of the properest young boyes . . . they painted *white*"; the formal explanation is found in the margin, "Their solemn Sacrifices of children, which they call *Black-boyes*"[45] (author's italics in both quotes). But Purchas had the last word after all. In the *Pilgrimes* Smith's marginal note is "transmogrified" into, "Their solemne making of black-berries."[46]

IV: The Magnum Opus—The *Pilgrimes* of 1625

(with engraved title page, some copies dated 1624, in four folio volumes)[47]

It has been estimated that two-fifths of the entire work were taken from Hakluyt and his *Nachlass*.[48] The part of Volume IV chosen for comment (the Ninth Book and the first part of the Tenth) amounts to five percent of the whole. This is both manageable as to size, and typical as to Purchas' handling of the material, though Purchas has drawn upon Hakluyt very little.

Briefly and broadly summarized, of the twenty chapters of the Ninth Book, twelve are based on or quoted from printed books which can be consulted today, seven apparently are from lost manuscripts, and one is an exhortation prepared by Purchas himself. Of the Tenth Book, two-thirds of the first part come from printed books, two folio pages only are from "amongst M[aster] Hakluyt's papers," and the remainder from manuscript material collected by Purchas personally, including a few short bits that may have had their origin in printed material.

To look into the matter in greater detail: Purchas had already stated in Chapter XIII of the Eighth Book that he would not print the entire original charter of April 10, 1606, because of later revisions and because he was more interested in things done "there" than "here [in London]." But he also would not print the "Articles and instruction two days after dated, signed and sealed," presumably for the same reason.[49]

This is Purchas' first sin of omission in the Ninth Book. No copy of any articles or instructions dated April 12, 1606, is known to exist, although "Instructions" dated November 20 have survived, in abridged or much later copies. As for the original charter, the official copy is to be consulted in the Public Record Office to this day.[50] Parenthetically it can be added that although Purchas' brief extract contains the correct latitudinal limits of the projected colonies, neither he nor John Smith was overcareful in citing them.

The first manuscript narrative in Book IX is a "Discourse" written by George Percy that contains much interesting information supplementary to Smith's (and, later, William Strachey's). At the same time it bears evidence of Purchas' habit of slashing rather than editing. The very second paragraph, for example, mentions a "blazing star" on February 12, 1607, followed by a landfall at Martinique on "the three and twentieth day," which must refer to March. Also, a marginal note states, *The next day Cap. Smith was suspected for a supposed Mutinie, though never no such matter.*[51] On the basis of other sources we may conjecture that "the next day" refers to the fleet's call at Great Canary Island, but we still do not know when *that* was. Several later passages hint at more arbitary cutting, but the worst of all is at the end of the "Discourse," where another marginal note tells us, *The rest is omitted, being more fully set downe in Cap. Smiths Relations.*[52]

Purchas is generally kinder to Smith than to many of his other sources, sometimes even exhibiting judicious editing. For example, in Chapter III, taken from Smith's *Map of Virginia,* he omits the Indian vocabulary prefixed to the book, while in Chapter XIII of the Eighth Book, containing James Rosier's account of George Waymouth's New England voyage of 1605, he adds an Indian vocabulary which is missing in the printed book.[53] We are grateful.

Purchas' handling of William Strachey's "True Reportory" also seems fair, but in the case of his extracts from Samuel Argall it is impossible to judge for lack of evidence.[54] Nevertheless, it is unfortunate that there is so little from Argall. He evidently was a keen observer, and his pithy style is a relief from the exuberant verbosity of his confreres. There is also regrettably little from John Rolfe, Alexander Whitaker, Thomas Dermer, George Sandys, and others—some of them barely mentioned. This, however, may not in every case be Purchas' fault. In any event, it is a pity that many, many letters that were available to Purchas but not used found their way to a wastepaper box to make room for scores of pages extracted, often carelessly, from books readily to be had then, and generally to be found in more than one library today.

Turning briefly to Bermuda, after summarizing or extracting material from the addition to Silvester Jourdain's *Discovery of the Barmudas,*[55] Purchas printed the first two-thirds of *A Plott or Mappe of Bermudas or the summer Islands made by Richard Norwood,* which was entered in the Stationers' Register on January 19, 1621-1622, but of which no printed copy seems to survive. The John Carter Library, however, has a contemporary manuscript entitled "Insularum de la Bermuda Detectio," which is unquestionably the same work, thus making possible a comparison of texts. With its aid, it can be clearly stated that, though John Smith also drew on Norwood in his *Generall Historie,* Book V, Purchas made a more accurate copy.[56]

Nevertheless Purchas, ever true to his habits, cut off the last third of Norwood's work with, "But we will give you a larger Historie of the Creatures from Captaine Smith, in the next Chapter."[57] But here Smith himself had to draw (not for the first time) on Nathaniel Butler's "Historie of the Bermudaes," a manuscript which, in Butler's hand, constitutes Sloan MS 750 in the British Museum today. Lovers of quaint stories of treasure hunts may enjoy in it the tale of "a boat with a choyce gang" who risked their lives "upon a golden errand," to find only "some smale aspersions of [Spanish] dollars," worth about £20.[58]

Book IX ends with quotations from an anoymous letter of mild complaint from Virginia,[59] an account of the French in Maine and Nova Scotia,[60] and Purchas' own discourse, called "Virginia's Verger."[61] This godly tract, of some fifteen thousand words in defense of Virginia, is Purchas at his most Purchasian—bombastic, pietistic, wordy and euphuistic.

Book X again relies heavily on John Smith's works and other printed sources, but two folio pages came from Hakluyt's collections,[62] as already mentioned, and the remainder draws on manuscript material collected by Purchas himself. It seems to be the work of a tired or bored man.

Yet Purchas was able to pull himself together for a theatrical climax. He bethought himself of more glorious days, peopled by "our English Debora, Queene Elizabeth," Sir Francis Drake, the ill-fated Earl of Essex, Sir Walter Ralegh, and other heroes of the Elizabethan heyday. Introduced by seven lines of poetry such as only he could write, Purchas closed his mammoth *Pilgrimes* with the manuscript "Relation" of the Azores expedition of 1597, written in 1607 by Sir Arthur Gorges for Prince Henry. Then, at last, came the "Conclusion of the Worke," a valedictory in praise of England, Virginia, and King James.

"Amen, O Amen."[63]

NOTES

1. Samuel Purchas, *Hakluytus Posthumus, or Purchas His Pilgrimes,* 4 vols., London, William Stansby for Henry Fetherstone, 1625 (in some copies, 1624; rpt. 20 vols., Glasgow, James MacLehose and Sons, Ltd., 1905-1907). All footnote references are to this edition, hereafter referred to as *Pilgrimes; STC* 20509 (*STC* here and hereafter refers to *A Short-title Catalogue of Books Printed in England, Scotland, & Ireland . . . 1475-1640,* compiled by A.W. Pollard & G.R. Redgrave, London, The Bibliographical Soceity, 1926, photogr. rpt., 1969; rev. ed. in preparation).

2. See *Pilgrimes,* I, xxi-xxvii; for further biographical notices, see Bolton Corney, *Curiosities of Literature Illustrated* (2d ed., London, 1838), 93-111, which mentions earlier summaries of Purchas' life; and four recent studies: George Bruner Parks, *Richard Hakluyt and the English Voyages* (New York: American Geographical Society, 1928; 2d ed., F. Ungar Publishing Co., 1961); Edward Lynam, *Richard Hakluyt & His Successors* (Hakluyt Society, 2d ser., XCIII [1946]); Loren E. Pennington, "*Hakluytus Posthumus,* Samuel

Purchas and the Promotion of English Overseas Expansion" (*Emporia State Research Studies*, 14, no. 3, 1966); and C.R. Steele, "From Hakluyt to Purchas," in D. B. Quinn, ed., *The Hakluyt Handbook* (Hakluyt Society, 2d ser., CXLIV-CXLV [1974]), I, 74-96. Note that the name *Purchas* was spelled more phonetically as Purkas, Purkis, etc., by his contemporaries, and was derived from Old French *purchas*, "pursuit," used as a name for couriers. There seems to be no basis for the common modern pronounciation as a homophone of "purchase, buy." Purchas' motto, as stated on the title page of the *Pilgrimes*, was: "ADVena sVM ego et peregrInVs In terrIs sICVt patres," with reference to *Psalms* 39:12, and *Hebrews* 11:13: "I am a stranger and a pilgrim in the world as were my forefathers." The capitals, rearranged, give the year, "A[nno] MDCVVVIIII [MDCXXIV]." despite the date "1625" which appears on most surviving copies. Some, however, are dated 1624.

3. Richard Hakluyt, title as stated, 3 vols., London, George Bishop, Ralph Newberie, and Robert Barker, 1598-1600; *STC* 12636.

4. Samuel Purchas, title as stated, London, William Stansby for Henry Fetherstone, 1613; *STC* 20505; hereafter referred to as *Pilgrimage*, with date of edition in parentheses.

5. George Abbot, title as stated, 3d ed., London, [T. Judson] for J. Browne, 1608; ; *STC* 27.

6. Edward Lynam, ed., *Richard Hakluyt & His Successors* (see n. 2, above), 51; hereafter referred to as Lynam, *Hakluyt*.

7. Subsequent edition, same title, years as indicated, *STC* 20506, 20507 (and for 1626, 20508).

8. Lynam, *Hakluyt*, 53.

9. *Ibid.*, 55.

10. *Pilgrimes*, I, xliv-xlv.

11. Lynam, *Hakluyt*, 59-60.

12. *Ibid.*, 60.

13. *Ibid.*, 61.

14. *Pilgrimage* (1613), 632.

15. *Ibid.*

16. Robert Johnson, *The New Life of Virginia: being the second part of Nova Britannnia* (London, Felix Kyngston for William Welby, 1612); *STC* 14700.

17. John Smith, *A Map of Virginia . . . Whereunto Is Annexed the Proceedings of Those Colonies . . .*, two parts (Oxford, Joseph Barnes, 1612); *STC* 22791.

18. Thomas West, Baron De La Warr[e], *The Relation of the Right Honourable the Lord De-La-Warre* (London, William Hall for William Welby: 1611); *STC* 25266.

19. *Pilgrimage* (1613), 634.

20. *Ibid.*, 635.

21. Ibid., 636.

22. Ibid., 638.

23. John Smith, *A True Relation of Such Occurrences As Hath Hapned in Virginia . . .* (London, John Tappe to be sold by William Welby, 1608); *STC* 22795. The reference could not be to R[ichard] Rich's *Newes from Virginia* (London, Edw. Allde to be sold by John Wright, 1610); *STC* 21005.

24. For the various issues of the title page, see Joseph Sabin [et al.], *A Dictionary of Books Relating to America*, 29 vols. (New York, 1868-1936), XX, 254-55. For a reprint of the British Museum copy in question, with notes, see Philip L. Barbour, ed., *The Jamestown Voyages Under the First Charter, 1606-1609*, Hakluyt Society, 2nd ser., CXXXVI-CXXXVII (1969), I, 165-208, with further elaboration in the forthcoming Barbour edition of John Smith's *Complete Works*.

25. *True Relation*, sig. C3^r, and *Pilgrimage* (1613), 638.

26. *Pilgrimage* (1614), 756.

27. Ibid., 760.

28. Ibid.

29. Robert Browning, "Pippa Passes," Part I.

30. *Pilgrimage* (1614), 761.

31. Ibid., 762.

32. Ibid., 764.

33. Ibid., 766. For notes on the accounts by Percy, Smith, and White, see Barbour, *Jamestown Voyages*, I. 145-46 and 147-50.

34. "Published by aduice and direction of the Councell of Virginia," (London, printed for William Barret, 1610); *STC* 24833. It was entered for publication November 8, 1610, "under the hands of Sir Thomas Smithe [treasurer of the Virginia Company], Sir Maurice Barkley [member of the Council], Sir George Coppin [the same], and Master Richard Martin [lawyer for the Company], and the Wardens" (Edward Arber, ed., *A Transcript of the Registers of the Company of Stationers of London, 1554-1640 A.D.*, vol. III, privately printed [London, 1876], 448.)

35. *Pilgrimage* (1614), 768.

36. John Smith, *A Description of New England: . . .* (London, Humfrey Lownes for Robert Clerke, 1616); *STC* 22788.

37. *Pilgrimage* (1617), 939; (1626), 830.

38. This survives in three known manuscript copies. The latest and most convenient edition is that published as: John Rolfe, *A True Relation of the State of Virginia Lefte by Sir Thomas Dale Knight in May Last 1616* (Charlottesville: University Press of Virginia, 1971).

39. *Pilgrimage* (1617), 950; (1626), 839.

40. Ibid., 952 and 841, respectively.

41. *Pilgrimes*, XIX, 118.

42. *Pilgrimage* (1617), 954; (1626), 843.

43. Smith, *Map* (first part), 32.

44. *Pilgrimage* (1617), 955; (1626), 843.

45. John Smith, *The Generall Historie of Virginia, New-England, and the Summer Isles: . . .* (London, John Dawson and John Haviland, 1624), 36.

46. *Pilgrimes*, XVIII, 451.

47. See n. 1.

48. George Bruner Parks, *Richard Hakluyt and the English Voyages* (New York: American Geographical Society, 1928, 1930; rpt., 1961), 227.

49. *Pilgrimes*, XVIII, 359-60.

50. See Barbour, *Jamestown Voyages*, I, 24, and 34n.

51. *Pilgrimes*, XVIII, 404.

52. Ibid., 419.

53. At least in the copies that have come to the author's attention.

54. *Pilgrimes*, XIX, 5-67. The rest of Purchas' Section IIII [sic] is from another source. See the general index, Vol. XX, for references to Argall.

55. See *Pilgrimes*, XIX, 171-206, for Purchas' account, in which he specifies that Smith borrowed from Captain Nathaniel Butler, a statement overlooked by General Sir J. Henry Lefroy when he edited Butler's "The Historye of the Bermudaes" (Hakluyt Society, 1st ser., LXV [1882], i-iii). Silvester Jourdain's *A Plaine Description of the Barmudas now called Sommer Ilands* ... (London, William Stansby for William Welby, 1613) was an expanded second edition of his A Discovery of the Barmudas ... (London, John Windet, sold by Roger Barnes, 1610); *STC* 14817 and 14816 respectively.

56. Richard Norwood, "Insularum de la Bermuda Detectio," in *John Pory's Lost Description of Plymouth* ... , ed. Champlin Burrage (Boston: Houghton Mifflin, 1918).

57. *Pilgrimes*, XIX, 192.

58. Ibid., 199, and Lefroy, *Historye of the Bermudaes*, 67-68.

59. *Pilgrimes*, XIX, 207-11.

60. Ibid., 211-17.

61. Ibid., 218-67. There is a manuscript copy (holographic?) of this at Chatsworth, among the MSS of the Duke of Devonshire. (The author inspected this a number of years ago and believes it is in Purchas' hand.)

62. Ibid., 400-405.

63. *Pilgrimes*, XX, 135.

HENRY NORWOOD AND HIS VOYAGE
TO VIRGINIA

Leota Harris Hirsch

It is puzzling that one of the most engaging narratives in all of seventeenth-century American literature still remains virtually unknown except to a coterie of scholars. Yet this narrative, Henry Norwood's *Voyage to Virginia*, is a fast-paced adventure story that can capture even the twentieth-century reader with its deft blending of the real, the vivid, and the gothic, graced with a romantic touch, and spiced with wit and humor. Why does Norwood's *Voyage to Virginia* continue to be, except in isolated instances, either overlooked or underrated? Its general neglect is a disservice not to Southern partisans but to the whole of early American literature. Norwood's narrative is a glistening microcosm of a number of early writings that, when viewed freshly and when freed of preconceptions, reveal characteristics indicative of a new dimension of this early period. It is a dimension that indicates a broader, richer, and more accurate base for seventeenth-century American literature than has yet been recognized.

Before embarking on a revaluation of Henry Norwood and his writing, some major deterrents must be dealt with. The most pervasive has been aptly called the "New England monopoly."[1] Serving this monopoly is the great amount of New England material available in proportion to that from the South. This far greater quantity encompasses not only the writings themselves but sub-

53

stantial biographical and critical data. It would be erroneous to challenge the New England quantitative dominance of seventeenth-century writing. Their colonists wrote prodigiously and they often wrote compellingly. An earned dominance is not the same as an accrued monopoly. Yet this is what persists.

The onus of this monopoly is not in its regional bias but in its concomitance: the widely accepted conviction of a Puritan unity of vision in seventeenth-century America. I suggest that the theory of a Puritan unity for this era is based in large part on the fact that what is generally offered for consideration is limited to a unified body of "Puritan" material. We have been basing our judgments on those New England writings that are primarily clergy-dominated and issued from a clergy-controlled press. What of the secular voice? What did the laymen, who after all comprised the majority of the seventeenth-century settlers, think and feel? A sound starting point may be found in the predominantly secular South. There, the writers are planters, adventurers, soldiers, merchants, indentured servants, explorers, governors—along with a few clergy. In this secular-dominated environment there are characteristics quite different from the accepted "norm." It is significant that these characteristics, discussed below, are not confined to Norwood's *Voyage* and other Southern writings. They can also be found in New England writings that are now bypassed, such as John Saffin's lyrics; or they can be looked upon loosely as "non-Puritan," as, for example, Edward Taylor's opulent, sometimes erotic imagery.

When these "non-Puritan" New England writings are placed alongside Norwood's narrative and other substantial writings of the South, it readily becomes apparent that seventeenth-century American literature has more than a Puritan unity. It has such dualities as the introspective and the sensuous, the drama of the soul and the play of the world, the intense and the genial, the holy and the human. This is a view that would extend D. H. Lawrence's well-known theory of "doubleness"—or contrariety—of the American writer.[2] His study of classic American writers begins with Benjamin Franklin, but this "doubleness" appears in the seventeenth century as well. If we are not to sacrifice historical perspective, as well as a fuller perception of our literary beginnings, we need to give this dual vision of the seventeenth century more recognition.

That a theory of duality is useful in enlarging our perception of seventeenth-century literature as a whole can perhaps best be seen in capsule form in the dichotomy of Anne Bradstreet's work. Even more than Edward Taylor's poetry, which for all its rapturously sensuous outpourings is still Puritan in its theological emphasis, Anne Bradstreet's best poems are considerably at odds with the established New England tradition. Her early imitative verses express the Puritan dogma, but it is generally agreed they are inferior to her later "domestic" poems. These, however, her son considered "too intimate"[3] for Puritan New England, and they were not published until the nineteenth century. Very endearing are the verses upon her daughter's recovery from sickness, her son's departure for England, the poignant sense of loss after the burning of their house, and—perhaps most appealing—those with the beautiful aura of her abiding love for her husband. Most will agree with Samuel Morison that at its best, Anne Bradstreet's poetry is "human, simple, yet inevitable in language . . . [and] devoid of religious dogma."[4] These qualities are more akin to the human dimension pointed up in the Southern writings, yet they were penned by a woman whose father and husband were both Puritan governors of Massachusetts. That they were withheld is indicative of the strength of the clergy-dominated outlook. That they were written is indicative of the dualities existing even in the Puritan stronghold of Massachusetts.

A revaluation of seventeenth-century American literature, then, must grapple not only with the New England "monopoly" and the widely held conviction of a Puritan unity, but it must also confront a third major deterrent, particularly pertinent to Norwood's *Voyage*: the primary writings of the early South are not readily available. To find many of the writings one must have access to rare books and pamphlets and have an unflagging diligence in tracking down scattered sources. If there is to be an appreciable advance in their recognition they must be made more accessible for appraisal. As Jay Hubbell observed regarding the neglect of Southern literature, there was in the nineteenth century a considerable bias on the part of Northern critics and literary historians, but in the twentieth century the main reason for most Northern historians' inadequate treatment of the Southern writers has been the difficulty of finding materials. "It was far easier to discuss intelligently the writings of Cotton Mather and of Jonathan Edwards than it was the work of Henry Timrod or William J. Grayson." [5]

Certainly this is true of Henry Norwood's *Voyage to Virginia*. Despite being heralded as "the literary masterpiece of the second half of the century" [6] in Howard Mumford Jones's excellent treatise, the *Voyage* has not been reprinted in full for well over one hundred years. [7] Yet it outranks the omnipresent John Smith offerings for fast-paced narration lively with dangerous adventures. The *Voyage* is related with a more engaging tone because of Norwood's wit and his flair for dramatic immediacy heightened by his use of oral rhythms and graphic details. Norwood artfully draws the reader into a vivid sharing of the wonder and horrors of his experiences, while Smith seems often intent on promoting Smith as the hero of each episode. Can the strange neglect of *Voyage to Virginia* be attributed in part to the supposedly shadowy existence of its author? We are prone to interrelate the writer with his writing, especially in early American literature where it is often the stature of the man more than the writing itself that accords him literary recognition. With this proclivity we are reluctant to chance an approval of a work in which the author is perhaps not safely adjudged.

There need be no such reluctance regarding Henry Norwood, for he is not a shadowy figure. There are a number of official documents covering some forty years, after his *Voyage* and until his death, that attest to his notable and varied career. Indeed, for a period in the 1660s Norwood was impressively addressed as "Esquire of the body of His Majesty, Treasurer to the Colony of Virginia, Colonel of a regiment and Lt. Governor of the City and Garrison of Tangier and Commander in Chief of all His Majesty's Forces in Africa." [8] When the scattered fragments of information concerning Henry Norwood are assembled, there emerges a man with charismatic qualities. The verve, ability, and style that characterize the tall, broad-shouldered narrator of the *Voyage* [9] are evident throughout his life. He proved to be an able governor and

military leader. And for all his cultivation of the aristocratic cavalier adept in social graces, he was a high-spirited Hotspur, vigorous
in action. He was an adventurer keen for come-what-may opportunity, yet a man of deep loyalties and abiding friendships. Although by strange omission he is not to be found in the venerable
Dictionary of National Biography or *Dictionary of American Biography*, enough data exist to establish Henry Norwood as a not
insignificant—and certainly an engaging—personage. If added to
the existing data one allows a measure of careful conjecture, a
substantial biographical sketch can be drawn.

Henry Norwood, born in Somerset in 1615, was the second son
of Sir Henry Norwood and Elizabeth Rodney, daughter of Sir
John Rodney, whose descendant would become a distinguished
admiral. [10] When Henry was less than two years old his father died,
and it was his grandfather William Norwood who became the mentor of his boyhood. [11] That there was a close and loving relationship
for the seventeen years until his grandfather's death and that the
relationship would remain of lasting regard is indicated by the
provisions of the will made when the writer-adventurer had become a septuagenarian. The tenor of these provisions and the direction of the will's most substantial bequests point to Henry
Norwood's strong attachment to family continuity. This would
suggest, although the records are scant during his early years, that
he may have attended Oxford, following the tradition approved by
his grandfather, who had sent to Oxford Henry's father, also a
younger son. After completing his education, Henry problably
went into the royalist army since at the close of the first civil war
he had already earned the rank of major, as we learn from his
Voyage narrative.

Following what he calls the "unparallel'd butchery," the assas-
sination of Charles I, Norwood was one of the many royalists who
"did fly from their native country, as from a place infected with
the plague." Norwood is refreshingly open in stating that he chose
Virginia to shun the "hot contagion" of England, and there to
seek his fortune. He had the additional "encouragement" of
knowing the colony was governed by his "near relative" Sir William Berkeley, a second cousin on his mother's side. He was joined
in this venture, begun in September of 1649, by two other royalist

majòrs, one of particular note, Major Frances Morrison. It is in part through his friend Morrison that Norwood would maintain his lengthy and not unimportant participation in Virginia affairs. Morrison, for some twelve years, acted as deputy for the quit rents due Norwood as Treasurer of Virginia. It was this same Frances Morrison who helped to write, with something of Norwood's skill, the lively account by the royal commissioners concerning Bacon's rebellion against Governor Berkeley in 1676.

It seems quite appropriate that the best of Henry Norwood's writing and the most substantial document concerning him is *Voyage to Virginia*, for his involvement with Virginia was to be the cornerstone of all that lay ahead for Norwood. He was to have many voyages spanning three continents, and he was to return to the colonies for several residences. But it was his first voyage to Virginia in 1649-1650 which captured his imagination and drew him into more than twenty years of participation in Virginia affairs.

Norwood's Virginia narrative is radiant with literary characteristics seldom noted in the era's usual voyage tales. Particularly apparent are his wit and his artful skill in evoking the sensuous pleasures he experiences. This sensuous characteristic is first evident early in the narrative when he describes how the scarcity of drinking water brought their ship into the harbor of Fyall Island. Norwood revels in the courtesies tendered to the captain, himself, and several of his companions. He tells of his delight, after the ship's confined quarters, in strolling about the orchards on the island, in picking and eating at will the succulent peaches. This delicacy was later surpassed by a banquet replete with excellent wines and "a handsome plenty of fish and fowl, several ways cooked" (p. 146).

The highlight of the Fyall interlude is a romantic vignette of a lovely Portugese noblewoman who graces the banquet with her presence. Tall she was and finely shaped, with a very clear skin: "her eyes and hair vying for the blackness and beauty of the jet" (p. 147). Norwood lingers over her charming and modest ways, reluctant to take his leave. But once on his way he makes the darkness more mysterious by alluding to the lurking nearness of the *Pycaroes*, or land-pirates. Back on board the ship, the "caress-

ing" mood is dislodged when he views the crew's drunken debauchery. Norwood wonders wryly whether the replenishment of
their fresh water was sufficiently balanced by the effects of the
more strongly charged "water."

The worldly humor that interlaces Norwood's writing is another
characteristic seldom noted in seventeenth-century American literature. Sometimes his wit provides a fresh touch to the usual tales
of storm terrors and other dangers. When one crewman, Tom
Reasin, was striving during a severe crisis to accomplish an almost
impossible task in saving the ship, Norwood relates that to encourage him the more, all passengers promised to reward his service by
subscribing amounts of tobacco for him when God should enable
them to arrive in Virginia. "The proportions being set down, many
were the more generous, because they never thought to see the
place of payment" (p. 150). During another terror, "while the seas
were enraged" and the gale kept increasing, Norwood's eye for the
picturesque captures the astonishing appearance of hordes of por-
poises so prodigious in number they seemed to cover the whole
surface of the tumultuous sea. The oldest seamen looked upon this
"as of bad portent, predicting ill weather," upon which Norwood
quips, "in our case, who were in present possession of a storm,
they appeared too late to gain the credit of foretelling what should
come upon us in that kind" (p. 149).

Norwood's wit in this action-packed story is enhanced by a
Franklinesque charm of deftly serving up sardonic observations of
himself as well as of others. In one passage, after the catastrophe
of being abandoned on a strange shore with no provisions for his
small group, Norwood tells of coming upon a tribe of Indians who
soon began to regard him as the leader. "They did me the honour
to make all applications to me, as being of largest dimensions, and
equip'd in a camlet coat glittering with galoon lace of gold and
silver, it being generally true, that where knowledge informs not,
the habit qualifies" (p. 159). Again, with a detachment as disarm-
ing as it is personable, he tells of parting with the coat when the
Indian king wanted it as a pledge of affection. Norwood found it
amiable to "honour the compliance of this particular because he
was the first king I could call to mind that had ever shew'd any
inclinations to wear my old cloaths" (p. 167).

Equal to his flair for the light touch is his skill in vivid realism. During the ever-increasing perils of punishing gales which damaged the ship and ruined their provisions, the famine became so stark that the passengers and crew "now were glad to make" the former-ly troublesome rats their "prey to feed on; and as they were insnared and taken, a well grown rat was sold for sixteen shillings as a market rate" (p. 153). Later, on January 5, 1650, after the treachery of the captain left Norwood and eighteen other passen-gers stranded on an island, their plight became even more desper-ate. As the hazardous days stretched on, so little hope was left that when one of the women had "the envied happiness to die," Norwood advised the other two women "to endeavor their own preservation by converting her dead carcase into food." With chill-ing matter-of-factness he adds, "as they did to good effect" (p. 157).

In dramatic contrast to the lean telling of their gothic terrors is the sensuous eloquence with which Norwood tells of their rescue by the Indians. Throughout this portion of the narrative Norwood lauds the Indians' compassionate care and consideration, especially to the sick among the group. It is difficult to accept Kenneth Murdock's charge[12] of Norwood's cavalier snobbery, for there is the same sensuous largesse to his account of a poor fisherman's hospitality as there is to the kindness of an Indian queen. Consider Norwood's fervent declaration after being cared for by the fisher-man. "I can never sufficiently applaud the humanity of this In-dian, nor express the high contentment that I enjoyed in this poor man's cottage." Although it was made only of mat and reeds and the bark of trees fixed to poles, "it had a loveliness and symmetry in the air of it, so pleasing to the eye, and refreshing to the mind, that neither the splendour of the Escurial, nor the glorious appear-ance of Versailles were able to stand in competition with it" (p. 161).

With the same sensory flourish he tells of an Indian queen who, although very plain and not young, showed in all her considera-tions for the well being of "us poor starved weather-beaten crea-tures" such charity and generosity that her graces "in our opinion, transcended all other beauties in the world" (p. 162). And later, again in the presence of an Indian queen, he basks in the delight of "a lusty, rousing fire" while he dines on wild turkey boiled with oysters. With an elegant sweep very much like his portrayal of the poor fisherman's house, he declares the dish was so savoury it "would have passed for a delicacy at any great table in England, by palates more competent to make a judgment than mine" (p. 166).

This portion recounting their relations with the Indians casts further question regarding Norwood's snobbery, for here the troublesome actions and the "inordinate fears" of Major Stephens enter the narrative. As clearly as Norwood has given recognition to the courage and ability of the crew-worker Tom Reasin, he as firmly denounces the upperclass Stephens for his rancorous apprehension of the Indians' every move, and further, because "his habits on shore were scandalously vicious, his mouth always belching oaths" (p. 166). Norwood observes that such a one as Stephens would not be worthy of mention, except that he was "such a strong confirmation . . . that true innate courage does seldom reside in the heart of a quarrelling . . . hector" (p. 166).

This moral exemplum, reminiscent of Bradford's handling of the Merrymount episode in *Plymouth Plantation*, is related to another characteristic of Norwood's narrative, a strong God-consciousness. It is strange that this characteristic is not given recognition even in a recent specialized work, "Colonial Shipwreck Narratives: A Theological Study."[13] As Richard Beale Davis has pointed out, although the article purports to be a "discussion and 'complete' listing of such narratives of the seventeenth and eighteenth centuries" yet it "exclude[s] such narratives as those of Henry Norwood and William Strachey which have theological overtones and undertones."[14] Indeed, the God-consciousness in Norwood's *Voyage* is so genuine-sounding that were some of the portions of God-centered diction set forth without identification they would readily be considered "typical" of New England Puritans. Of the twenty-some passages with frequent reference to God's providence and with prayers to God the Almighty, two excerpts must here suffice. One relates to their arrival at the Jenkin Price house "thro the infinite goodness of the Almighty":

Being thus brought into safe harbour by the many miracles of divine

mercy, from all the storms and fatigues, perils and necessities to which
we had been exposed by sea and land for almost the space of four
months, I cannot . . . [say] in more proper terms, than the words that
are the burthen of that psalm of providence, *O that men would therefore praise the Lord for his goodness, and for his wondrous works unto
the children of men!* (p. 169).

And later, this passage, heightened in impact because it concludes
his narrative:

Thus (by the good providence of a gracious God, who helpeth us in our
low estate, and causeth his angels to pitch tents round about them that
trust in him) have I given as faithful an account of this signal instance
of his goodness to the miserable objects of his mercy in this voyage, as I
have been able to call to a clear rememberance (p. 170).

So ends Norwood's vibrant adventure story of his first voyage
to Virginia. It is an artful blending of the sensuous, the genial and
the starkly real, yet with a pervasive God-consciousness characteristic of the era. Delightful as a literary work, the *Voyage* narrative
also provides authoritative biographical details concerning Norwood during the year 1650. It was mid-February when he finally
arrived at Governor Berkeley's home, and for several months Norwood enjoyed a comfortable hospitality at Greensprings. Then in
May, with funds advanced by his cousin, Norwood set sail for
Holland, there to petition Charles II for the appointment of Treasurer of Virginia. Successful in his suit, he returned to Virginia,
presumably to settle, but any such plans were abandoned when
the colony came under the control of Cromwell in 1652.[15] Norwood, an ardent royalist, devoted the next years to the various
uprisings aimed at the restoration of Charles II. Twice he was
arrested but managed to escape imprisonment until 1655 when he
was taken to the Tower.[16]

Cromwell wanted Norwood and several other strong activists far
removed from England and so ordered them shipped to New Jersey as prisoners, thereby putting them beyond the reach of habeas
corpus. For some reason Norwood was singled out from the group
and was relegated to shabby treatment within the Tower. There
can be some gratitude for this neglect since it produced a most
adroit letter, one of the few by Norwood extant in entirety. Writ-

ten to John Thurloe, then Secretary of State, the letter confirms Norwood's easy way with metaphors and his ability with prose rhythm. There is a sureness of tone, also. Neither obsequious nor demanding, the petition hones throughout to a firm and fair-minded stance. Characteristic of Norwood is the vigorous thrust for action; if he is not to be given a hearing he would sooner be "throwne away" into however unhappy an exile rather than languish longer. Norwood writes:

> Although I have beene loath to rub the sore, whilst the stitches were tender, that some unjust insinuating persons have made uppon me, yet by the favour of this worthy gentleman (with whom I have the honour of an alliance) I crave leave, after 23 moneths silence once more to aver, that if it were impartially enquired into, nothing could be more apparent, then of the truth of armes being the best commoditie Virginia vends. But, Sir, because I know you have reason to prefer the oath of another to anything I can say in my owne defence, I shall not hope to endeavor to recover your charitable opinion, by contradicting a plausible evidence (how true God and mine owne conscience best know) but doe most humbly apply myself to the bounty of your goodness in furthering the inclosed, which onely speakes the sad relation of my present condition; and that my desires by this address may not seem (in respect to the conjuncture) to promote any sinister end, or malignant designe (very alienate to my temper) I shall chuse (if his highness deny my petition) much rather to be throwne away in exile into those deserts, where I never had health nor content, then to languish here under soe great prejudice and clamorous necessity as I am, and long have been too sensible of. In that case, I shall onely aske a little liberty uppon bayle to make some preparations necessary to soe long a voyage; to procure which if I obteyne the favour of your good word, I shall be obliged readily in all places and conditions to acknowledge myselfe, with very great respect, sir, your most gratefull and humble servant. . . . [17]

It might well be that Henry Norwood wrote his *Voyage to Virginia* while confined in the Tower for the long months that his petition went unanswered. Three passages in the narrative indicate that it was written a considerable time after the events took place. The first refers to the happy-ever-after state of the two women who had been in the stranded group. Norwood tells us "they lived . . . to be well married, and to bear children, and to subsist in as plentiful a condition as they could wish" (p. 161). Another reference concerns the expertise of the Indian guide Jack "who afterwards lived and died my servant" (p. 167). The third passage pays tribute to Berkeley's generous provisions, not only to his kin, but to Norwood's friends, Major Fox and, especially, Major Morrison. It was Morrison whom Berkeley placed in command of the fort, "which was profitable to him whilst it held under the king, but did advance him after to the government of the country, wherein he got a competent estate" (p. 170). It seems plausible that the enforced confinement in the Tower led to Norwood's setting down his adventure-packed experiences of that first voyage to Virginia. And perhaps it explains why this man of action produced only one literary work, despite his evident flair for writing.

This, of course, can only be conjecture. As to verifiable facts, it is on record that Norwood was finally shipped to New Jersey as a prisoner. But he was released in 1659 after a House of Commons debate questioned the legality of Cromwell's procedure.[18] Norwood was directed to post a five hundred pound bond securing the condition that he would not return to England without leave. His banishment was royally lifted when Charles II was restored to the throne. Norwood's position became a favored one with the Restoration. In April of 1661 he served at the King's coronation as Esquire of the Royal Body, after which he received a grant for life of the office of Captain of Sandown Castle.[19] More to his liking for action, he was promoted to Lieutenant Colonel and commissioned to join Lord Rutherford's regiment at Dunkirk. Shortly thereafter, Rutherford left him in charge as deputy governor, a post which he kept until November of 1662 when Dunkirk was sold to France at the King's order.[20]

Norwood's fourth residency in America was considerably more auspicious than his third, when he had been a prisoner in New Jersey. And if it did not have the dramatic adventuring of his initial voyage to Virginia, it surely found him a more distinguished personage than the young major whose second Virginia residency was cut short in 1652 when Cromwell gained control of the colony. Now, twelve years later, he was a lieutenant colonel engaged in the successful capture of New Amsterdam, promptly renamed New York. So competently did he serve his commander Colonel Richard Nicholls, both in military matters and in overseeing the colony, that Nicholls wrote the Duke of York to recommend the appointment of Norwood as governor. Nicholls seems to have recognized the same vigorous and genial qualities Norwood evinced during his earlier experiences in Virginia, for he observed that Norwood's "temper would be acceptable both to the soldiers and country." [21] Norwood's service as governor of New York missed fruition by a narrow margin of chance. Before Nicholls' letter could have reached the Duke, Norwood had already been granted a warrant to raise five hundred men for Tangier, and was soon thereafter commissioned lieutenant governor of that exotic province. The double lure of potential profit and power connected with Tangier made it a fertile ground for financial-political intrigue. That Norwood held his key position for three tumultuous years attests yet again to his innate abilities as a leader wherever he might find himself.

Norwood's various writings of this period, although only excerpts are extant, show his characteristic geniality and wit. Of a number of his letters listed in the Dartmouth papers, two in particular are calendared with some detail. One is to Colonel William Legge about his son George, whom Norwood christened "gentle George" (later created the first earl of Dartmouth):

> You please me to the purpose in the newes of gentle George. . . . Had Ned Vernon told me these tidings I should have held it apochrifa for his sake alone, but gentle George has ever watch'd Ned's countrywoman and made her gentle too; yet (raillarie apart), I thinke from my heart the woman has the better on't. God give them both joy. [22]

Another Norwood letter in the Dartmouth collection refers to his "uneasy kind of life" in Tangier but gives no details because "there is no present remedy but patience, which because it is an ingredient I leaven all my meat and drinke withall, you may hope to see me retourne laden with abundance of virtue, a meere saynt." [23]

That the convivial "saynt" still had a keen eye for the picturesque as in his Virginia narrative is evident in his spicing his official report from Tangier with the colorful account of receiving a horse, a camel, and a young lion from Ben Ali Gayland, Prince of West Barbary. [24] A review of the official reports by the men who governed Tangier before and after Norwood indicated that only the zestful Norwood ever brightened the routine documents.

It was primarily his Tangier ventures that brought Norwood

into more than a casual relationship with the indefatigable Samuel Pepys. For all of Pepys being far better known than Norwood, it is misleading to accept without qualifications, as has been done,[25] his heated charge that Norwood's Tangier reports in 1668-1669 had an "insolent and ironically prophane stile."[26] Unfortunately the report is not to be found, but with all of Norwood's extant writings giving evidence of a literate grace, Pepys' charge seemed inconsistent enough to prompt a careful scrutiny of his richly human *Diary*. By noting pertinent entries in context with the Tangier venture, it appears quite likely that Pepys' assessment of Norwood's style was based more on financial than literary considerations. For some time preceding this Tangier report, Pepys, a profit-sharing member of the Tangier Commission, had noted in his *Diary* occasions when various men promised him higher profits in the Tangier venture if they could be appointed to replace Norwood. With the very ambitious Pepys ever intent on augmenting his income (his concern for money was such that he even expressed heartfelt thanks to God at the death of one to whom he owed a yearly sum),[27] his not deriving a prospective three hundred pounds per annum could well have been cause enough for him to fault Norwood.

Supporting his view regarding the Pepys-Norwood relationship at the time of the entry in question is the tenor of Pepys' evaluation of those who handled Tangier affairs before and after Norwood governed this colony. Pepys found grievous fault with all of them, Thomas Povy, Colonel Fitzgerald, Lord Middleton, and even his patron, Lord Sandwich. Indeed, in over one hundred entries regarding Tangier management—covering a span of ten years—almost the only laudatory reference one finds that is not later retracted is to himself: "I have good reason to love myself for serving Tangier, for it is one of the best flowers in my garden."[28]

A more important consideration that brings into question the objectivity of this very human and volatile man of affairs is the decided change in his attitude to Norwood after he decided not to pay what he owed him. This matter "do stick in [his] mind," notes Pepys, and it keeps vexing and annoying him. There is a much different regard for Norwood before this non-payment. During the several years earlier, the entries concerning Norwood convey him to us as a highly personable and convivial gentleman. On October 12, 1660, Pepys attended Sir Batten's venison party "where dined withal . . . Sir Edward Brett and Major Norwood, very noble company." Another entry in 1662 notes a gathering in Coventry's Chamber at St. James that was "very merry, Major Norwood being with us." Two years later on the occasion of a Tangier dispute between Norwood and the then governor Colonel Fitzgerald, Pepys favors Norwood while denouncing Fitzgerald as "most imperious and base." [29] However, this favoring of Norwood might stem here more from Pepys' usual disapproval of whoever was in charge at Tangier. It is not until the dispute between Norwood as governor and Giles Bland as mayor of Tangiers that Pepys denounces Norwood's report for its "insolent and ironically profane stile." Despite Bland's appearance before the Tangier Commission to personally plead his case, with Norwood being represented only by his written report, the dispute was settled in Norwood's favor. Pepys berates Bland for spoiling his case by "illtelling it," adding, "If he had known how to tell a man's tale he could have mastered Norwood." [30] Obviously Norwood did know how to "tell a man's tale" in his report—no small feat for any writer. One wonders, then, to what degree a financial vexation might have prompted Pepys' sharp criticism of Norwood, particularly when during this same period the King directed it be recorded that Norwood's Tangier proceedings were "well pleasing to His Majesty." [31]

Affairs in Virginia continued to involve Norwood even during his governing of Tangier. England's principal Secretary of State, then Sir Joseph Williamson, turned to Norwood during the summer of 1667 for a briefing of the various grievances stirring within the Virginia colony. Norwood's report, characteristically lucid and compact, gives evidence of a firm knowledge of the issues and attitudes of that colony. [32] It is tempting to speculate what might have happened had Norwood been appointed successor in Virginia as Berkeley recommended in 1667. But this was not to be. Instead Norwood continued as lieutenant governor of Tangier until 1669, when he returned to England. Involvement with Virginia continued to influence Norwood's life, for it was largely the accumulated quit rents that enabled him to acquire from his cousin the ancestral Leckhampton Manor estates in Gloucestershire. But though he thereafter enjoyed the graces of a country gentleman's life, he did not lose the zest and resiliency that characterized his Virginia adventures.

The next two decades found him serving in either an elective or an appointive office, among them justice of the peace (1670), mayor of Gloucester (1672), and member of Parliament (1675-1678). All the while he did not neglect his lifetime appointment as alderman, conferred by Charles II. Even into his seventy-third year, shortly before his death, he was active in government affairs. [33] But it was his connection with Virginia that offers the most telling indication of Norwood's continuing vitality and resourcefulness. In the tangled political directives granting Virginia quit rents to Lords Arlington and Culpepper in 1672-1673, without Norwood's prior grant having been rescinded, the two lords, apparently unwilling to risk an open challenge with the personable Norwood, "found it expedient" to offer him a one-third share of the quit rents. [34] Far more striking is Norwood's masterful stand before the Lords of Trade and the Commissioners of the Treasury in 1681. Auditor General Blathwayt insisted that Norwood be held accountable for all of what he deemed "missing" rents of the preceding ten years.

It is no judgment on the right or wrong of the issue to enjoy the scene suggested by the account of the hearing. On one side was Norwood, now in his late sixties. On the other was Blathwayt, supported by the full roster of the influential Lords of Trade and the Treasury Commissioners. There is no complete transcript of the hearing, but the summarized results record that Norwood "vigorously resisted the demand and successfully maintained his position that the quit rents had been 'granted' by the Crown." [35] This provocative summary indicates that Norwood still had the verve, style, and ability which were his some thirty years before, when he embarked on the Virginia adventure that was to shape his whole future.

For all the color and even drama of his life, Norwood's last wishes were for simplicity. He asked to be buried in his ancestral burying place of Leckhampton "without pomp," near where his grandfather William Norwood was buried. It is here that we can glimpse how strong the bond with the grandfather who reared him must have been, for his will directs that the two graves be covered by a single flat stone "on which shall be engraven 'here was buried the body of William N. esq. who died 23 Sp. 1632 as also the body of Henry the youngest son of Henry N. who died [blank] 16[blank].' " Another indication of deep feeling for family tradition is that although he provided a lifetime annuity for his bachelor brother Charles, he chose to settle the Leckhampton manor and estate upon a first cousin, William Norwood, his closest relative with legal issue. It was a bequest that was to perpetuate itself into the twentieth century.[36]

The personal bequests of Henry Norwood's will are particularly revealing as a glimpse of his warmth, and something of his cultured grace. In part, too, a measure of the man can be gauged by the caliber of his friends. Norwood willed to the Honorable Andrew Newport "as a mean acknowledgment of the greatest friendship I ever knew" his "callash" (a fashionable carriage), three particular paintings and any other three pictures of his choice. The two men were friends for over three decades, both as young royalists actively involved in the various attempts to restore Charles II to the throne, and later as members of parliament together.[37] Another legatee was William Longueville, who was noted for combining two of Norwood's skills: financial acumen and literary flair. Through William's success in conveyancing, he recouped the family fortune lost by his spendthrift father, Sir Thomas Longueville, but despite his immersment in the world of commerce, he retained a lifetime delight in letters. A liberal benefactor of the poet Samuel Butler, Longueville was considered to have a discourse that was "fluent, witty and literate."[38] There is an impressive image in the bequest that Norwood's gold pocket clock be left to Sir Anthony Kirk, one of the Lords Commander of the Great Seal of England, but the remembrance given to a James Halsall is more endearing, betokening many convivial hours. To him went the "old black table given me by my Lady Mordant which mean as it is may give him occasion to remember two old friends." Norwood's friendship with the beautiful Lady Mordaunt reached back to the years when as a young cavalier, he, Andrew Newport, and others were led by Sir John Mordaunt in serving the cause of Charles II. Mordaunt, later made Baron of Reigate and then Viscount of Avalon, held key posts during the Restoration period.[39]

To his cousin Thomas Norwood, Henry Norwood left "all my books" while to Cornelius Norwood, Fellow of Oxford, he assigned ten pounds to buy such books as had been promised him. Since ten pounds was a not inconsiderable sum to spend on books in those days, the larger bequest of "all my books" would indicate that Henry Norwood had a fairly sizable library. Generous provisions were made not only within the Norwood family but also to the young people on his mother's side, among them to Henry, son of Captain Anthony Rodney, whose grandson would become a distinguished admiral; to his nephew the minister Seymour Kyrton; and to the Honorable Mrs. Jane Berkeley. It can be seen from this document, the last before he died, that Henry Norwood was a man of strong loyalties and cultured tastes, and that his preserved friendships were of a caliber that reflects well on the measure of his character.

It is true that as an ardent royalist and a convivial, worldly man he does not fit within the generally accepted New England "Puritan" mold. But it does not in any sense diminish the rightful dominance of the Puritan tradition to suggest that we do a disservice to our early literature if we continue to neglect the zestful human dimension of the primarily secular and Southern writings, represented by a narrative as delightful, witty, sensuous and adventure-filled as Henry Norwood's *Voyage to Virginia*.

NOTES

1. Howard Mumford Jones, *The Theory of American Literature* (Ithaca: Cornell University Press, 1948), 87.

2. David H. Lawrence, *Studies in Classic American Literature* (1923; rpt. New York: Viking Press, 1964).

3. Samuel Eliot Morison, *The Intellectual Life of Colonial New England* (Ithaca: Cornell University Press, 1956), 219.

4. Ibid., p. 222.

5. Jay B. Hubbell, *The South in American Literature, 1607-1900* (Durham, N.C.: Duke University Press, 1954), vii.

6. Howard Mumford Jones with the aid of Sue Bonner Walcutt, *The Literature of Virginia in the Seventeenth Century*, second ed. (Charlottesville: Virginia University Press, 1968), 96.

7. Norwood's narrative first appeared in Awnsham Churchill, *A Collec-*

tion of Voyages and Travels, vol. 6 (London, 1732), 145-170; all references to the narrative are from this edition. There were two more Churchill editions between 1744 and 1752; the *Voyage* also appeared in *An entertaining account of all the Countries of the known World*, third edition (Sherborne, 1752). The next and last publication in full was in Peter Force, *Tracts*, 3, no. 10 (Washington, 1844). It has been 130 years since *Voyage to Virginia* has been published in its entirety.

8. Public Record Office, *Calendar of State Papers, Domestic, 1667-8* (London: Eyre and Spottiswoode, 1893), 21.

9. Norwood's physical description is drawn from comments within the *Voyage* narrative, such as his being of "largest dimension"; his being able to row like a veteran seaman as his hands had been well seasoned by pumping water from the damaged ship three hours a day for many weeks; his remarkably strong constitution leading to his being selected "father" of the stranded group because of the "health and strength it had pleased God to preserve unto me above my fellows"; and his ready acceptance of greater toil and risks since "God's wonderful mercy" had made him "the strongest to labour."

10. J. H. Tyre, "Col. Henry Norwood of Leckhampton, Co. Gloucester," *Transactions of the Bristol and Gloucestershire Archeological Society*, 47 (1926), 113-14. For Admiral George Rodney, see the DNB.

11. Based on the provisions of Norwood's will, dated Sept. 4, 1689 as printed in Fairfax Harrison, "Henry Norwood," *Virginia Magazine of History and Biography*, 33 (1925), 9-10.

12. Kenneth B. Murdock, "The Colonial and Revolutionary Period," Part I in *The Literature of the American People*, ed. Arthur Hobson Quinn (New York: Appleton-Century-Crofts, 1951), 22-23.

13. Jane Donahue, "Colonial Shipwreck Narratives: A Theological Study," *Books at Brown*, 23: 101-34.

14. Richard Beale Davis, "Literature to 1800," *American Literary Scholarship: An Annual, 1969*, ed. Albert Robbins (Durham, N.C.: Duke University Press, 1971), 140.

15. Tyre, 116.

16. Ibid.

17. Letter written Dec. 18, 1656 in John Thurloe, *A Collection of the State Papers of John Thurloe*, vol. 5 (London, 1742),427-28.

18. Tyre, p. 117.

19. Ibid.

20. Public Record Office, *Calendar of State Papers, Domestic, 1661* (London: Eyre and Spottiswoode, 1860), 85, 313.

21. Letter of Col. Richard Nicholls to Duke of York, Nov. 1665 in Public Record Office, *Colonial Papers, America and West Indies, 1661-68* (London: Eyre and Spottiswoode, 1860), no. 1094.

22. Letter of Dec. 4, 1667 in *Historical Manuscripts Commission*, vol. 2, app. 5, *Dartmouth Papers* (London: Eyre and Spottiswoode, 1887), 16.

23. Ibid., Letter of Jan. 18, 1664-1665, 11-12.

24. *State Papers, Domestic, 1667-8*, 21.

25. Tyre, 120.

26. *The Diary of Samul Pepys*, ed. Henry B. Wheatley, vol. 2 (New York: Random House, 1893), entry Jan. 29, 1669.

27. Ibid., vol. 1, entry Feb. 9, 1664-1665.

28. Ibid., entry Sept. 26, 1664.

29. Ibid., entry Dec. 15, 1664.

30. Ibid., vol. 2, entry Dec. 14, 1668.

31. *State Papers, Domestic, 1667-8*, 531.

32. *Colonial Papers, America and West Indies, 1661-9*, no. 1532.

33. Tyre, 120.

34. Public Record Office, *Calendar of Treasury Books, 1681-85* (London: Hereford Times Limited, 1916), 305.

35. *Colonial Papers, America and West Indies, 1681-85* nos. 202, 232.

36. Captain J. H. Tyre, who served in Washington during World War I, was a descendant of the Gloucestershire Norwoods. See Harrison, 2.

37. "Newport, Andrew," *Dictionary of National Biography* (Oxford: 1921-22), 14, 355-56.

38. Ibid., "Longueville, William," 12, 126.

39. Ibid., "Mordaunt, John," 13, 853-55.

TO CAESAR FRIEND OR FOE?: THE BURWELL PAPERS AND BACON'S REBELLION

W. H. Ward

I

The comic spirit did not surface so often in the literature of seventeenth-century America that we should part willingly with any manifestation of it there or with any scrap of knowledge about those remarkable individuals who managed to serve it in such inhospitable circumstances. Sadly, however, in the case of the most extensive and most engaging of the accounts of Bacon's Rebellion, we have been at least partially deprived on both counts: the one surviving copy of the manuscript, called the "Burwell Papers" after its earliest recorded owner, is incomplete, and of the putative author of the waggishly pedantic chronicle, few biographical facts are discoverable. But whoever and whatever else he may have been, the shadowy Virginian was indisputably a singular fellow, an American character whose irascible wit and eccentric idiom would have put him in easy company with such New English sojourners as Thomas Morton and Nathaniel Ward.

That the author was John Cotton of Queen's Creek, York County, Virginia, is an inference drawn almost completely on the basis of evidence contained in a letter first printed in the Richmond *Enquirer* on September 12, 1804 and later included among Peter Force's *Tracts*.[1] Bearing the signature "An. Cotton," this brief, apparently contemporary report of the insurrection shares so many correspondences of phraseology with the longer history now ascribed to the Queen's Creek planter that a derivative relationship between the two items is beyond question. The former refers to a certain Colonel Page as "one that my Husband bought of Mr. Lee" (p. 10); the latter calls the same man "once My Sarvant."[2] With these identifications in mind, literary detectives, most recently Lawrence C. Wroth[3] and Jay B. Hubbell,[4] have begun their steps with the epistolary account and have followed a trail through colonial records which ultimately led them to the conclusion that the signatory to the letter was the wife of John Cotton, the figure to whom they therefore attributed the more expansive but clearly kindred version.

Amidst the general assent to the theory of Cotton's authorship, the sole voice of protest has been that of Howard Mumford Jones,[5] who strikes at the very root of the attribution by questioning the authenticity of the "An. Cotton" letter, as well as that of the note "To his Wife, A. C.," which was printed with it by the *Enquirer*. Jones variously argues that the name of John Cotton's wife was Hannah rather than Ann, that the "ostensible occasion" of her letter is "suspicious," that "An." may even be an abbreviated form of a masculine name, and, finally, that the short missive "To his Wife" is so rhetorical as to be incredible as a communication between husband and wife. Summing up, he declares, "The guess may be hazarded ... that Virginia never saw a gifted literary woman named 'Mrs. An. Cotton,' but that, for some reason now unknown, some literary hack or even some person without literary training found it profitable to condense awkwardly the Burwell material."

Certainly, the discrepancy involving the Christian name of Mrs. Cotton constitutes a problem which has been too lightly regarded by those who have championed her husband as the author of "The History of Bacon's and Ingram's Rebellion, 1676." The records of Hungars Parish, Northampton County, do list her as "Hannah" (and "Hanna").[6] If, therefore, we are to accept her unreservedly as the "An. Cotton" whose name appears on an account of the rebellion, we must assume either that these baptismal records are inaccurate or that her true name was Hannah and that she was familiarly known as "Ann" or "Anna." The notion that "An." may be a masculine abbreviation is insupportable, however, in the face of the writer's clear reference to "my Husband." Moreover, by showing that John Cotton was acquainted with one Christopher Harris, Francis Burton Harrison[7] has produced a plausible "Mr. C. H." (the addressee of that letter) and has thereby strengthened the probability that Mrs. Cotton's account is genuine. And there are at least two reasons why we should not be overly troubled by the artificial tone of the paragraphs "To his Wife." The first and most important of these reasons is that we evidently possess only a fragment of the document, the *Enquirer* having stated that it was publishing only an "extract" from the now lost original. Thus the writer's magniloquent pronouncements on life are printed out of context and, lacking any preface, must seem even more precipitously bombastic than they really are. Further, that such rhetoric should be found in a personal letter becomes more easily acceptable when one considers the character of the other document ascribed to the same man. We should not be startled to find that the stylistic idiosyncrasies which saturate his chronicle of the rebellion appear in his personal communications as well. Indeed, we might expect it.

Jones' objection that the "An. Cotton" letter borrows tropes and allusions "scarcely suggesting a feminine pen" is presumably based on the assumption that a provincial dame would have no interest in or knowledge of such things as sixteenth-century jest books or the metaphorical possibilities of millstones and wild animals. But the activities farther north of Mistresses Bradstreet and Hutchinson bear sufficient witness that the colonial housewife was occasionally attracted to intellectual areas customarily reserved in that time for males. There is also one facet of the condensation that seems distinctly feminine: although the Burwell narrative is frequently ribald, sexual humor and incident is wholly absent from the letter.

Although Jones' suspicion that the short account is an imposture ought not to be dismissed hastily, one feels compelled to observe that the ascription of the item to some anonymous "literary hack" raises far more questions than it answers. Nor can we regard the letter as specifically a précis of the Burwell Papers, for the "An. Cotton" material offers some few facts (such as the names of the "cheife men" who subscribed to Bacon's Middle Plantation oath) which appear never to have been present in the text of the unique manuscript now extant. The hypothetical forger, then, would either have had to perform supplementary research for the sake of some relatively minor details or have used another, fuller text of the history as his source. Notwithstanding Ebenezer Cooke's apparent employment of a more complete version, it is evident that copies of the chronicle were rare even in the eighteenth century; and this very rarity contributes to the unlikelihood that the letter to Mr. C. H. is spurious. So, while the ascription must remain somewhat provisional, the case for Cotton's authorship is, for the present, stronger than the objections that have been lodged against it.

It is possible that Mrs. Cotton's letter is the older of the two accounts and that her husband's narrative represents an expansion of it. This, indeed, is the surmise of Wroth, who finds in the Burwell chronicler's "leisurely handling" of his material an indication that the rebellion has been over for some time.[8] But the impediments to this chronological ordering are formidable. If we entertain the assumption that the letter came first, we must also assume that Mrs. Cotton herself was often given to the same stylistic quirks that so distinctively characterize her husband's account. Clearly, it is much easier to believe that the rhetorical flights in her work were borrowed from his than it is to credit the idea of his finding these quaint tropes in her letter, incorporating them into his version, and larding the mixture with a great many similar figures of his own devising. The curious sort of mind that created the Burwell history is simply too uncommon for us to accept that it was possessed by both man and wife. And, despite Wroth's suggestion that Cotton postponed writing, the allusion to Governor Berkeley's "Proclamation of June last" (p. 96) confirms that the history was composed no later than June 1677. Because the conclusion of the manuscript is lost, it is impossible to determine at what point Cotton actually left off. In its present state, the narrative terminates with the execution of William Drummond, who went to the gallows on January 20, 1676/7. One may therefore infer with confidence that the narrative was written during the first six months of that year.

Present in Ebenezer Cooke's "History of Colonel Nathaniel Bacon's Rebellion" is compelling evidence that the Burwell Papers, even in their original entirety, did not comprise a full text of the history as Cotton wrote it. Wroth has shown that the "old, authentick Book" upon which the eighteenth-century Poet-Laureate of Maryland based his Hudibrastic burlesque was Cotton's narrative, for the Virginian's eccentric phrases and odd recollections are scattered liberally throughout the poem. But Cooke also provides details which, though credible and of the sort Cotton relished, are missing from the Burwell Manuscript and from the Robert Beverley *History of Virginia* mentioned by the versifier in Canto I. That this additional material was derived from a fuller Cotton text is conjectural, yet it seems the most probable explanation. Cooke relates, for example, that the soldiers of the loyalist leader Giles Brent deserted their commander and went over to Bacon, "Adoring here the Rising *Sun*, / As in the *East*, they say, 'tis done" (II, 230-31). Mrs. Cotton's letter likewise reports that these men defected, "resolveing with the Perssians to go and worship the rising sun, now approaching their Horisson" (8). Her brief account cannot have served as Cooke's source, and the rising sun motif is absent from the Burwell version. This situation forces the inference that the allusion to sun-worship did occur in the text of the Cotton history from which the Marylander was working.

Cooke's treatment of the Baconian siege of Jamestown features a number of unique details which may well have come to him in the "old, authentick Book."' He avers, for instance, that even though Bacon allowed his loyalist female hostages to withdraw from their station before the trenches, the insurrectionist had their white linen outclothing "Stuck artificially on Poles" (II, 62) in order to give the appearance that the rebel works were still shielded by captive women. Further, with a salty archness of the sort frequently encountered in the Burwell Papers, Cooke confesses that he is at a loss to suggest where the ladies may have slept, "Unless with Nat, a Nap they took / In Tent, as black as Chimney Nook" (II, 70-71). A more substantive inclusion describes the charge led against the dissidents by one Hubert Farrill, who, according to the poem, had ordered his men to fall prone upon the ground for protection when they saw him do so:

> THEN marching on, a Ball from *Nat*
> Laid *Farrell* on his Belly flat;
> Which b'ing observ'd by *Farrell's* Bands,
> They all fall flat upon the Sands,
> Thinking he did it, as the Token,
> Of what he just before had spoken . . . (II, 113-18).

In the resultant confusion, all chance of success was lost. Bacon himself speaks of the wounding of Farrill in a letter collected by the Royal Commissioners,[10] but the strategic significance of the occurrence is revealed only in the poem.

These incidents seem entirely plausible, yet one is perturbed by their absence from all known manuscript and printed sources except Cooke's poem itself. No signs of excision are evident in the Burwell "White Aprons" episode (pp. 68-69), nor is Farrill mentioned in that portion of the prose account which deals with the fight at Jamestown (pp. 70-71). Cotton does describe Farrill's death in a subsequent engagement, referring to him at this point as "one Hubert Farrill" (p. 89), a designation which implies that his name has not arisen before. Later, however, there is injected the possibility that, although he agreed to direct the raid in which he died, Farrill "was not, at this time, fully cured of those Wounds he receved in the Salley at Towne" (p. 91). This remark, with its perfunctory allusion to the officer's earlier shooting, is so offhand as to suggest that the exact circumstances of his previous misfortunes may have been reported in a section deleted from the Burwell narrative. Cooke's satire also furnishes numerous names and minor facts which do not appear in the Burwell version. The surviving manuscript notes, for example, that after first balking at signing Bacon's oath, the people of Gloucester County finally agreed to it at "another meeting, and in another place" (p. 74). The poem, on the other hand, relates that their compliance was obtained "At *Warner's* House" (II, 272), referring to the Abingdon Parish home of Colonel Augustine Warner. Similarly, the Burwell text reports that, while paying "his oblations in the Temple of Venus," Captain Thomas Hansford was apprehended "at the Howse where Coll: Reade did once live" (p. 80), but the poem speaks of the place as belonging to "Auborn" (III, 48)—possibly the Richard Auborne who was appointed to a clerkship by the House of Burgesses in June 1680.[11] Moreover, Cooke's intimation that the insurgent captain was "By *Auborn's* wanton Wife betray'd" may shed some light on the identity of Hansford's fellow-worshipper.[12]

Obviously, none of the foregoing is meant as even a beginning toward a reconstruction of Cotton's original narrative on the basis of the contents of Cooke's poem. Admittedly, it is conceivable that such details as Farrill's lucklessness before Jamestown and Hansford's betrayal by a woman either came to the poet from some source unheard-of by the twentieth century or are the products of his own imagination. Nevertheless, these touches are so much of the intimate (and mostly non-essential) sort which manifestly fascinated John Cotton that their presence in Cooke's copy of the planter's history is a clearly legitimate conjecture. By the same token, the very similarity of character between Cooke's unique details and those which abound in the prose manuscript suggests that even if Cotton's chronicle in its original state should come to light, the literary estimates of it would not have to undergo much revision. Although the increased richness of a full text would be most welcome, the essential spirit and idiom of the work appear to have been fortunately preserved by its unknown abridger.[13]

II

Cotton's prose style has drawn a variety of critical responses, but only Hubbell, who calls it "a kind of belated Euphuism,"[14] has made a serious attempt to analyze the historian's mode of expression. The manuscript's lack of real stylistic homogeneity is doubtlessly one factor which makes a satisfactory description difficult to achieve. This facet of the history is perhaps best understood by viewing it as utilizing a basic narrative style from which Cotton sometimes departs for the purpose of creating desired effects. His fundamental constructions generally conform to what has been denominated the "loose and free" style:

> The sentence proceeds in virtually a series of main statements, each developing from the last. These are linked together in one of three ways: parataxis combined with juncture; coordination introduced usually by such words as "and," "but," "nor," "neither," or "for"; and a kind of quasi-subordination, where the link-word is usually "as," "that," "where," or "which." The punctuation, carefully inserted at the link points, follows the syntax of its time, not that of the present day.[15]

Cotton does not characteristically make use of parataxis with juncture, but the latter two structures are regular features of his sentences when his concern is with simple narration rather than discursive elaborateness:

> When that Grantham arived amongst these fine fellowes, he was receved with more then an ordnary respect; which he haveing repade with suteable deportment, he aquaints them with his Commission, which was to tell them, that there was a peace Concluded betwene the Governour and there Generall; and since him self had (in som measures) used his indeviours, to bring the same to pass, hee beg'd of the Governour, that he might have the honour to com and aquaint them with the terms; which he saide was such, that they had all cause to rejoyce at, then any ways to thinke hardly of the same; there being a Complete satisfaction to be given (by the Articles of agreement) according to every ones particuler intress; which he sum'd up under these heads (p. 94).

An almost obsessive employment of balance and antithesis is the most distinctive trait of Cotton's prose. From the very beginning of the fragmentary narrative, his enthusiasm for opposing phrases and ideas against each other is plain, as when he reports that a group of besieged Indians "were resalve, before that there spirits were downe, to doe what they could to keepe there stores up. . . . And all though they were by the Law of Arms . . . prohibited the hunting of wilde Deare, they resalved to see what good might be don by hunting tame Horsses" (p. 47). The dilemma of Bacon caught between his Indian foes and Berkeley's potential Gloucester recruits is similarly expressed in antithetical terms: "He knew that to have a certaine enimy in his front, and more then uncertaine friends in his reare, portended no grate security from a violent death, and that there could be no grate difference betwene his being wounded to death in his brest, with bows and Arows, or in the back with Guns and Musquit bullits" (p. 57-58).

It was this feature, together with Cotton's fondness for alliteration, assonance, and consonance, which led Hubbell to call him a "belated Euphuist";[16] but even in his most ornate passages, such as the following one which Hubbell quotes, the planter does not display sufficient balancing of word sounds and pursuit of structural repetitions to qualify as a thorough Euphuist:

> But he [Major Lawrence Smith] perceveing that the Gloster Men did not weare (in there faces) the Countinances of Conquerers, nor there Cloathes the marks of any late ingagement (being free from the honourable Staines of Wounds and Gun shott) he began to hope the best, and the Gloster men to feare the worst; and what the properties of feare is, let Feltham tell you, who saith, That if curage be a good Oriter, feare is a bad Counceller, and a worss Ingineare. For insteade of erecting, it beates and batters down all Bullworks of defence: perswadeing the feeble hart that there is no safety in armed Troops, Iron gates, nor stone walls. In oppossition of which Passion I will appose the Properties of it's Antithesis, and say That as som men are never vallent but in the midst of discourse, so others never manifest there Courage but in the midst of danger: Never more alive then when in the jawes of Death, crowded up in the midst of fire, smoke, Swords and gunns; and then not so much laying about them through desperation, or to save there lives, as through a Generosety of Spirit, to trample upon the lives of there enimies (p. 88).

The specific fashion in which Cotton deals with the aphorisms in the excerpt above reinforces the observation that he prizes and practices antithesis more than any other device. First he cites Feltham's paradigm on the properties of fear, which are exposed by means of contrasting them metaphorically with the properties of courage ("a bad Counceller, and a worss Ingineare" as opposed to "a good Oriter"). He then announces that he himself will undertake to characterize the properties of courage, the antithesis of Feltham's subject. But Cotton's explanation too is structured antithetically by the opposition of bravery "in the midst of discourse" to bravery "in the midst of danger" (with the alliteration of the "d"words adding to the balanced effect). Thus he expounds upon the major fear-courage antitheses, one Feltham's and one his own.

The mental and syntactical complications which such a cluster of antitheses entails forces Cotton to abandon the "free and loose" sentence pattern which straight narration permits. To compensate for the added length and complexity of some of the members, he lessens the number of members per sentence, coming more often to full stops so as to enable his reader to digest the passage in manageable units. If one substitutes semicolons for the full stops, it becomes apparent that the structure of the excerpt is, after all, not so different from the constructions he often adopts in unadorned narration. Coordinative words such as "and" and "for" are seen to fulfill their accustomed function in the "free and loose" arrangement. Infrequently, however, when Cotton wishes to repeat the same basic antithesis in more than one way, the forced shortening of the sentences becomes extreme, and the result is an uncharacteristically tight "curt" style: "The Lion had no sooner made his exitt, but the Ape (by indubitable right) steps upon the stage. Bacon was no sooner removed by the hand of good providence, but another steps in, by the wheele of fickle fortune. The Countrey had, for som time, bin guided by a company of knaves, now it was to try how it would behave it selfe under a foole" (pp. 77-78).

A typical method by which Cotton generates humor is his technique of selecting some distinguishing fact about a character and playing upon it in his commentary on that figure's behavior. The pattern is exemplified by Cotton's inferring from the execution of Captain Farlow, a gentleman "acquainted with the Mathamaticks," that "the Asstrolabe, or Quadrant, are not the fitest instruments to take the altitude of a Subjects duty" (p. 83). This strain of wit, which is born of the same associative mental processes that form the intellectual basis of metaphysical poetry, is again on view in Cotton's treatment of Captain Drew, the miller-turned-rebel who found himself in command of a threatened garrison: "This Whisker of Whorly-Giggs, perceveing (now) that there was More Water coming downe upon his Mill then the Dam would hould, thought best in time, to fortifye the same, least all should be borne downe before he had taken his toule" (p. 95). The historian's metaphors spring too readily out of his subjects to match the cerebral *tours de force* of which the true metaphysicals were capable, but his tendency to make figurative extensions of actual objective qualities is, at bottom, only a less daring form of conceit.

As Chaucer concocted the pilgrimage to Canterbury in order to focus on the pilgrims themselves, so Cotton extracts from Bacon's Rebellion a gallery of diverse individuals whose characterizations he sometimes effects in terms of beast fables or *fabliaux*. He is most drawn to the incidental and the bizarre; and he delights in such trivia as the joke of the York Fort gunner, who, after the loyalist rout at Jamestown, "did proffer to purchase, for any that would buy, a Collonells, or a Captains, Commission, for a chunke of a pipe" (p. 70). Like George Alsop, Maryland's early poet-chronicler, Cotton displays a lively interest in provincial sexual mores, shedding crocodile tears over the plight of the wretched prostitutes "who seeing so many Men going to kill one another, began to feare that if they staide behinde, for want of doing they might be undon (there being but a few left at hom, excepting ould men, to sett them on worke,) and so chose rather to dye amongst the soulders, then to be kep from there labour, and so dye for want of exercize" (p. 72). Cotton's contemporaries could not, of course, have missed the bawdy wordplay with "dye." He takes the same salacious pleasure in relating Hansford's capture in the temple of love; confiding that Richard Lawrence, a prominent Baconian, often availed himself of "the darke imbraces of a Blackamoore, his slave" (p. 96); and observing that a Mrs. Howard "was not so much concern'd that her Son in Law was made a prissoner, as her Daughter was vext, to see they had not left one Man upon the Plantation, to comfort neather herself nor Mother" (p. 85). Mrs. Cotton excludes all of these anecdotes and intimations.

One inevitably comes to the question of Cotton's own political attitude toward the rebellion, but his patent inconsistencies on this head make his true feelings hard to discern. He is convinced that Berkeley's prideful refusal to stop the costly erection of useless frontier forts was both a political and military blunder arising from the testy old governor's determination to brook no challenge of his policies. Bacon, though "passionate" and "rash," performed a necessary function in moving unilaterally against the Indians;

and in doing so he incurred the enmity of Berkeley's circle, who "began (som of them) to have Bacons Merits in mistrust, as a Luminary that thretned an eclips to there riseing gloryes" (p. 53). These grasping advisers, Cotton declares, were responsible for the proclamation against the young firebrand as a rebel. Neither does he profess to understand why Berkeley issued a similiar edict later against Bacon and sought "to raise the countrey upon him" (p. 56) when the general's only apparent objective was that of neutralizing the Indian threat. It is only when Bacon's adventure turns to "Al-a-mode Rebellion" at Middle Plantation that Cotton firmly withdraws his approbation, for the middle-class planter is not prepared to see Virginians fire upon British soldiers no matter what the domestic situation. He is outraged by the burning of Jamestown and attributes the death of the archrebel to "an admireable and ever to be cellibrated providence" (p. 74). Yet even as he seems to take satisfaction in the demise of the general, Cotton respectfully notes that it came about because "he subjected him selfe to all those inconvenences that, singly, might bring a Man of a more Robust frame to his last hom" (p. 75). The narrative essentially takes the position that Bacon's commission was probably due him and was properly used until he went to the extreme of defying England herself. This radical action, together with Ingram's unlawful assumption of the nontransferable commission, invested the loyalist faction with "indubitable pretences against a usurped power" (p. 91) by the time that active hostilities ended.

But merely to understand the foregoing is not to apprehend the informing spirit of the Burwell Papers. Cotton is far more concerned with registering his comments on human vagaries than with delving into the moral perplexities of the uprising; he is more at pains to exercise his wit than to prove his skill as a political analyst. This is not to say, of course, that he does not sometimes take seriously the tragic effects of the revolt. His indignation at Bacon's destruction of the capital and at Berkeley's heartless treatment of Major Cheseman's wife (p. 81) is entirely unfeigned. He is perfectly willing, however, to depart from his previous position on a topic when a desirable literary effect can be obtained by the departure. Within the same paragraph, he cites Bacon's "rash proseedings" then declares him possessed of "those induments which constitutes a Compleate Man (as to intrincecalls), wisdom to apprehend and descretion to chuse" (p. 53). Cotton's description of the battle at Jamestown is sheer comedy. The ill-fated loyalist infantry, he recounts, "(like scholers goeing to schoole) went out with hevie harts, but returnd hom with light heeles" (p. 70). Yet two paragraphs later the erstwhile humorist is full of distaste for war as he depicts how Bacon set his cannon "to worke (playing som calls itt, that takes delight to see stately structurs beated downe, and Men blowne up into the aire like Shutle Cocks) against the Ships" (p. 71).

These blatant contradictions and Cotton's treatment of the two camps of antagonists comprise part of the key into the historian's peculiar genius. On the whole, his judgments upon the warring factions are remarkably evenhanded, especially so in view of the fact that he himself lived through the disruption at close quarters. He indicts Bacon for his treasonous excesses but plainly admires him as a heroically magnetic figure; he charges Berkeley with maintaining a clique of parasitical favorites but accords him due respect as the king's vicegerent. In short, the narrative reflects a completeness of unity between its style and its attitude toward the subject matter that is thoroughly extraordinary. The antithetically balanced units in Cotton's rhetoric are mirrored thematically in his opinions, which also achieve an equipoise resultant from the tension exerted on each other by opposites of the same value.

Were Cotton's prose style and narrative procedures insufficient to persuade one that the primary aim of his memoir is literary entertainment, the presence of the two poems in his work should help to confirm that this is so. "Bacons Epitaph, made by his Man" and "Upon the Death of G: B. [General Bacon]" (pp. 75-77) are diametrical reactions in verse to the passing of the insurgent chief, and, considering the ambiance in which they were written, they are of surprising quality. [17] Both poems, written in couplets of iambic pentameter, contain enough accentual variation to avoid monotonousness, and Cotton's judiciously sparing use of end-stopped lines argues him a poet of some practice and facility.

The "Epitaph" opens with a ten-line apostrophe to personified Death in which the pro-Bacon persona mournfully prophesies that the general's removal will result in the extinguishment of liberty and the return of "Caoss" to the land. Having finished this initial address, the speaker directs his words to the reader and introduces a line of thought which has both figurative value and implicit relevance to the dissatisfaction of the Virginia commons with their government:

> If't be a sin to thinke Death brib'd can bee
> Wee must be guilty; say twas bribery
> Guided the fatall shaft. Verginias foes,
> To whom for secrit crimes just vengance owes
> Disarved plagues, dreding their just disart
> Corrupted Death by Parasscellcian art
> Him to destroy. . . .

Herein the Berkeley cronies are accused of the ultimate political fix: the suborning of Death himself through black magic. As he is pictured in this hyperbolic elegy, Bacon would not be out of place with Marlowe's Tamburlaine and Dryden's Almanzor. But it is not only the rebel's martial prowess that the speaker finds super-human. While the armed might of Caesar altered "the outward frame" of the world, Bacon's commanding tongue "Could subdue / The ruged workes of nature." For those who see Bacon as a prototype of George Washington, the persona of the "Epitaph" proves himself a gifted seer with the prediction that

> none shall dare his Obseques to sing
> In disarv'd measures, untill time shall bring
> Truth Crown'd with freedom, and from danger free,
> To sound his praises to posterity.

The final four lines of the piece are given over to a favorite motif of Cotton's, that of legal terminology. This closing section is aes-thetically the weakest, however, for Bacon's recourse "unto a higher Court" is too much a cliché to be effective. Also poetically amateurish is his dual use of Caesar in the "Epitaph." Having already compared the exploits of the insurrectionist to those of the actual Roman commander, Cotton ends the panegyric to Bacon with a reference to the dispute over "Whether to Ceaser hee was friend, or foe." This mixing of the actual historical Caesar with "Ceaser" as a depersonalized metaphor for government itself constitutes one of the few instances when Cotton's poetic invention plays him false.

Angry in tone and viciously aggressive in its attack, "G: B." snatches up the last line of the "Epitaph" and fires back hotly,

> Whether to Ceaser he was Friend or Foe?
> Pox take such Ignorance, do you not know?
> Can he be Friend to Ceaser, that shall bring
> The Arms of Hell, to fight against the King?

For the first twenty-four lines, rhetorical questions serve as the basic argumentative weapon for the anti-Bacon persona, and the structure of the poem is largely founded on the loyalist speaker's refutation of points made by the companion piece. To the suggestion that Death has been bribed, he replies only that loyal men "honour all / That lends a hand unto a T[r]ators fall." After likening the elegist to a minister who has been well paid to eulogize "incoffin'd filth and excrements," he momentarily strikes a purely metaphysical pose and paradoxically admits to grief:

> Yet that wee Grieve it cannot be denide,
> But 'tis because he was, not cause he dide.
> So wep the poore destresed Ilyum Dames
> Hereing those nam'd, there Citty put in flames. . . .

To round off this second poem, Cotton combines legal jargon with the personification of Death, two more borrowings from the "Epitaph." In the view of the loyalist speaker, however, the court of Judge Death is the only one with which Bacon need concern himself. And the irreversible verdict is already in:

> The Braines to plot, the hands to execute
> Projected ills, Death Joyntly did nonsute
> At his black Bar. And what no Baile could save
> He hath commited Prissoner to the Grave;
> From whence there's no repreive. Death keep him close
> We have too many Divells still goe loose.

It seems quite unlikely that these pieces reflect a change of mind about Nathaniel Bacon on Cotton's part. Certainly, Bacon himself can have done nothing to influence any such alteration, for both poems were composed after the young insurgent had gone to his secret grave. The prose narrative was also written months after Bacon had succumbed to the "bloody flux," but it too contains both praise and censure of him. It appears far more probable, rather, that the pairing is simply another manifestation of Cotton's pleasure in challenging his own wit, another deliberately contrived demonstration of his sophistic ability to defend either side of a question. Whether he shared the intellectual delight in dualism which fostered "L'Allegro" and "Il Penseroso," or whether he was animated by the same "spirit of contradiction" that Boswell perceived in Dr. Johnson, the Burwell chronicler was no small-minded man to be shackled by consistencies, foolish or otherwise. Taken together, the "Epitaph" and the reply stand as the supreme indulgence of his passion for balance and antithesis.[18]

NOTES

1. "An Account of Our Late Troubles in Virginia. Written in 1676, by Mrs. An. Cotton, of Q. Creeke," in *Tracts and Other Papers, Relating Principally to the Origin, Settlement, and Progress of the Colonies in North America, from the Discovery of the Country to the Year 1776*, ed. Peter Force (1836; rpt. New York: Peter Smith, 1947), I, no. 9, 1-11. Hereafter the text is cited parenthetically.

2. [John Cotton], "The History of Bacon's and Ingram's Rebellion, 1676," in *Narratives of the Insurrections, 1675-1690*, ed. Charles M. Andrews (New York: Scribner's, 1915), 97. Hereafter the text is cited parenthetically from this edition, presently the most widely available.

3. *"The Maryland Muse* by Ebenezer Cooke: A Facsimile, with an Introduction," *Proceedings* of the American Antiquarian Society, NS 44 (1934), 299-306. "The History of Colonel Nathaniel Bacon's Rebellion in Virginia. Done into Hudibrastic Verse, from an old MS" is hereafter cited parenthetically from this edition.

4. The best source for the known facts of Cotton's life, as well as information regarding the work of others who have postulated his authorship of the chronicle, is Hubbell's "John Cotton: The Poet-Historian of Bacon's Rebellion," in *South and Southwest: Literary Essays and Reminiscences* (Durham, N.C.: Duke University Press, 1965), 205-27. This study constitutes a revision of Hubbell's earlier "John and Ann Cotton of 'Queen's Creek,' Virginia," *American Literature*, 10 (1938), 179-201.

5. *The Literature of Virginia in the Seventeenth Century*, 2d ed. (Charlottesville: University of Virginia Press, 1968), 108-109n.

6. See *William and Mary Quarterly*, 1st Ser., 18 (1910), 179; 22 (1913), 41.

7. "Footnotes Upon Some XVII Century Virginians," *Virginia Magazine of History and Biography*, 50 (1942), 289-99.

8. Wroth, "*Maryland Muse* Introduction," 304.

9. Wroth, who made a tabulated comparison of the poem's narration of the rebellion with those in the three major contemporary accounts, is mistaken in his assertion that Cooke's handling of the Jamestown siege marks the only point at which he brings forth detail that is not to be found in the Burwell manuscript ("*Maryland Muse* Introduction," 301). Mr. Thomas R. Adams of the John Carter Brown Library has informed me in a letter dated February 16, 1973 that Wroth's tabulation has unfortunately disappeared from the library's files.

10. See Andrews, *Narratives*, 133-34.

11. *Journals of the House of Burgesses, 1659/60-1693*, ed. H. R. McIlwaine (Richmond: Virginia State Library, 1914), 122.

12. There are also two relatively long passages wherein Cooke supplies a letter and an oration (II, 275-93; III, 274-309) which, judging from the contrary indications at the corresponding points in the Burwell text (74, 92), almost certainly were never in Cotton's history and which may be inventions of the poet. It is remotely possible that the nautical jargon which garnishes Cooke's rendering of Captain Thomas Grantham's admonitory speech to Ingram and his men was suggested to the poet by Grantham's own memoirs, in which he recalls having told these rebels that continued resistance would leave them "entirely Shipwreck'd" (*An Historical Account of Some Memorable Actions, Particularly in Virginia*, 2d ed. [1716; rept. Richmond: Carlton McCarthy, 1882], 20).

13. In the opinion of Hubbell, who acknowledges his indebtedness to Morgan P. Robinson for the conclusion, the Burwell Papers are an eighteenth-century manuscript ("Poet-Historian," 206).

14. Hubbell, "Poet-Historian," 212. Also see Moses Coit Tyler, *A History of American Literature, 1607-1765* (New York: Putnam, 1878), I, 73; and Jones, *Literature of Virginia*, 112. Though the essay directs most of its attention to the manuscript's poetic eulogy on Bacon, the prose style is also briefly considered in Hans Galinsky, "Kolonialer Literaturbarok in Virginia: Eine Interpretation von *Bacons Epitaph* auf der Grundlage eine Forschungsberichtes," in *Festschrift zum 75. Geburtstag von Theodor Spira*, ed. Helmut Viebrock und Willi Erzgraber (Heidelberg: Carl Winter, Universitatsverlag, 1961), 260-308.

15. Ian A. Gordon, *The Movement of English Prose* (London: Longmans, 1966), 114-15.

16. I am indebted to Professor Percy G. Adams of the University of Tennessee for pointing out to me originally that the designation of Cotton's style as Euphuistic is inadequate.

17. In the belief that the author of the chronicle is also the author of these poems, I entirely concur with Hubbell, who is uncertain whether they should be taken "as radically divergent expressions of Cotton's changing conception

of Bacon or as a poetic debate" ("Poet-Historian," 211-17).

18. To the general encomium embodied in this collection of essays, I wish to add my personal thanks to Professor Richard Beale Davis of the University of Tennessee, under whose direction and with whose generous aid I initiated my first study of the Burwell history.

ROBERT BEVERLEY: COLONIAL ECOLOGIST AND INDIAN LOVER

Wilbur R. Jacobs

"Robert Beverley, Provincial Rebel," might also be the title of this essay. My proposition is that Beverley, from the fragments of data that have come down to us, was an argumentative individualist, who, having had bad luck in love, in politics, and in lawsuits over land, became a semi-recluse. His indignation helped him to see his fellow-Virginians in a different light from the usual; he depicted them in a book as lazy, ungrateful oafs living in a land of plenty that they were spoiling by their improvements. It was the aboriginal Indian, Beverley argued, who knew how to enjoy the fruits of the land, but he, like the beautiful natural world in which he lived, was polluted by contacts with whites. In fact, if one reads Beverley's book closely, he will conclude that the Indian man and certainly the Indian woman were better products of God's handiwork than the white people.[1]

But let us go back to the beginning of the story to see how this theme helps to explain Beverley and the remarkable history he wrote in 1705, *The History and Present State of Virginia.*[2] For some clues to explain some of his attitudes, we must go back to Beverley's parents. Robert Beverley, Sr. was à frustrated "cavelier" who emigrated from England to Virginia in the middle of the seventeenth century. He married the daughter of an English merchant, and raised a family of a half dozen boys and girls (though most of them seem to have died off and left their thousands of acres of tobacco land to Robert, Jr., the historian). As if fighting Cromwell's Puritans were not enough, Robert Beverley, Sr. became involved in the thick of a hubbub in which a local planter's vigilante gang burned tobacco fields in protest against the policies of Governor Thomas Culpepper. These obstreperous planters were even selective in their burning: they fired the sweet-leaved tobacco fields, apparently the favorites of Governor Culpepper, who was outraged. In his *History*, though he does not mention his father, Robert Beverley, Jr. unleashes scalding criticism on Culpepper, who persuaded the Virginia assembly to pass an act providing for a fine of £500 and a year's jail sentence "upon any Man that shall presume to speak disrespectfully of the Governor."[3]

Apparently this is just about what Robert Beverley, Sr. did. The Governor waived his imprisonment, however, providing that he ask for pardon on bended knee and post a £2000 bond promising good future behavior. This humiliation broke the old man's heart. He died shortly afterwards in Virginia at the time his son, Robert Beverley, Jr. (born about 1673), was in England finishing his schooling.[4]

The young man seems never to have forgotten that cruel treatment accorded his father; at least that is my contention. He vowed that he would have his day with any tyrannical governors sent to lord over Virginia. He prepared for a career of vengeance as a government clerk, a position that gave him abundant experience in writing (one wonders how Beverley came to be such a skilled stylist for his elegant simplicity shows a kind of genius at work), and in observing government operations. He was a scrivener at first in the office of the provincial secretary. Then he rose to Clerk of the Council, and finally had the prestigious post of Clerk of the General Assembly.

Meanwhile, the young Beverley grew to middle age. He married Ursula, the innocent, sixteen year old daughter of William Byrd I. She died leaving Beverley with a son, William, who is said to have had a more agreeable personality than his father. Beverley, in these middle years, seemed to be rising in political office, temporarily representing Jamestown in the Burgesses during the years 1700-1702 and 1705-1706.[5]

In this period of his life, however, Beverley's very wealth and prestige appear to have soured him. A contemporary described him in a courtroom as being curt and arrogant in manner. He undoubtedly missed his wife, for he never remarried, living alone with his son in solitary splendor. The princely estate left to him by his father was called Beverley Park. With the addition of some 6,000 additional acres inherited from brothers, Beverley was one of the biggest landholders in the province. But still the crusty planter was not satisfied. His favorite recreation was land speculation and fee collection from offices he held in the government. When involved in a particularly stubborn property settlement, he finally decided to go over the heads of local authorities to appeal his case personally in England.[6]

While in London, however, Beverley's disgust with Virginia affairs involved him in more trouble. He unwisely cooked his own political goose by writing several indiscrete letters back home which found their way into official records. His imprudence evidently angered a powerful Virginia governor, Francis Nicholson, whom Beverley accused (in the first edition of his *History*) of setting himself up as a kind of "Vice-Roy." Nicholson, who likewise had a temper, managed to frustrate Beverley's plans for office holding for some years to come. Meanwhile, Beverley lost his lawsuit in England.[7]

Everything happened at once, but there was still one way to uncap Beverley's explosive resentment. This was to write a book proving to the world what a "Machiavellian" rascal Nicholson really was. In the process, Beverley could put old Governor Culpepper in proper historical perspective. The idea of the book, however, came not from Beverley's frustrations, but rather from an unexpected invitation extended to him to read a draft revision of John Oldmixon's *British Empire in America*. The Oldmixon draft, Beverley tells us in the preface of his book, was a mess, filled with errors, exaggerations, and gaps of narrative. As Beverley wrote, "the Account was too faulty and too imperfect to be mended."[8]

And so he decided to write his own book, one that was "plain and true," though he modestly told his reader that the "Method and Stile" might not please as much as he desired. As Louis B Wright pointed out in his excellent sketch of Beverley, the Virginia planter set out to shock his fellow Virginians and at the same time persuade all his readers that he was giving them an accurate account. In a spirit of playfulness he began his work by telling the reader, "I am an *Indian,* and don't pretend to be exact in my language; But I hope the Plainness of my Dress will give . . . kinder Impressions of my Honesty. . . . Truth desires only to be understood." [9]

It was in the first edition of his *History* (1705) that Beverley fully vented his spleen by splashing uncomplimentary remarks about Culpepper and Nicholson throughout his chapters. In later years, after he had mellowed, he attempted to soften his remarks in a second edition of 1722, but added little and left us with a kind of marshmallow narrative. For this reason we turn to his first, unrevised edition for the best appraisal of his work. [10]

Regardless of his motives in writing, Beverley's accomplishment as an ethnologist was not duplicated by any other English colonial historian of his day. New England Puritan writers of the time filled their historical works with predestination hocus pocus which portrayed the Indian as a Devil's demon. Beverley, by contrast, gave the world an urbane, critical portrait of the Indian based upon close observation and examination of works of other authors, including John Smith, Father Louis Hennipen, and Louis Armand, Baron de Lahontan. Moreover, when Beverley relied on these authors, he acknowledged his sources by quotations. For the sake of securing accurate information on Indian religion, Beverley placated a native informant with plenty of "Cyder" which loosened his tongue on the subject of Indian physicians, priests, and conjurers. [11]

What distinguishes Beverley's picture of the Indians is his portrayal of them as a people with a culture which had much to offer whites. The central, or third part of his book, discusses in rich detail their wampum, agriculture, religion, weapons, tools, houses, recreation, medicines, and marriage customs. This is concluded with an appraisal of the European impact in undermining the agreeable, natural, relaxed lifestyle of the Indians. Other sections of the book cover the early history of Virginia, its colonial trade, commerce, and natural products, as well as government and politics about the year 1705. The historical sections going back to the Roanoke colony are not without minor errors in fact.

With these facts in mind let us comment on the basic themes that Beverley stressed. They gave him a chance to write a book showing the world what kind of place Virginia really was. For him the province was an ecologically balanced natural garden of incredible riches, but the white "Inhabitants" were incapable of appreciating what they had. "They spunge upon the Blessings of a warm Sun, and a fruitful Soil, and almost grutch the Pains of gathering in the Bounties of the Earth." In fact, these Virginians were so slothful, Beverley writes, that "tho' their Country be over-run with Wood, yet they have all their Wooden Ware from *England*; their Cabinets, Chairs, Tables, Stools, Chests, Boxes, Cart-Wheels, and all other things, even so much as their Bowls, and Birchen Brooms, to the Eternal Reproach of their Laziness." [12]

One has the impression that the Virginians were such a collection of indolent louts that they scarcely deserved the beautiful country they had wrested from the Indians. Though they had a college, a Church of England ("establisht by Law. . . . Yet liberty of Conscience is given to all other Congregations pretending Christianity, on the condition they submit to all Parish duties"), a governor, council and assembly, a corpus of laws, and a militia; some snakes, frogs, plus a few Chinches, Seedticks, Red-Worms, and "Musketas"; a fine climate, and vast fertile lands for planting—though they had all this—the Virginians, Beverley argues, were unappreciative and undeserving.

Expanding his argument, Beverley clinches his case against his fellow Virginians by accusing them of damaging the great New World garden. Lazy as they were, the whites were capable of destroying the ecological balance. Native Indians, Beverley tells his readers, stored up nuts, corn, and "Fruits of the Earth in their Season," and indulged in "the Pursuit of their Pleasure." "And indeed all that the *English* have done," he argues, "has been only to make some of these Native Pleasures more scarce (i.e., by killing off wildlife), by an inordinate and unseasonable Use of them; hardly making Improvements equivalent to that damage." In surveying what happened to the Indians after the arrival of the Europeans, Beverley once again states that though the Virginians made "Alterations, I can't call them Improvements." [13]

Having put down his countrymen in favor of the Indians, Beverley goes on to show how the English took over the greater part of the Indian country and thereby made everything less plentiful; there was less wildlife, less land for Indian cultivation, less wilderness for gathering wild nuts, fruits, berries, and seeds. In addition, the whites "have introdc'd Drunkenness and Luxury amongst them, which have multipl'd their Wants, and put them upon desiring a thousand things they never dreamt of before."[14]

Not only were the whites of Virginia stupid and cruel in their treatment of Indians in Beverley's lifetime, but they had also carried on a foolish policy of racial discrimination which caused great bloodshed down through Virginia's early history. In an extended section on intermarriage in his book, Beverley says that because Virginians refused Indian mates, jealousy, misunderstanding, and war resulted. Very often the Indians proposed intermarriage, stating "that the English were not their friends if they refused it." Indeed, the marriage of Pocahontas and John Rolfe in 1614 brought about a firm peace that joined hostile Powhatan to the Jamestown settlers. This theme, interestingly enough, was copied by Beverley's brother-in-law, William Byrd II, who pointed out in his *History of the Dividing Line* that Indians were husky and strong and would improve the white race by intermarriage. And besides, wrote Byrd with a twinkle in his eye, "after all that can be said, a sprightly Lover is the most prevailing Missionary that can be sent amongst these, or any other Infedels."[15]

The argument about the Indians being excellent physical specimens made by Byrd is also taken from Beverley's *History*. Intent upon demonstrating the natural beauty of the Indian people, Beverley praised their physiques:

> The *Indians* are of the middling and largest stature of the English; They are straight and well proportion'd, having the cleanest and most exact Limbs in the World: They are so perfect in their outward frame, that I never heard of one single *Indian* that was either dwarfish, crooked, bandy-legg'd or otherwise mis-shapen.[16]

The children, Beverley noted, were very perfect specimens, and this did not result from the Indians' killing off "weak and misshapen" infants. But it was the women who captivated Beverley (one wonders why he did not take an Indian wife for himself in those lonely years of middle life). They were, he writes, "generally

Beautiful, possessing an uncommon delicacy of Shape and Features, and wanting no Charm but a fair Complexion." Nor did these lovely creatures sell their bodies for wampum beads. Such stories, Beverley assures us, were untrue. There were misconceptions about Indian "Damsels" because they were so "full of spirit, and from thence are always inspir'd with Mirth and good Humour. They are," he says with admiration, "extremely given to laugh . . . frolicksom, but without any real imputation to their Innocence."[17]

Certainly Beverley's picture of the tidewater Indian people has a modern tone. His views closely accord with those of many of today's authorities on Indians.[18] Beverley's Indians did practically nothing to disturb the beauty of the natural wilderness in which they lived. Tragically, these agreeable native people were dispossessed by a lazy, greedy, slothful tide of whites. One is driven to the conclusion in analyzing Beverley that his disillusionment and anger with whites enabled him to transcend his own ethnocentricity to give us a favorable picture of Indian society.

The fact that Beverley mellowed in later years and actually cultivated a friendship with the amiable Governor Alexander Spotswood (who shared Beverley's love of the land and gave him commissions in the government so he could begin again to collect fees),[19] does not detract from the intrinsic value of Beverley's work. But it does show that he was not as crusty as he pretended to be, especially when he was willing to soften his criticisms of fellow Virginians in the second edition of his book. We may conclude, perhaps, that the Virginians were not as oafish as Beverley said they were, and his Indians were not quite as noble as he portrayed them to be. Nevertheless, we still thank him for giving us a witty, urbane, and authoritative view of old-time Virginia. If he exaggerated a bit, what other writer of history can say that he has not done the same? One has the impression that Robert Beverley loved those Indians as much as he loved Virginia and the fees and land profits that came his way. Judging from the fortune he acquired, Beverley's love of the Indian was deep and abiding.

NOTES

1. The psychological explanation offered here can be supplemented with an argument based on the concept of identification. Using theory set forth by Erik Erikson in his book, *Identity and the Life Cycle* (New York: Inter-

national Universities, 1959), it is possible to suggest that Beverley identified with his father's "hurt" and became an opponent of English colonial governors. At the same time he praised the culture of the Virginia Indian people who had been dispossessed and harassed by settlers: Beverley even went so far (as noted in this paper) to say he was an Indian himself. In the idealized Indian he could find and even assert his injured self and family. When he talked about Indian people being beautiful, mirthful, physically well-proportioned, he also set forth his personal ideals of what he would like to be. See Erikson, *Identity and the Life Cycle*, a small book of three essays (especially 30-37) and the discussion of negative identity (129 ff.). I am particularly indebted to Professor Peter Loewenburg of UCLA for assistance in making this evaluation of Beverley's personality.

There is also the possible explanation, offered by Louis B. Wright in his edition of Robert Beverley, *The History and Present State of Virginia* (Chapel Hill: University of North Carolina Press, 1947, xix-xx) that Beverley wrote a promotional description of Virginia and her native people in order to attract European settlers who might purchase his lands. However, the above psychological explanation seems to me to have a greater element of truth. In any case, Beverley's *History* shows he was well acquainted with utopian literature and pastoral poetry (he was educated in England) which portrayed the ideal of an innocent man (and sometimes a woman, too), living in an ideal landscape. Beverley's picture of the Indian as a natural man living in an unfallen state was reminiscent of the biblical Eden. Beverley was also probably indebted to John Locke (and possibly Hugo Grotius) who, it will be recalled, placed man in a state of nature as the starting point for treatises on government. Professor Lester A. Beurline, of the University of Virginia, has convinced me in conversations and in correspondence that Beverley's *History* was partly the product of these literary influences.

2. Citations to Beverley's *History* are from L. B. Wright's edition, cited above, which reproduces the text of Beverley's History published in 1705. Wright used the copy owned by the Huntington Library, Rare Book No. A 1705 9793. Beverley is identified on the title page and an accompanying engraving of the arms of Virginia as "R.B. gent" and "a Native and Inhabitant of the Place."

A French translation was published in Amsterdam in 1707 (Hunt. Lib. Rare Book No. A 1707 11204. This volume was reprinted in 1712 and 1718.) and in Paris (Hunt. Lib. Rare Book No. A 1707 11958); and a revised English edition was published in London in 1722 (Hunt. Lib. Rare Book No. A 1722 9852). In all these editions Beverley is identified as "R.B. gent."

In the nineteenth century, Charles Campbell, the Virginian historian, wrote an introduction to a reprint of the 1722 edition, *The History of Virginia in Four Parts by Robert Beverley* ... (Richmond, Virginia, 1855).

3. Wright, ed., *Beverley's History*, 88.

4. This argument is set forth by Charles Campbell in his 1855 introduction to Beverley's history. Campbell ed., Beverley's *History*, pp. 2-3. Al-

though Campbell offers no documentation, his interpretation is plausible and generally accords with the views of other writers. And the kind of treatment given the father of the historian seems to have been in England a frequent substitute for a gentlemen's punishment.

5. One of the best summaries of Beverley's life is Fairfax Harrison's "Robert Beverley, the Historian of Virginia," *Virginia Magazine of History and Biography*, 36 (Oct. 1928), 333-44. For the above biographical data, see 333-38.

6. L. B. Wright, ed., Robert Beverley, *History*, xiv-xv; Farifax Harrison, "Robert Beverley," 337-42.

7. L. B. Wright, ed., Robert Beverley, *History*, xv, 86, 97, 99-100, 103-11. Although Beverley had harsh words for Nicholson's "Despotick Administration," he did give the governor credit for certain accomplishments such as instituting "Olympick Games." Such accomplishments were, however, part of a scheme to make the governor popular with the people. Ibid., 98.

8. This statement and other criticisms of Oldmixon's work appear in the preface of Beverley's revised edition of 1722, *The History of Virginia in Four Parts* . . . (London, 1722).

9. L. B. Wright, ed., Robert Beverley, *History*, 9.

10. Ibid., xxvii, 356-59.

11. Ibid., 200.

12. For the above quotations, see ibid., 319, 295.

13. Ibid., 156.

14. Ibid., 233.

15. For an expanded discussion of the commentary by Beverley, Byrd, and other early writers on Indian-white intermarriage, see W. R. Jacobs, *Dispossessing the American Indian* (New York: Charles Scribner's Sons, 1972), 114-19, 159, 209n., 210n.

16. L. B. Wright, ed., Robert Beverley, *History*, 159.

17. Ibid., 159, 171.

18. An appraisal of earlier New-World writers who commented upon the Indian is in J. H. Elliott, *The Old and the New World, 1492-1650* (Cambridge, England: At the University Press, 1969), 32 ff. Certainly Beverley does not suffer by comparison. For a description of the culture of the Virginia Indians see Nancy O. Lurie's "Indian Cultural Adjustments to European Civilization," in Roger L. Nichols and George R. Adams, eds., *The American Indian Past and Present* (Waltham, Massachusetts: Xerox College Pub., 1971), 42-60. Much of what Dr. Lurie details in this penetrating essay confirms the accuracy of Beverley's portrait of Indian people. See also, W. R. Jacobs, *Dispossessing the American Indian*, 1-15, 107-72.

19. Fairfax Harrison, "Robert Beverley," p. 339. Beverley dedicated his *Abridgment of the Publick Laws of Virginia* . . . (London, 1722) to his friend, Governor Spotswood. Hunt. Lib. Rare Book No. A 1722 Y 19445.

STYLE, SUBSTANCE, AND SELF IN WILLIAM BYRD'S FAMILIAR LETTERS

Robert D. Arner

If Solomon sends lazy people to the ants to learn industry, all authors should not be ashamed to go to the bears, to be instructed never to produce any offspring of theirs until they have brought it into shape fit to be seen.

William Byrd to Peter Collinson, July 18, 1736

Considering their value as commentary on his published works and their intrinsic interest as literature, it is more than a little surprising that the letters of William Byrd of Westover have not as yet appeared in a collected edition.[1] Perhaps the chief reason that such a volume has been slow in coming, apart from the difficulty of locating the letters, is the result of an overemphasis upon the first part of the previous statement. The diaries (despite the large gaps they leave in Byrd's life), the two histories, and the journals have seemed sufficient to give us a comprehensive view of his mind and art; the letters have been consulted mainly as supplementary materials, evidence to corroborate or, in a few cases, to qualify what we already know about the master of Westover from his published writings. Accustomed to reading correspondence mainly for its historical or biographical information, we tend too easily to forget that in his personal correspondence Byrd was indulging his talent for what some critics of the English eighteenth century have termed "the exemplary form of the period." [2] This is not to suggest that he wrote letters with an eye to their eventual publication— time and again he disclaims any such intention[3]—but rather to note that, unlike the diaries, they represent a form of private literature meant for an audience other than himself, a reader whom he usually-ly knew well and to whose interests and intelligence he shaped his prose; whatever his intentions, the letters were, in a sense, "pub-lished." [4]

Oliver W. Ferguson has observed that Jonathan Swift, an almost exact contemporary of Byrd's and the author of volumes of let-ters, carefully studied "the particular attitude he struck in each, and the tone appropriate to that attitude" even though he may not have polished each paragraph. [5] His description seems equally appropriate to Byrd's epistolary art and provides a convenient point of departure for an investigation of his letters.

The rise of the letter as a literary form in the eighteenth century was facilitated by the increasing efficiency of the English postal system, which helped to insure letter writers that their products would arrive safely and would be read, thus indirectly influencing the care with which epistles were likely to be composed. It was stimulated by the publication of English editions of French letters, notably Dennis' and Dryden's *Voiture* in 1696 and Boyer's *Letters of Wit* in 1701, by collections of English letters such as Swift's edition of Sir William Temple's *Letters* in 1700, and by a host of letter-writing manuals that began to proliferate during the final decades of the seventeenth century. [6] It was also endorsed by the example of ancient authors, among whom the most prominent authorities on epistolary style were Cicero, Seneca, and Pliny. Ac-cording to Howard Anderson and Irvin Ehrenpreis, Cicero viewed the familiar letter as "an escape from formality, a release from the sort of rules associated with 'higher' kinds of literature"; he advo-cated both informal subject matter and informal diction. Seneca, on the other hand, "wished letters to be more profound" and distinctly literary, though he felt that profundities should not be "set forth as philosophical expositions in full dress." Pliny was traditionally seen as the mediator between these two points of view, but, as Anderson and Ehrenpreis note, on the fundamental issue of naturalness of style no mediator was really needed. Cicero and Seneca agreed that the prose of familiar letters should be informal, but disagreed on how best to achieve that informality.[7]

To pass from these theories into Byrd's letters is to enter a much less self-consciously literary world, though it would probably be a mistake to assume that he was not familiar with French practices, English paradigms, and classical prescriptions. But he did not, as Pope did, refer either to *Voiture* or Cicero in his letters, nor did he attempt any systematic formulation of what he thought a letter should be. We can, however, glean a few attitudes from his correspondence. At times, he seemed to prize letters as a means of self-expression, a release from psychological tensions, although he never went so far as to consider them a medium for private confessions. Safe behind the rhetorical mask of a lover's self-denial, for instance, he wrote to "Zenobia," a correspondent not otherwise identified: "Rather than you shou'd be out of humour at my Writeing, I'll deny my troubled mind that offensive way of easing its pain" (*ASD,* p. 266). The closest he came in an epistle to baring the side of himself he reserved for his diaries was in a long letter to Mrs. Dunn ("Dunella"), in which he complained of the behavior of Mrs. (or Miss) J-f-r-y, whom he had in a moment of sympathetic weakness installed at Westover as a companion for his first wife. "Dear freind [sic]," he asked, "ought a person with such unsociable qualitys, to be suffer'd in the Family of any man that loves Peace and order, and will assert the soveraignty of his House-hold" (*ASD,* p. 295). Even on this occasion, he appears to have had an ulterior motive, for in a later letter which has disappeared he asked her to come to Westover as a governess. He retracted the offer when John Custis, his brother-in-law, wrote to him with a bad report of her character (*ASD,* pp. 290-91, n. 2).

In certain trying circumstances, Byrd also valued the opportunity that letter writing gave him to gather his thoughts, recollect his emotions in relative tranquility, and put the best words in the best order. Thus when John Orlebar, a Master in Chancery and an emmissary from Miss Mary Smith—the "Sabina" Byrd pursued so assiduously during his second stay in London—called on him with her command not to write to her any longer, the master of Westover sat silent through most of the interview. The next day he wrote explaining his reticence:

I was then so surpriz'd and disconcerted at what you told me, that tis
no wonder I was out of all condition of returning my answer. Besides
there are so many unlucky mistakes happen in delivering of verbal
answers, that the surest way will be to send you mine in writeing ("To
Olibari," April 1, 1718;   ASD, p. 339).

We have as well the evidence of his diary (April 16, 1718) that he
spent long hours attempting to verbalize his feelings for Miss
Smith's perusal,[8] so that we may take him seriously when he exclaims to her: "How short do weak words fall of reaching the
sprightly sentiments of the heart!" (ASD, p. 304). In the letters
to "Sabrina," he faced with full consciousness the problem con-
fronted by every serious literary artist, the indequacy of language
to convey powerful and unique emotions.

There were happier times for Byrd both in England and America, and during these periods he found the letter a means of entertainment for his reader and himself. It was a surrogate for conversation, and, like the "informal" talk of the drawing room or coffeehouse, it was expected to be polite, witty, amusing, and urbane.[9] It bridged the gaps between personal interviews, com-
municating news and gossip that the writer knew was of interest to
his recipient. It could manage to be entertaining even when saying
nothing:

I dont know yt any body has done a very Wise thing or a very foolish
one, tho most of the Parlt men are in Town, since I had ye honour of
seing you, and God knows nothing but those 2 extreems will entertain.
As for moderate matters and ye common occurances that happen
amongst this wicked Generation I wou'd not robb the Coffee-houses
and Visiting-days for fear they shou'd be left destitute of conversation
("To Facetia," n. d.; ASD, p. 201).

The parenthetical irony of this passage, which invites us to wonder whether Parliamentarians belong to the wise or the foolish, at
the same time assures us (syntactically) that there are men of both
sorts in government; it is matched by a more pervasive ironic
commentary on the content of the familiar letter: "God knows
nothing but those 2 extreems will entertain." This is as much a
shared joke between two friends as is the remark on Parliament or
the ironic proposition that letters, as substitutes for conversation,

could replace the tête-à-tête. The two are related social arts, not identical ones, and both writer and reader are aware of the definitive limits of each. Yet in his ironic way, Byrd is serious enough about the comparison to return to it, probably a full thirty years later, in a letter to his "Cousin Taylor":

It's now the fourth time this year I have broke in upon . . . [your] meditations, which is pretty fair for one who lives quite out of the Latitudes of news and adventures, nor can pick up one dark scandal to season a letter withal. 'Tis a mighty misfortune for an Epistolizer not to live near some great city like London or Paris, where people play the fool in a well bred way, and furnish their neighbours with discourse. In such places stories rowle about like snow-balls & gather variety of pretty circumstances in their way, till at last they tell very well and serve as good entertainment for a country cousin. But alas, what can we poor Hermits do, who know of no Intrigues but such as are carried on by the amorous Turtles, or some such innocent Lovers? Our vices & disorders want all that wit & refinement which makes them Palatable to the fine world, nor can we dress up the Devil so much to all advantage as to make him pass for an angel of light. Therefore, without a little invention, it would not be possible for one of us anchorites to carry on a tolerable correspondence, but like French Historians, where we don't meet with pretty incidents, we must e'en make them, & lard a little truth with a great deal of Fiction.[10]

The rest of the letter, which tells the story of an "Italian Bona Roba" not deemed suitable for modern pages by some twentieth-century editors,[11] continues in the same vein. The long preamble, Byrd protests, was designed to insure Mrs. Taylor that the anecdote is not of a "poetical sort" (*Writings*, p. 395) but wholly true, and he persists in this obvious prevarication even down to his final sentence, where he solemnly signs himself hers "without one word of a lye" (*Writings*, p. 395).

Without a doubt, this is one of the most amusing and delightful letters to be found in any literature, and it is so largely because of the disguised skill with which Byrd establishes his speaking voice in the passage quoted above. He adopts the character of an Epistolizer proud of his ability to write three letters about nothing in one year and proves his claim by producing a fourth, but then, like a true confidence artist, he asks his reader to buy wares he has already advertised as worthless. His second masquerade, that of a hermit or an anchorite, exaggerates both his innocence and his actual living conditions, at the same time that it comments ironically on a prevailing British attitude toward the colonies and the veracity of the Epistolizer; how, after all, would an otherworldly anchorite know that familiar correspondence ought to be seasoned with scandal? Selected images advance the humor—a story's rolling about like a snowball is a good example—and are aided by the informality of the sentence structure itself and by the comic stress laid on certain key words. The final "withal" in the first sentence, for instance, seems a perfect touch to characterize the Epistolizer, as does the beginning of the fourth sentence ("But alas") and the verb "lard" in the final statement.

Behind the mask of the Epistolizer, who laments the innocence of his rustic retirement, stands Byrd himself, employing one of the most familiar motifs of Horatian satire, the contrast between the purity of the country versus the corruption of the city, to comment upon what in another letter he called "the Onions and Fleshpots of Egypt [London]" (To Charles, Earl of Orrery, July 5, 1726; *VMHB*, 32:27). His pose permits him to have it both ways, to present a satiric criticism of London and Paris even while he exposes the boredom of the pastoral evironment, and his performance in larding "a little truth with a great deal of Fiction" unites the two worlds. The entertainment value of his story, like that of the stories written to him by his city cousin, depends upon an accumulation of "pretty" circumstances; both contain a significant amount of invented and fabricated material.

Obviously, a warm and friendly human relationship underlies this letter. The writer shares with his reader a humorous appreciation for the foibles of "French Historians" and a background in classical literature; the prose characterizes Mrs. Taylor almost as fully as it does Byrd. So, too, we understand the nature of the relationship Byrd had with another correspondent, Lord Boyle, from the tone of his letters to his titled English friend. One begins with a comment that is also pertinent to Byrd's concept of the function of letters:

> The Historical Epistle which You did me the Honour to send me, of the 30th of June last, gave us great Entertainment. Every thing is described with so much life and propriety that I fancyed the Objects

themselves present before my eyes. I could imagine I saw Miss Die Chapman bridle up and look happy when the Queen of France seemed gracious, and put on her disappointed Face when Her Majesty withdrew her Smiles. I could also figure your Lordship performing the friendly Office of picking up some of Lord Windsor's Effects, and others of them droping [sic] while he was bowing low for the trouble he had the misfortune of giving you. I could also paint the sprightly Colonel nodding over his Draughts, and cracking a stale Joke for the hundred and fiftieth time, while some of the Company took the liberty to laugh, not so much at the Story as at the Historian (February 2, 1726/27; *VMHB*, 32: 28).

In comparison to the letter to Mrs. Taylor, this is a straightforward account, one of the purposes of which is to insure Lord Boyle that his letter arrived safely.[12] Yet a similar warmth is present in both letters, toned down by a sense of respect for his Lordship which is registered by the greater degree of formality of the style. Byrd's variation of his verbs—for instance "imagine," "figure," and "paint"—lets his correspondent know that the writer has gone to some lengths not to be repetitious or boring and becomes, in fact, a substitute for the manners that would have been displayed on the occasion of a personal interview between the two men. By focusing his opening remarks on the contents of the Lord's last letter and on his own responses to them—here again the verbal variations come into play—he is able to pay his Lordship a graceful compliment on his writing ability, one that means even more coming from a writer who is himself the master of an easy, smoothly elegant style.

Byrd's appreciation of the scenes depicted in Boyle's letter takes us to the heart of the comic world of the familiar epistle. As Anderson and Ehrenpreis note, "the letter borrows constantly from the drama: the writer arranges, if he can, a scene revealing the oppositions inherent in the actors as well as the reason for them. Thus the letter can take on the fascination of the theater. . . ." A related effect is the establishment of a comic perspective shared by writer and reader, one that depends upon the writer's comprehensive view from above of the situation, his reader's personality, and the relationship that exists between them and himself in the act of writing. "Humor," the two critics continue, "is the simplest way for a man to suggest that he stands outside himself."[13] Byrd's comments on Boyle's letter testify that Boyle has successfully achieved both of these effects, the creation of comic scenarios and a personal comic distance which he is able to convey to his reader.

The humor of many of Byrd's letters, and particularly of his love letters, is in some ways more private than the comedy Boyle's letters evidently possessed, largely because in them he attempts to describe not situations but states of mind. The letters are stylized, for the most part, in accordance with the general formula he shared with one of his male correspondents, a "Seignor Punchino," when he offered the other writer some good-natured criticism:

> I believe while you were favouring me . . . [with] this Letter, you dreamt you were writeing to your Pastorella, so many sweet things were never said to a Man since Jupiter writ to Ganemede. . . . Consider that tho tis pardonable for a man in love to be out of his wits when he talks to his Princess: yet he shou'd quit his flights and his hyperboles upon other occasions, and condescend to use the common sence and common Language of men (*ASD*, p. 253).

Among the flights and hyperboles which Byrd found useful in his amorous correspondence, none is more important than the hyperbolic speaker, whose tone of voice exaggerates and ironically qualifies the emotions of the writer. For convenience in discussion, the role Byrd chooses to play in each letter might be designated his "persona," although the voice is really an extension of his personality rather than a mask for it;[14]The hyperbolic speaker differs from the persona of the playful letter to Mrs. Taylor in being less complicated and complex. We see a striking usage of it in his letter to "Babbina," which borrows from the epic the device of beginning *in medias res* and the motif of divine control of human affairs and character; from the romance and the epic, Byrd borrows the hero, whose heroic qualities are immediately diminished by a comparison with a puppy. A reference to Homer's account of the battle between the pigmies and the cranes (*Illiad*, III, 1-5), one of the favorite allusions among writers of mock epics, which Byrd manages to remake into a version of Leda and the swan, adds to the mock epic dimensions of the letter, and the whole is held loosely together by the kind of "illogical logic" that would have done credit to Tristram Shandy. The epistle is both short enough and amusing enough to warrant quoting in full:

> This is now the 9th day I have been blind wth an excess of Passion for the brightest of all the Fairys your self. Oh unhappy Hero that I am! What a misery t'is, that Puppys shou'd begin to see after that time and Lovers not? Sure the Gods never conferr'd so much perfection, delightful Madam, within so small a compass. You are an abridgement of Female excellence, and tho nature has drawn your dear person in little, yet she has drawn your fine qualitys in great. In that Speck of Entity she has inclos'd spirit enough to animate a machine as bulky as Mrs. Ireton or the Dutch-woman. With what transport have I beheld that lively spirit ready to fly away wth the clogg of china-mould that composes your delicate body. If the blast breath'd in at your nostrels, or back side after your conception had been never so little stronge[r] you must have been under a necessity of hanging a young Fellow about your alabaster neck, to keep you from being mounted to the upper Regions. Dearest Madam, figure to your self that such an accid[ent] may happen stil in a windy day, and make discreet provision against it by ... joining to your dainty person about ten stone more of wholesome flesh and bloud, which may fix you down securely to the Earth and guard you from the fate which many of your Kindred the Pigmies have suffer'd before you, by being snatcht away by Cranes and Hurricanes. Now I must tell you precious Madam, that I find my self much about the Weight I prescrib'd to you, and if you wou'd have the goodness to use me in the capacity above mention'd I swear to you by my manhood, an oath I use only upon solemn occasions, I wou'd stick as close to you
> As twineing Ivy round a bashful Tree (*ASD*, pp. 197-98).

This letter moves amusingly and with perfect balance between the flesh and the spirit. "Babbina," for all her delicacy, is still a creature of the flesh subject to human passions, as the reference to her birth, her nostrils, and her backside establishes. It is effusions such as these that convinced Pierre Marambaud, Byrds's latest and in many ways most thorough biographer, that in these early affairs Byrd's "reason was less engaged than his heart."[15]

One would not wish to challenge that assertion too strenuously, but it should be modified by an awareness of Byrd's own comments on the style suitable for love letters and by a recognition of the potential for the creation of a persona even in a familiar letter.

Byrd suits his style and content to his true feelings and to the character of the woman he addresses, of course, but that is only another way of saying that his roles are flexible and various. With one woman who was evidently his conquest already, Mrs. B----s ("Cleora"), he feels free to include a scatalogical allusion, decently dressed, to be sure, in respectable language (*ASD*, p. 363). For "Seignora Incognita," who had apparently sent him an unsolicited and frankly invitational missive, he adopts the role of a morally offended skeptic in order to challenge her to perform what she has promised (*ASD*, pp. 255-56). To "Preciosa" he writes with a self-assured tone, informing her that he has it in his power to convert her resentment into passionate love and that she will be "glad to love me in the end"; he then concludes with the ironic subscription, "Your Slave" (*ASD*, pp. 271-72). To "Monymia," he is by turns mentor and ardent suitor (*ASD*, pp. 229-34; 241-42). In all cases, these roles provide him with a vantage point to view himself from above even as he is protesting the total blindness of his passionate involvement.

Only in the correspondence with Miss Mary Smith ("Sabina") does Byrd's comic distance break down, in part because, as Marambaud suspected, he seems to have been genuinely more deeply involved in this affair than in the others, and in part as a result of Miss Smith's insistence that he give over his "Romantick" style ("To Veramour," January 23, 1717/18; *ASD*, p. 315) in favor of a more straightforward prose. On February 24 of the same year, Byrd promised to comply with her request, but he could not wholly forbear indulging his taste for analogies. "Suppose a Person ill of the small Pox," he wrote in what must have been a painful reminiscence of his first wife's death, "shou'd suffer a freind [sic] to converse so nearly with him as to give him the distemper, wou'd it not afterwards be a very odd piece of discretion to desire him to keep his distance?" (*ASD*, p. 343). Despite the ironic understatement in such a phrase as "a very odd piece of discretion" and the potential for distance in the role of an ill lover, a role he had played to perfection in his letter to "Parthenissa" (*ASD*, pp. 213-14),[16] he could not separate himself from his emotions; the character of the distempered lover expresses too nearly his own state of mind to function as a hyperbolic pose. It is psychologically descriptive, almost a metaphor, rather than a dramatic role. At last Byrd's pride came to his rescue, although even then the ambivalent fluctuation between half-prayerful humility and wry irony suggests that he had not yet found a place to stand secure above his experience and, like Troilus at the end of Chaucer's poem, look down on his own folly:

> That you dealt very unjustly & very dishonourably by me your own father confesst sufficiently, when he call'd you Jilt & other names of infamy for haveing given me so much encouragement. Now for him after being convinct of this to drive on another match is something so profligate towards you, towards the man that is dealing for you, and towards me y^t am injur'd, that civility wants a proper name for it. But as for your conduct Madam, tho all the world must condemn you, yet you may plead in your excuse the Violence of the temptation. There is a vast Estate with which a fine Lady cant possibly be miserable. Then your man has so bright an understanding, so sweet so engaging a temper so polite a behaviour, and has a constitution so uninjur'd by excess and disaster that he may well dazzle your Eys and make you forget all the Rules of Truth & Justice. . . . However I forgive you, and may Heaven forgive you too. Tho I cant forbear telling you that in the midst of this dreadful prospect I must stil hope you will act as a woman of sence & honour and not disappoint the flattering hopes you was pleas'd to give me (May 6, 1718; *ASD*, pp. 355-56).

The letters to "Sabina" belong not to the world of comedy, as most of Byrd's other familiar letters do, but rather to the world of the epistolary novel. They do not depend upon a firmly established or at least clearly defined human relationship existing anterior to their composition, but record a process of discovery of personality—the "diminishing fact behind the public facade," to use Anderson and Ehrenpreis' phrase. Like the early novel, they reveal the subtleties and nuances of love through a consistently maintained point of view that gradually develops the character of both reader and writer, and they accomplish this even while preserving the effect of spontaneity.[17] In an odd way, they even complement one of the themes of Richardson's *Pamela* (1740), at least as Fielding interpreted that novel, for they inform us that a woman in the marriage market is likely to hold out for the highest bidder. One has only to compare their handling of this theme with the letters to "Clarinda" (*ASD*, pp. 236-41), which abound in generalizations about the temptation to marry for money and titles, to become aware of the much greater degree of personal involvement that motivates the correspondence to "Sabina" and the greater depth of insight into human nature that Byrd brought out of his experiences with her.

In accordance with his own rules as he expressed them to "Seignor Punchino," Byrd abandons hyperbole and hyperbolic speakers when he addresses correspondents other than the women he attempted to woo with varying degrees of seriousness. Gone, too, are all but the vestiges of the carefully balanced clauses and witty turns of phrase that characterize the style of many of those letters. He employs instead a naturally graceful, fluid prose that responds to the rhythm of his ideas rather than to the mechanical principles of balance and antithesis. For content, he draws upon the kinds of situations and arrangements of characters that he had found so entertaining in Lord Boyle's letter. One of the best of this kind he wrote to "Lucretia," apparently an English kinswoman (*ASD*, p. 282, n. 2), describing a stagecoach journey he had recently taken. The episode could have served Fielding as a model for Chapter Twelve, Book I of *Joseph Andrews,* and aims at a similar unmasking of pretensions. It is an excellent genre sketch superior in some ways, particularly in its handling of speech, to the more famous portraits of North Carolinians in his *History of the Dividing Line.*[18] As is often the case with Byrd's humor, the laughter depends upon the reader's discovery that things are exactly the opposite of what they seem to be or ought to be. The "Country Parson," who wears the robes of the Prince of Peace, turns out to be a child of wrath, and the sexually fastidious Prude who is shocked to see a woman's elbow displayed in public has "had a child by her Uncles coachman, and made this Journey on purpose to meet him at one of the Inns by the way" (*ASD*, pp. 286-90).

For the aristocratic Byrd, there was little difficulty in attaining a comic perspective on his fellow wayfarers and little risk that his relative would not share his views. Occasionally, however, the effort to achieve distance and to communicate his view to his reader must have cost him a good deal more trouble. In what is perhaps his most famous and most controversial letter, addressed to

Charles, Earl of Orrery on July 5, 1726, he makes himself the hero of his own comic situation and is both a character in the action and a commentator on it. Somewhat in the manner of his letter to Mrs. Taylor, the epistle makes use of traditional pastoralism and the contrast between London, where the atmosphere is loaded with "Fogg and Smoake" (*VMHB*, 32: 27), and Virginia, where "fine Air and a Serene Sky" keep the citizens in "Good Health and Good Humour" and reconcile "a Man to himself" and his "misfortunes" (*VMHB*, 32: 26). After a long rehearsal of the virtues of Virginia, in the course of which Byrd portrays himself seated "Like one of the Patriarchs" surrounded by "my Flocks and my Herds, my Bond-men and Bond-women," he comes to the point: "Thus My Lord we are happy in our Canaans if we could but forget the Onions and Fleshpots of Egypt" (*VMHB*, 32: 27). The vices of London, he asserts, kept him too long "from the more solid pleasures of Innocence and Retirement" (*VMHB*, 32: 28).

These are precisely the sentiments we should expect a venerable patriarch to deliver, and we need to be careful not to make either too much or too little of them. They are, first of all, merely consistent with the role Byrd has chosen to play in this epistle, and if they may also be taken as an index to his progress in becoming an American or to his substantial contributions toward the creation and definition of a set of myths—the myth of the Garden and the ideal of the patriarch-philosophe, by which the antebellum South would live and die—they are, as well, the wistful expressions of a man who badly misses London and suffers in his silent exile.[19] They must be considered both in the literary context of Horatian satire and Virgilian pastoralism and in the company of other letters which Byrd devoted to the same subject of life in Virginia. The complex Horatian irony of the epistle to Mrs. Taylor has already been noted; for the rest, in only one letter, dated June, 1731, and directed to Lord Boyle, does he frankly endorse the ease and "innocence of the Patriarch" (*VMHB*, 32: 35). Otherwise, as Pierre Marambaud pointed out, Byrd knew too well what the realities behind his pose were, the rigors of the climate and the wilderness, the regimen of life on the plantation.[20] His letter to Mrs. Pitt (*VMHB*, 9: 237-39) of January 6, 1735/6, paints a different portrait of the weather in Virginia, and his epistle to the same Earl of Orrery, dated May 27, 1728 (*VMHB*, 32: 33-34) describes a different sort of American landscape. He counters the glib assertion in the pastoral letter previously referred to that Virginia's governors "may be Tyrants in their nature, yet they are Tyrants without Guards" (*VMHB*, 32: 27) by practical political analysis addressed to the same correspondent:

> we are not so apt to spoil our Governors as they are in the other Plantations, because we never compliment with one Penny more than their established Income. We dare not be generous to those who are Good, for fear of setting a Precident for those who are Bad. Most of the Colonies have been imprudent that way. They have done extravigant things for Governors they have been fond of, which has afterwards been made a Rule for their Successors tho' never so disagreeable (February 3, 1727/28; *VMHB*, 32: 31).

Because Byrd could not help becoming a Virginian when his intended "Pilgrimage in this New World" ("To John, Earl of Orrery," July 20, 1732; *VMHB*, 32: 36) lengthened into permanent residence, and because he was so fully aware of the paradoxes inherent in his pastoral pose, his American letters acquire a special significance for the student of American literature and culture, a value quite apart from their excellence as examples of the familiar epistle. The fact that the genealogy of his patriarch is more literary than factual does not mean that we can dismiss him as the product of Byrd's imagination, for, as Leo Marx assures us, the idea of America is intimately connected with traditional Horatian and Virgilian modes of thought and feeling.[21] In the patriarch, Byrd is attempting to find an "American" voice for a select, sophisticated London audience, a role which, while pretending to accept prevailing British definitions of Virginians, in reality mocks those views. Most visitors to the colony, Pierre Marambaud notes, reported that the life of the planter was one of "independence, luxury, leisure, and loneliness."[22] But that, saving only the loneliness, was not a true portrait, as Byrd and his privileged correspondents well knew, and he could count on their appreciation of his irony when he adopted the role in his letters.[23]

There is another way to approach the meaning of Byrd's pastoralism. Although George Core assures us that no significant discrepancies exist between Byrd's public and private selves,[24] it is clear that the master of Westover felt other tensions. He belonged both to the provincial world of Virginia and the sophisticated world of London, and the interesting thing about the voice of the Horatian hermit and patriarch is that it enabled him to create an ideal middle landscape and an ideal speaker in which the opposing values of nature and civilization, retirement and culture, wish and history could be reconciled. By striking a balance between expression and objectivity, he has solved as well one of the most pressing literary problems of his age: the projection of a public personality in a private document.[25]

The Biblical overtones with which Byrd's Horatian patriarch speaks suggest another sort of wish-image—the idea of a Promised Land—that he had to reconcile with the facts of life in Virginia and his longing for London. Nor are these the only "American" accents to be heard in the letters. Early in his career as an epistolizer, he had ironically claimed an "Indian Sincerity" ("To Panthea"; *ASD*, p. 196) as the hallmark of his prose, possibly in an attempt to validate the naturalness of his language in keeping with prevailing attitudes about the ideal prose of the familiar letter. Many years later, he told Peter Collinson that the manuscript of his *History* was merely an "Indian Scribble" (July 18, 1736; *VMHB*, 36: 354), this time making a defense for more serious literary purposes. But although Virginians might affect to be Indians in their writing, as Robert Beverley had in his Preface to *The History and Present State of Virginia*, they were nonetheless transplanted Englishmen—not American natives. On this point Byrd insisted even while making use of the popular misconception in a striking reference suggestive not only of the passage from youth to manhood but also of cultural rebirth. Writing to the Earl of Orrery, he compared his voyage to America to the experience of an Indian who has undergone the ritualistic loss of memory in "the Ceremony of *Husquenawing*" (*VMHB*, 32: 25), but assured his reader that even such an ordeal could not make him forget the Earl's kindnesses and the world of London. The roles that he adopted for the entertainment of his English friends constantly remind us that he never did, even as they allow him comic distance on his own situation. Knowing both literature and London equally well, he was able to maintain a point of balance and to see both sides of his life simultaneously.

The world of London is never far in the distance even in Byrd's letters to American correspondents. To Benjamin Lynde of Salem, Massachusetts, he writes one of his best letters, dated February 20, 1735/6, and filled with reminiscences of their adventures in the English capital (*VMHB*, 9: 241-44). To Sir John Randolph, he speaks of plays he has seen in London and begs news from the Old World (January 21, 1735/6; *VMHB*, 9: 239-41). The letter to Randolph, also one of Byrd's best, abounds in comic miniatures, from the picture of the great lawyer knee-deep in the mire of Virginia's back roads (which Byrd compares to the muddy roads of Sussex) to gentle satires at the expense of Randolph's dignity and a local actor's lack of talent. Warm and intimate in its tone and lacking any speaking voice not identifiable as Byrd's own, the letter is firmly rooted in the soil of Virginia but displays as well a yearning for the Mother Country. Byrd's great regard and open esteem for his friend and his enjoyment of the conversation they have recently shared holds the epistle together tonally and masks its cultural ambivalence.

Life in Virginia and the struggle to become a Virginian form a large part of the drama of Byrd's American letters and are, therefore, both directly and indirectly, reasons for the high literary quality of these epistles. Byrd's need to rely exlusively upon the letters to sustain transatlantic friendships and to bridge large gaps in communication with pithy news and friendly gossip, together with his increasing psychological and literary maturity, might also be cited as reasons for their superiority to most of his earlier letters. Generally speaking, his correspondence tends to fall stylistically as well as chronologically into three periods, with the letters of his early stay in London (before 1705) evidencing the greatest degree of artificiality in style and sentiment; apparently influenced by Senecan models, they often come perilously close to the literary exercises he turned out during the same period, although they manage to retain their generic qualities as letters mainly through our sense that they are intended for a particular reader. The correspondence belonging to the second London residence, as exemplified by the letters to "Sabina," displays greater naturalness and sincerity, but in its absorption with private emotions and states of mind sometimes verges on the confessional mode of modern letter writers.[26] With a few exceptions—the letter to "Lucretia" is one—the American letters (1726-1744) are both more interesting and better examples of the familiar letter as a literary form.

Taken together, Byrd's epistles reveal facets of his personality not fully explored in the diaries or disclosed in his more public writings. For this reason alone they will continue to be read, but we can accurately interpret the evidence they offer only if we keep in mind that they are also literature. In them, Byrd has the opportunity to work out the relationship between objectivity and subjectivity; to take, in specific instances, a long step towards solving, temporarily and only for himself, the central literary problem of his age: the resemblance of persona to personality. The letters allow us to see Byrd from both perspectives simultaneously, as they also permitted him to distance himself from experiences even while he was recording his impressions, more or less immediate and spontaneous, for someone else. Once we have all the letters before us in a collected edition, we should be able to see their literary qualities still more clearly, and to this writer at least it seems a reasonable prediction that they will then take their place, next only to the histories, as Byrd's most important contributions to American literature.

NOTES

1. According to Pierre Marambaud, *William Byrd of Westover, 1674-1744* (Charlottesville: University Press of Virginia, 1971), 282, an edition of the letters is currently underway under the expert editorial guidance of Louis B. Wright. Marambaud, (282-87) prints an excellent bibliography of Byrd's known letters. A brief discussion of Byrd's letters may be found in Richard Beale Davis, "William Byrd: Taste and Tolerance," *Major Writers of Early American Literature*, ed. Everett H. Emerson (London and Madison: University of Wisconsin Press, 1972), 162-67.

2. Howard Anderson and Irvin Ehrenpreis, "The Familiar Letter in the Eighteenth Century: Some Generalizations," *The Familiar Letter in the Eighteenth Century*, ed. Howard Anderson, Philip B. Daghlian, and Irvin Ehrenpreis (Lawrence and Toronto: University Press of Kansas, 1966), 282.

3. Most especially in the letters to "Sabina," in which he manages to

retain a measure of self respect through his repeated insistence that he will show her letters to no one, even though he feels that the possession of them gives him the power to put an end to her engagement to Sir Edward Des Bouverie. See, for example, "To Sabina," May 6, 1718, in *Another Secret Diary of William Byrd of Westover, 1739-1741*, ed. Maude H. Woodfin and Marion Tinling (Richmond: The Dietz Press, 1942), 354-56. Hereinafter, *ASD*.

4. William H. Irving, *The Providence of Wit in the English Letter Writers* (Durham: Duke University Press, 1955), 14, goes well beyond this claim, contending that the familiar letter was above all else "literary, and though it was in most cases written for and sent to the person whose name appears on the superscriptions, it was written with a larger audience in view and finally by the author's connivance or the connivance of friends after his death found its way to that larger audience." That Byrd took the time to make copies of his letters and in some cases reread and rearranged them, as he did with the letters to "Sabina" (*ASD*, 299, n. 3), would seem to lend some support to this position, but in general my arguments accept the more modest view of D. L. Hobman, "Letters as Literature," *Quarterly Review*, 292, No. 601 (1954), 358: "It is exactly this conjuring up of another human being, this sense of another presence . . . which distinguishes letters from all other forms of literature."

5. " 'Nature and Friendship': The Personal Letters of Jonathan Swift," *The Familiar Letter*, 16.

6. On the British postal system, see Howard Robinson, *The British Post Office* (Princeton: Princeton University Press, 1948), 81; R. W. Chapman, "The Course of the Post in the Eighteenth Century," *Notes and Queries*, 183 (1942), 67-69; and Irving, 30. In chapters 2-3, pp. 57-137 of his study, Irving deals with French models and English letters before the eighteenth century. By far the best study of letter-writing manuals, complete with an extensive bibliography, is Katherine G. Hornbeak's *The Complete Letter Writer in English, 1568-1800*, Smith College Studies in Modern Languages, 15, Nos. 3-4 (1934).

7. Anderson and Ehrenpreis, 270-72; Irving, 31-56. See also *Tatler*, Nos. 30 and 87, and *Spectator*, No. 542.

8. *William Byrd of Virginia: The London Diary (1717-1721) and Other Writings*, ed. Louis B. Wright and Marion Tinling (New York: Oxford University Press, 1958), 107.

9. Anderson and Ehrenpreis, 274-76; Herbert Davis, "The Correspondence of the Augustans," *Essays in English Literature from the Renaissance to the Victorian Age Presented to A. S. P. Woodhouse* (Toronto: University of Toronto Press, 1964), 195-212; rev. and rpt. in *The Familiar Letter*, 1-13.

10. "To Mrs. Taylor," (October 10, 1735) *The Writings of "Colonel William Byrd of Westover in Virginia, Esqr.,"* ed. John Spencer Bassett (New York: Doubleday, 1901), 394-95. Hereinafter, *Writings*.

11. "Letters of the Byrd Family," *Virginia Magazine of History and Biog-*

raphy, 9 (1902), 229. This journal, hereinafter designated *VMHB* and referred to in the text by volume and page numbers only, printed a substantial number of Byrd's letters and, along with *ASD*, is the major source of the primary materials consulted in this essay.

12. Overseas and even intracolonial deliveries were not as reliable as those in London, as we may gather from Byrd's comments in his letters to Benjamin Lynde (*VMHB*, 9: 242) and Captain Parke (*VMHB*, 9: 244).

13. 280-81.

14. Ferguson, 27-31, makes a similiar point about Swift's letters.

15. Marambaud, 24.

16. The role depended both upon dramatic and romantic conventions and included the standard "longing look" and "pale countenance" (*ASD*, 214) counterfeited by Hamlet, among other theatrical lovers. Byrd began the epistle: "I sigh enough to blow out all the candles in the room" (*ASD*, 213).

17. Anderson and Ehrenpreis, 281-82.

18. For another brief discussion of this letter, see Willie T. Weathers, "William Byrd: Satirist," *William and Mary Quarterly* 4, 3d ser. (1947), 32-3; Weathers notes the resemblances between this sketch and Byrd's portrait of the North Carolinians. Kenneth Lynn, *Mark Twain and Southwestern Humor* (Boston: Little, Brown & Co., 1959); rpt. as "The Style of a Gentleman," *Critical Approaches to American Literature*, ed. Ray B. Browne and Martin Light (New York: Thomas Y. Crowell, 1965), I, 51-52, comments on Byrd's failure to render the speech of the North Carolinians.

19. These views are most cogently argued in review essays by George Core, "Two Views of Colonel William Byrd," *Southern Literary Journal*, 4 (1972), 117-21; Carl R. Dolmetsch, "William Byrd II: The Augustan Writer as 'Exile' in His Own Country," *Virginia Quarterly Review*, 48 (1972), 145-49; and Lewis P. Simpson, "William Byrd and the South," *Early American Literature*, 7 (1972), 187-95.

20. Marambaud, 147.

21. Leo Marx, *The Machine in the Garden: Technology and the Pastoral Ideal in America* (New York: Oxford University Press, 1964), esp. chap. 1.

22. Marambaud, 147.

23. For John Boyle's reputation as a wit and a letter writer, see Irving, 254-57; the sophistication of the fourth Earl of Orrery (Charles) is demonstrated by his role in exposing the "Phalaris" letters.

24. Core, 120.

25. Anderson and Ehrenpreis, 282.

26. On this point, see D. L. Hobman, 362-64.

THE REV. SAMUEL DAVIES' ESSAY SERIES:
THE VIRGINIA CENTINEL, 1756-1757

J. A. Leo Lemay

PART ONE: THE ESSAY SERIES

In the twentieth century, the Virginia Centinel essay series has been known to scholars only because essay No. 10 contains an early attack upon the Virginia Regiment commanded by George Washington, and because this essay caused Washington and many of his best officers to consider submitting their resignations.[1] But in the early nineteenth century, the series was remembered primarily for its literary artistry. The first historian of American printing and the first person to attempt to write a more than parochial literary history of America, Isaiah Thomas, recorded in his *The History of Printing in America* (1810) that William Hunter's *Virginia Gazette* "published in 1757, many well written essays, under the signature of *The Virginia Centinel.*"[2] The reason that such books as Martin Christadler's on the early American essay or Jay B. Hubbell's literary history of the South do not mention the Virginia Centinel is simply that only the infamous No. 10 is generally known to exist.[3] Just a few issues of the *Virginia Gazette* from the 1750's are extant, and the only Virginia Centinel that survives in the *Virginia Gazette* is No. 10. But eighteenth-century newspapers commonly reprinted articles, poems, and essays of special interest, and ten of the nineteen known numbers of "The Virginia Centinel" may be found in the newspapers of other colonies.[4]

The first number of "The Virginia Centinel" appeared in the *Virginia Gazette* of April 30, 1756 (no longer extant). This most popular number of the series was reprinted five times: *The New York Gazette* of June 14 (which noted the date and place of its source), the *Boston News Letter* of June 24 and July 1, the *Connecticut Gazette* of June 26, the *Boston Evening Post* (evidently copying the *New York Gazette* text) of June 28, and the *Maryland Gazette* of August 12. Unfortunately, all reprints are incomplete, invariably omitting what the *New York Gazette* called the author's apology "for himself as a public Centinel," and only the *New York Gazette* (the text cited), the *Boston News Letter*, and the *Maryland Gazette* contain the prefatory poem on public spirit, and the epigraph.

The essay was popular in other colonies for a combination of reasons. Paradoxically, it appealed both to the developing American nationalism of the colonists and to the provincialism and chauvinism of the individual colonies. The American colonies were caught in an unofficial war with the French. The war had called forth, in 1754, Benjamin Franklin's editorial and snake cartoon ("Join or Die"), as well as his Albany Plan for the unification of the colonies.[5] Virginia bore the brunt of the earliest attacks, but New England, New York, Pennsylvania, and Maryland were also affected. The *New York Gazette* omitted the Centinel's apology because it was "of little Moment in the animating of our Countrymen"—an effect almost as necessary in the more northern colonies as in Virginia. But the other colonies must also have enjoyed the lashing that the Virginia Centinel bestowed upon the lack of "Public Spirit" in Virginia. New England especially (where the Centinel essays were most popularly reprinted) considered itself, with good reason, the most courageous and public-spirited of His Majesty's colonies. Perhaps the *Maryland Gazette* reprinting of the essay as late as August was caused in part by the fulfillment of the dire April prophecies of war and ruination that were to come, "when such a Scene of Blood, Devastation and Terror opens before us in the approaching summer." The Centinel had predicted that if the people did not join the militia to protect the frontier, "this favourable Spot of the Globe, this Land of Plenty and Liberty, shall become a conquered enslaved Province of France, and the Range

of Indian Savages . . . principally owing to the Security or Cowardice of its present Inhabitants." The *New York Gazette* prefaced its
reprinting of the essay with "We should think ourselves blameable
were we not at this Time to give the following a Place in this
Paper." The Centinel's appeal for patriotic public spirit struck a
responsive chord throughout the colonies.

An original prefatory poem of seventeen lines in blank verse
exhorts the Virginians to fight the French and Indians:

> Friends! Countrymen! or, if a nobler Name
> Will fire you into Patriots, BRITONS! hear
> Your bleeding Country's Call——AWAKE! ARISE!
> Whether Ye shine in Life's meredian Blaze,
> Ennobled into Chiefs; or labouring, till
> The stubborn Furrow with an Hireling's Arm.
> Sturdy of Heart, and guileless. Bravely rise,
> In all the Manliness of Freedom rise;
> And guard your All from the rapacious Hands
> Of Avarice and Ambition——Where, Oh! where
> Is Public Spirit, Freedom's honest Heart,
> Her social Warmth; her Sturdiness of Limb,
> The hardy Front, the Majesty of Mein,
> The Arm Herculean?—Rouse, and fiercely drive
> Invasion from your Borders, keenly press
> Her routed Squadrons, and exulting stab
> The baleful Sorceress in every Pore.

The lines are competent eighteenth-century verse, typical of the
magazine and newspaper poetry of the time, but without special
intrinsic excellence. Since the thesis was presented in greater detail
and more persuasively in the accompanying essay, one can sym-
pathize with the editors who omitted the epigraph. Nevertheless,
the fact that the Centinel could and did write competent blank
verse is one clue to his identity.

The first Virginia Centinel essay exhorts the Virginians to fight
and exaggeratedly portrays the evils of the French and Indians;
but the last paragraph, which clinches the argument, is especially
interesting for its rhetorical structure, its praise of George Washington (hitherto unnoticed), its specific references, and its series of
historical examples proving that a comparatively small number of
French and Indians could conquer the Americans:

Dangerous as your Situation is, it is certainly in your Power, under the ordinary Blessings of Providence, to free your Country from its present Distress, restore its Peace and Safety. But whoever observes what little Disposition has appeared among us to exert that Power,—that even such an acceptable and popular Officer as Col. Washington, has not been able to enlist a sufficient Number of Men, in such a populous Colony as this, without Compulsion;—that the public Resentment has been so cool against those murderous Savages the *Shawaneese*, that it was with the greatest Difficulty an Handful of Men could be raised to attack them in their Towns,—that Multitudes have been unmanning themselves in Luxury and Pleasure, when the Cause of their Country called them to encounter the glorious Danger of the Field; and their Enemies were enterprizing, indefatigable and successful,——whover has observed such Things as these, it must strike a Damp to his Spirit, and alarm him with anxious Apprehensions. What avails the Superiority of our Numbers, or the Advantage of our Situation, above our Enemies, if we sit still, and do Nothing; a little Smattering of History will inform us, that a few hardy, resolute and enterprising Fellows, have often routed a much superior Number, and over-run Countries that had all these Advantages in the highest Degree. The little States of *Greece*, stood their Ground against all the Power of the vast *Persian* Empire, mortified the Insolence of *Xerxes*, and defeated the most numerous Army,† that ever was raised upon the earth. *Darius* with an Army of 5 or 6 Hundred Thousand Men was routed by about 30,000 Veterans under *Alexander* the Great; *Darius* losing about 100,000, and *Alexander* about 300: The *Hunns, Goths* and *Vandals*, savage Banditti, not unlike our Indians, over-run [sic] the vast *Roman* Empire, and crumbled it into Pieces, and the most powerful Kingdoms of Europe, at present are but Fragments of that unwieldy Body. *Charles* the XII. of *Sweden*, with 8000 hardy *Swedes* slaughtered and put to Flight 100,000 *Russians*, in their Intrenchments. These Instances are sufficient to mortify our Confidence in our Numbers and Situation; which will only render the Victory of our Enemies more signal and illustrious, unless we vigorously exert ourselves.[6] It is Courage, my Countrymen, it is Courage and good Conduct, Hardiness, Resolution and Unanimity, which determine the Fate of Nations, and decide the Victory in the Field. These manly Qualities, with the Concurrence of Heaven, would soon recover our sinking Land; but without them all our Hopes are but vain and presumptuous. Therefore away with sneaking Cowardice, dreaming Security and effeminating Pleasures; and put on the Man, the Patriot, the Hero.

---

†*About 6 Millions 2 Hundred and 83 Thousand, including Soldiers, Servants, Women, Sutlers, &c.* Herod, 1. VII, c. 60, 72, 87.

The motif of uncertainty concerning the outcome of the war, especially in conjunction with praise for Washington, must have reminded all Virginians in 1756 of the surprising and undreamed-of defeat of General Edward Braddock less than a year before. The first Centinel essay had a double-edged effect: it not only informed the public that Virginia and America would be lost to the English if the colonists did not manfully fight, but also reminded them of the heroic fighting of the colonials during the defeat of the British regular soldiers—thus subtly building the colonists' self-esteem while proving the necessity for courage.[7]

The next extant Virginia Centinel, "Virginia Centinel No. III," was reprinted in the *New York Gazette* (the text cited) for June 28, and reprinted from there in the *Boston Evening Post* of August 9.[8] The date of its appearance in the *Virginia Gazette* is not given. May 14 would have been its publication date if no intervals had occurred in the appearance of the essay series. Since the first few numbers of almost every new essay series in a colonial newspaper appeared regularly, it seems likely that the third Centinel was published in the *Virginia Gazette* on May 14 or May 21. After a prefatory epigraph from a speech by Cato in Sallust's *Catiline Conspiracy*,[9] the author states his subject: "As the Incursions and Barbarities of the Enemy upon our Frontiers have at Length forced us upon the Expedient of drafting the Militia, perhaps a few Thoughts upon that Subject, may not be unseasonable." Then, with the bludgeoning honesty that was to make the Centinel infamous, he attacked the past performance of the American militia: "Should we form our Ideas of a Country Militia from what we have hitherto seen in this Colony; I own we have little Reason to expect any Good from it." But then the author claims that the militia if "well armed and disciplined, and animated with a proper Spirit" could answer "all the Purposes of a standing Army, without the Expence to the Country." To prove his point, the learned Centinel pointed out that "*Soldiers by Profession*, are, comparatively, but a modern Invention; and many powerful Nations have had no other Defence, but the Country Militia." So the Centinel sketches the structure of the army of the Roman Commonwealth before turning to his own colony. "*Virginia*, upon an Emergency, could easily spare an Army of 10,000 Men to be drafted out of the Militia, without leaving our Families defence-less." Then, introducing a radical economic note, the Centinel said: "Nay, I dare affirm, there is that Number of Men, able to bear Arms in this Colony, who depend almost entirely upon the Labour of their Slaves, and do not so much as take the Care of Over-seers on themselves. And I am not sagacious enough to dis-cover, what mighty Loss it would be, either to the Public, or to their own private Estates, if [at this point the rhetoric calls for the reader to expect—and the contemporary Virginian to fear—that the Centinel will say that the deaths of such parasites would be no loss, but instead there is an anti-climax of reasonableness] such should spend a Campaign, or at least a few Weeks, in the Fron-tiers."

The Centinel next argues that the example of "Gentlemen of Fortune and Influence" would "propagate a Spirit of Patriotism and Bravery among the Populace." He claims: "I converse a good deal with this Order of Mankind; and from my Knowledge of their Dispositions, I can assert, that such an Example is more likely to excite them to exert themselves, and brave all Dangers for their Country, that all the Acts our Legislatures can make, and all the Wages, Premiums, &c., which they can propose." The Centinel says that he has heard some people argue: " 'What! shall we fight for Gentlemen? They have more to lose than we; and therefore, let them go out, and fight for themselves.' " Although the Centinel mocks this argument by referring to the story of the "Fellow that refused to pump in a leaky Ship,"[10] he nevertheless is again striking a radical economic note and telling the wealthy planters that they must fight.

The Centinel then praises Peyton Randolph, who was later to be the first president of the Continental Congress, and who, the *Virginia Gazette* of May 7 announced (reprinted in the *New York Gazette* of May 27), had formed a volunteer company of gentle-men to serve on the frontier: "While I am hinting this Patriot-Scheme to my Countrymen of Fortune, how agreeably am I sur-prised to find, that what I feared would be received as the roman-tic Project of a whimsical Patriot, has already been digested into a Plan of Association, and is about to be carried into Execution." The conclusion of this number exhorts the colonial Americans with a quotation from Cicero that anticipates President John F. Kennedy's Inaugural Address: "If every Man in this Colony, able to join in such a disinterested Scheme, would heartily concur in it, our Frontiers would soon be guarded with a numerous Army of brave Men, actuated by the most exalted Principles. And not an *Indian* Savage, or *Gallic* Slave, would venture near the Borders of so heroic a People; who have a Sense of an Interest besides, and superior to their own; and can understand that Mystery, advanced about 1800 Years [ago], by a *Roman* Patriot, 'That we are born for our Country, as well as ourselves.' "

The distinguishing characteristics of the author of the Virginia Centinel essay series begin to be apparent in this Centinel. He is evidently not one of the Virginia aristocracy, not one of the wealthy planters—and he reveals a degree of hostility and resentment toward that group. The attack on a standing army and praise of militia also imply that the author dislikes not only the British regular army (and such officers of disbanded regiments as Lawrence Washington, George's older half-brother) but also any American group such as the Virginia Regiment, which intended to serve through the crisis (rather than, like the militia, turning out for specific emergencies) and which hoped (or, at least, its officers hoped) to be incorporated into the British regular army. Also, the Centinel, without directly saying so, obviously resented the fact that the militia law favored the wealthy by allowing them to pay £10 for a substitute.[11]

The same issue of the *Maryland Gazette* (August 12, 1756) that published the first Virginia Centinel essay contained another essay "From the VIRGINIA CENTINEL" which, like the first, was not further identified, but unlike the first, was not reprinted by any other colonial newspaper. It may have been No. 2, but it does not seem logically to follow No. 1 or to precede or to follow No. 3. No. 9 of the series appeared in the *Virginia Gazette* on August 20, and our unnumbered essay does not seem to precede it, and besides it is probably reprinted in the *Maryland Gazette* too soon to be No. 8; therefore I believe that this unnumbered essay was No. 5, 6 or 7. As I shall show below, it paraphrases and quotes a sermon by another American minister, and treats the same subject as the Virginia Centinel, Nos. 17 and 18.

The unnumbered Virginia Centinel viciously condemns French Catholics, recounting the history of the massacres of the French Protestants, beginning with the St. Bartholomew's day massacre of 1572, and concentrating on the persecutions by Lewis XIV. The Centinel details the persecutions of the "*Hugonots* (as the Protestants are there called)." He claims that the "Prisons and Gallies were filled with such as had been apprehended, while attempting to fly the Kingdom. But notwithstanding the utmost Vigilance, *Voltaire* tells us, That about 500,000 made their Escape, in about three Years; and settled in *England, Germany, Holland,* and even in Places so distant as *Virginia*, and the Cape of *Good Hope* in *Africa*." The essayist says that the persecutions continue under the present King of France, Lewis XV, and quotes from recent letters written by French ministers. The Centinel concludes with an exhortation:

> What do you think of it, that *Virginia* should become the Scene of such Barbarities? The Thought must fire you into Heroes, and rouse all the *Man* within you, to keep such a cruel murderous Power far from your Borders. For my Part, I am a Lover of Peace, and neither Nature nor Education has formed me for War: But while such a Scene is before me, I could throw away my Pen, and take the Sword, and rather die in the Field, than submit to a Medley of *French* and Popish tyranny.

When it reprinted the "Virginia Centinel No. IX," the *Pennsylvania Gazette* (the text cited) of September 16 noted that the source was the *Virginia Gazette* of August 20. The *New York Gazette*, September 27, and the *Boston Evening Post* of October 11 also reprinted the essay, but the former omitted the source and the latter omitted not only the source but also the prefatory epigraph from Virgil, as well as the concluding signature "L." The ninth Centinel was occasioned by England's declaration of war with France. [12] The Centinel warns of "the fluctuating State of Kingdoms, and how seldom the Issue corresponds to human Expectations." He condemns the colonists for their "general Corruption of Manners," and specifically names their "Luxury, Sensuality, mutual Diffidence, Animosities, divided Interests, and selfish Pursuits." Anticipating Edward Gibbon, he reminds his readers that these faults caused the downfall of "*Babylon, Jerusalem, Per-*

sia, Greece, and *Rome.*" Then the Centinel contrasts the "happy Situation" of England and the English colonies with the weak condition of France and the French colonies, saying that this difference gives us reason "to hope, that these Commotions [may] terminate in our Favour." The last paragraph urges that "every Man in his Station, do all in our Power for this End." In the midst of a long and effective anaphora, the Centinel urges: "Let the Clergy especially, shock their Hearers with the Horrors of Popery; animate them with a publick Spirit, and the ardent Love of Liberty; and rouse them from their Lethargy with just Representations of their Danger." The Centinel concludes with King Henry's "Once more unto the breech" speech in Shakespeare's *Henry the Fifth,* III, i, 3-9, 15-17, urging the men to fight.

At the end of the ninth Virginia Centinel essay appears the signature "L." The ninth Centinel is the first one extant to conclude with an initial. Since, as we will see, two of the essays conclude "L. & V.," the purpose of the initial is evidently to credit a particular writer with that essay. The use of the initial(s) suggests that two persons collaborated on the essay series. Perhaps all of the original essays concluded with an initial (or with two), and these signatures were simply omitted by the papers that reprinted the early essays. But it seems unlikely that, with so many newspapers reprinting the first Centinel, they would all omit the signature. More probably, the identifying signatures only began after the first (or the first few) Centinel(s) had appeared. I suspect that one author ("L.") began the series and was joined by a collaborator before the ninth Centinel appeared. But it is possible that the essay series began as a collaboration and that the authors decided to distinguish their respective work after several Centinels appeared.

Although the condemnation of luxury and sensuality were standard themes in eighteenth-century English and American literature, the authors of such diatribes were frequently religious and were commonly dissenters. No doubt we can find some wealthy Anglicans and deists who are exceptions to this generalization—but such exceptions will often be found to have a special rhetorical purpose in advocating a Spartan discipline (e.g., Benjamin Franklin). By and large, such attitudes were more common among the

dissenters and middle-class than among the wealthy and aristocracy. The colonial Virginian laymen who can be identified with
long protests against luxury and sensuality are James Reid and
Landon Carter—both quite religious, and the former evidently a
Presbyterian.[13] The attitudes of the Centinel as revealed in the
ninth essay suggest that he was middle-class, religious, and a dissenter.

The infamous "Virginia Centinel No. X" appeared in the *Virginia Gazette* of September 3, 1756 (text cited). It was reprinted in
four papers: the *New York Mercury*, October 25; the *Pennsylvania
Journal*, November 4; the *Maryland Gazette*, November 25; and
the *Connecticut Gazette*, December 4—thus tying the Centinel No.
16 in popularity and coming behind only the five reprintings of
the first Centinel. After a prefatory epigraph from Virgil, the Centinel opens with a consideration of "The Profession of Soldiers,"
saying that "their Merit should not be invidiously depretiated;
their Foibles maliciously exaggerated; or their Conduct censured,
by Chimney-corner Politicians, who lie sneaking at Home, in glorious Ease, and know not their Circumstances, or the Reasons
upon which they act." But after the declaration, the Virginia Centinel penned a scathing denunciation of the Virginia Regiment,
and, by implication, of its leader, the young Colonel George Washington. Washington was so upset that he suggested resigning his
commission, and all the officers at Fort Cumberland threatened
the same. Richard Bland, who appreciated the difficulties of Washington and the officers in commanding an unruly small body of
temporary soldiers, answered the Virginia Centinel No. X; and
Washington himself wrote a reply and sent it to his brother, paying
ten shillings to have it published in the *Virginia Gazette*.[14] Here is
the Centinel's attack:

> No profession in the World can secure from Contempt and Indigna-
> tion a Character made up of Vice and Debauchery; and no Man is
> obliged to treat such a Character as sacred. When raw Novices and
> Rakes, Spendthrifts and Bankrupts, who have never been used to com-
> mand, or who have been found insufficient for the Management of their
> own private Affairs, are honoured with Commissions in the Army;
> when Men are advanced according to Seniority, the Interests and Influ-
> ence and Friends, &c, and not according to Merit; when the common
> Soldiers are abused, in a Fit of Humour or Passion, or through an

Ostentation of Authority; and in the mean Time, perhaps, tolerated or connived at, in Practices really worthy of Correction; when the Militia Men are brow-beat and discouraged in every noble Atchievement, as claiming a Share with the Soldiery in their Monopoly of Honour; when the Officers give their Men an Example of Debauchery, Vice and Idleness; when they lie sculking in Forts, and there dissolving in Pleasure, till alarmed by the Approach of the Enemy, who could expect to find them no where else; when instead of searching out the Enemy, waylaying and surprising them, obstructing their Marches, and preventing their Incursions, they tempt them by their Security and Laziness, to come in Quest of them, and attack them in their Fortifications.——When this is the Case, how wretchedly helpless must a Nation be? What useless Lumber, what an Incumbrance, is the Soldiery?

Conscius ipse sibi de se putat omnia dici

I would by no Means make the *Event* the Standard by which to judge the Measures taken, though this be undoubtedly the Standard of the Crowd. Successful Rashness will never fail of popular Applause, and unfortunate good Conduct will never escape Censure. But when nothing brave is so much as *attempted*, but very rarely, or by Accident, or for necessary Self-defence; when Men whose Profession it is to endure Hardships, and encounter Dangers, cautiously shun them, and suffer their Country to be ravaged in their very Neighborhood; then, certainly, Censure cannot be silent; nor can the Public receive much Advantage from a Regiment of such dastardly Debauchees.

After this denunciation, the Centinel quotes Shakespeare's *Henry the Sixth, part II*, III. i. 300ff. on cowards, and quotes Horace's Book III, Ode 2 (as well as Philip Francis' translation) on the "Discipline proper for Soldiers," before sarcastically commenting: "But it seems the Delicacy of modern Soldiers cannot bear such hardy Discipline. Their Ease and Pleasure must not be disturbed by the Fatigues and Dangers of the Field or Woods." The Centinel then turns to his favorite method of proof and amplification, the piling up of historical examples from the Bible and from classical historians, all showing that "Luxury and Sensuality have unmanned many an Army, and enslaved or ruined many flourishing Cities and Kingdoms." The Centinel concludes that "The Application of these Pieces of History is easy." The essay is signed "L. & V."

Because of this essay, the officers of the Virginia Regiment at Fort Cumberland wrote to Lt. Colonel Adam Stephen, in a letter dated October 6, 1756 (probably first published in the *Virginia*

Gazette), which was printed in the *Pennsylvania Journal*, November 4, 1756, that "unless we have ample Satisfaction for these so groundless and barb'rous Aspersions, we are one and all (at this Garrison) fully determin'd to present our Commissions to the Governor." The officers revealed that they believed that the Governor must have concurred with the opinion of the Virginia Centinel, for it was well known that sensitive contents of the Virginia newspapers had to have the governor's approval: "[we] desire that you will inform His Honor we expect that he will provide a Sett of Men for the Service, that will better answer the expectations of Our Countrey and of himself; we say Himself, believing The Printer wou'd never have dar'd to insert such a Paper in His Gazette without His previous Knowledge or Consent, in either of which cases He must have believ'd the Censures therein to be just."[15] The officers gave as their deadline for the apology, November 20, and bitterly concluded that they wanted to be justified to "the Neighboring Colonies, amongst whom we make no Doubt we are by this Time become a common Topic of Derision and Ridicule[,] a Favor we are to thank Our COUNTRY MEN for."

Governor Dinwiddie reassured the troops of his confidence; more importantly, a letter correcting the Centinel and praising the troops was written by the prestigeous Richard Bland.[16] Under the pseudonym "Philo Patriae," Bland pretended to be an objective British citizen and Virginia Colonist, writing a letter to his burgess, urging the support of the militia. Bland also established his ethos by pretending to be a less artful writer than the Centinel, though possessed of "Facts, and from them [of] . . . Truths, which the Centinel may not have adventured to." Bland hints that he had long ago "pointed out with a kind of prophetic Spirit, the fatal Consequences" of the British neglect of the French invasion of the frontiers, but he was "not regarded." So Bland traces the history of the niggardliness of the Virginia burgesses to fund men and material to meet the French and Indian invasion of the frontiers, and includes an aside scorning the conduct of Colonel Thomas Dunbar, who fled from the frontier with the British regulars after the defeat of General Braddock.

"Philo Patriae" condemned the short-sighted, niggardly actions of the Virginia legislators, mentioning particularly the limitations on the service of the militia ("restrained from marching more than five miles beyond the [frontier] inhabitants"). There are too few men to guard too long a frontier. He praises the officers, who have "behaved with remarkable Courage and Resolution; who have marched over vast Mountains; supported with invincible Patience, the rudest Fatigues; and shewed the most intrepid Valour in the greatest Dangers, and the warmest Desire to preserve their Country." Philo Patriae said that more money was needed from the legislators for troops and material, and that fewer restrictions should be put on the terms under which the soldiers would serve: "Generals and Commanders of armies must be left to act as they find it most expedient for their Country's Interest." And so he concluded with an implied threat to the colonial Virginia politicians by pretending to be "one of your Electors," writing to his good friend, a burgess.

Most Washington scholars have treated the Virginia Centinel as if he were completely jaundiced and as if his indictment had no semblance of truth. But complaints about the Virginia Regiment and especially about its officers circulated in private. The Rev. James Maury, in a letter of June 15, 1756, wrote that its bad reputation dated from General Edward Braddock's treatment of the regiment in the spring and early summer of 1755: "Such was the treatment which that unfortunate regiment received last campaign from the commander-in-chief, that no person of any property, family, or worth has since enlisted in it, and the Governor has filled up the vacant commissions and the new companies with raw, surly and tyrannical Scots, several of them mere boys from behind the counters of the factors here; thus, that regiment, from an exceeding good one, has degenerated into a most insignificant and corrupt corps." Maury had been instrumental in passing the militia act of 1756, and he was especially disappointed that "the salutary purposes of that act will be defeated, as the above complement of men will generally be made up of worthless vagrants, servants just out of servitude, and convicts bought with the fines paid by recusants; men utterly unacquainted with the woods and the use of fire arms, and, for these reasons, were there no other, unfit to be sent against the Indians." In the spring of 1756, Maury had served as a chaplain to the Louisa county militia and testified that he was "fully convinced . . . they would have followed *their* own officers with the utmost spirit to Duquesne, or any other place" but that "the bare suspicion that some of the officers of the [Virginia] regiment were to act over them as captains, had almost the same effect on the men as a spark of fire on a train of gunpowder. It raised such a fermentation, as Col. Washington's positive declaration that they should not be commanded by any officers but these lieutenants, could scarce allay."[17]

The author of the satiric "Dinwiddianae" addressed a ballad entitled "The Remonstrance" to Governor Dinwiddie, accusing him of cramming the "fighting list" with "Shop Keepers & Shavers." The satirist noted that the commissions in the Virginia Regiment "were at this time distributed with great partiality to those whose chief merit, was that of being his hon[o]rs Countrymen whilst many natives who had interest to raise men were manifestly neglected."[18] Even Governor Dinwiddie and the members of the House of Burgesses heard of the supposed misconduct of the officers and troops of the Virginia Regiment. Dinwiddie wrote Washington on April 8, 1756: "I hope the affairs of the Regiment are not in so bad a condition as represented here. The Assembly were greatly inflamed, being told that the greatest immoralities and drunkenness have been much countenanced, and proper discipline neglected; I am willing to think better of our officers and therefore suspend my judgment till I hear from you."[19]

Although the charges by the Centinel against the Virginia Regiment were neither new nor, necessarily, false—they startled because they were public and because they were applied too indiscriminately. The dutiful soldiers and officers (who were, by and large, personally brave and sober) justly felt outraged. Not only was the Centinel too indiscriminate in his bill of complaints, but he also seemed to be charging the Virginia Regiment with the common complaints against the English regulars. The Centinel's statement that "the Militia men are brow-beat and discouraged in every noble Atchievement, as claiming a Share with the Soldiery in their Monopoly of Honor" reflects the usual colonial feeling that the English regulars always attempted to take all the honor for every victory and every brave deed and to blame the Americans for every defeat and every instance of cowardice.[20] The Centinel has generally been charged with grossly maligning the Virginia Regiment, but it appears to me that he can only be found guilty of exaggerating, and of publicly stating what others were privately saying and writing.

Although the scathing condemnation of the nature of soldiers in the last extant Centinel (No. 19) may reply to various attacks on the Centinel by soldiers, the existing evidence indicates that the Centinel took little notice of the furor raised by his tenth essay. The "Virginia Centinel No. XI" was reprinted in only one paper, the *New York Gazette* for November 1, 1756, which neither notes when the original appeared in the *Virginia Gazette*, nor gives the concluding signature (which may, of course, have been omitted in the original printing). The Centinal discusses the nature of government, particularly praising the balance of power in the English system. The author quotes an epigraph from Cicero as well as citations from Tacitus on the excellence of the doctrine of the balance of power. Of course the Centinel could not refrain from his usual method of amplification, and so briefly surveys the "despotic" or "confused" governments of the rest of the world—but all this prefaces the danger of coming under the "despotic and lawless Power of France." An admirable use of an incremental refrain ("And must this be lost?—Yes, if our Sins and our Enemies prevail") builds up to the loss of "our Religion":

> We prize our Religion, the pure Religion of Jesus, streaming uncorrupted from the sacred Fountain of the Scriptures, as the richest Jewel in our Treasure. And must this be lost?——*Yes*, lost in the Rubbish of Superstition, Folly and Idolatry; enervated, debased by the Fopperies of Popery; expensive in their Use; worth nothing in the End, but to confound the Mind with Darkness and Delusion. Instead of worshipping GOD, we must worship the Priest, and his consecrated Wafer; and instead of one Mediator, have an Hundred. What makes this Ruin more dreadful is, that we shall be forced into this Sink of Corruption. It will not be Matter of Choice, but Necessity; tremendous Necessity! arising from Confiscations, Dungeons, Chains, and all the Horrors of the Inquisition!

The content and style are obviously melodramatic and highly rhetorical—but, together with the bluntness and vigor found elsewhere in the essays, the passage demonstrates why the Centinel was remembered by Isaiah Thomas (or by his source of information) as an artful writer. Without the genius of a Benjamin Franklin or a Thomas Paine for memorable, terse sentences, for an absolutely clear style, or for original expression, the Centinel nevertheless writes effective hortatory propaganda. The eleventh Centinel closes with a quotation on vice from that favorite mid-eighteenth century poet, Edward Young.

The sixteenth number of the Virginia Centinel was reprinted in four papers: in the *New York Gazette*, February 21, 1757 (omitting only the signature "L. & V."); the *Boston News Letter*, March 17 (omitting both the concluding examples and the signature); the *Pennsylvania Gazette*, March 17 (the text cited); and the *Boston Evening Post*, April 18 (omitting the prefatory epigraph). Unfortunately, none of the reprints notes from what issue of the *Virginia Gazette* the number is taken, but the dates of the reprinting, together with the fact that the eighteenth number of the Virginia Centinel did not appear in the *Virginia Gazette* until January 21, 1757, suggest that the sixteenth Centinel originally appeared sometime in December, 1756. This Centinel argues that disaster would result for Virginia and the other English colonies if the Cherokees, Creeks, Chickasaws and Choctaws joined with the Shawnee and the Delaware Indians against the English colonies; and conversely, argued that these Indians, as allies of the English, would be the best possible men to fight in the backwoods: "Our Frontiers have been ravaged principally by *Indians*; and *Indians* will always be found the most proper Persons to fight *Indians*."[21] Referring to the criticisms that followed his tenth Centinel essay, the author sarcastically says, "A military Gentleman (who has been pleased lately to animadvert upon the *Virginia*-Centinel with that Candor and Politeness which the *Centinel* always expected to find in the Army, The School of Politeness)[22] complains, that in a wide-extended Country, mountainous and woody, the sculking Savages could conquer thrice their Number, and cannot be met with but by Accident. In such Places their Brother-Savages would be the most proper Persons to discover and attack them. Not to add, that as they would expect no Wages, but only Clothes and Provision, and a few Presents, they would be a much less expence to our impoverished Country, than the same Number of our own Men."

The way to bind these nations of Indians to the English colonies, the Centinel maintains, is by trade. The epigraph quotes six lines from Edward Young proving that *"TRADE'S the Source, Sinew, Soul of All."* The Centinel claims that "public Interest *ought* to direct Nations in contracting Alliances," and that it was in the interest of Virginia and of the other English colonies to maintain alliances with the Indians by trade. The Centinel quotes Alexander Pope to prove that "Self-Interest is the ruling Passion of the World." And so the Centinel comes to his central thesis: "Now nothing can be more evident to us, nothing is more evident to them, nothing has been more frequently and explicitly declared by them, than that a beneficial Trade is their highest Interest; that they will, nay *must*, join with that Nation with whom they can carry it on the most advantageously; and consequently, that the *English*, and particularly *Virginia*, cannot possibly take so effectual a Method to secure their Friendship, as to establish a Trade among them. This is their Proposal; this is their Request; this they have themselves declared the most effectual Method to attach them inalienably to us." In proof of his assertion that the Indians desire the trade, he cites Sir William Johnson's "Treaty with the *Six-Nations* last Winter," two speeches by Cherokee chiefs, and Major Andrew Lewis' conference with the Cherokees. The Centinel ends on a note of exhortation and warning: "Therefore, this Winter is the critical Time; and if nothing be done, the Consequences are likely to prove fatal and remediless." Like the tenth Centinel, the sixteenth is signed "L. & V."

The Virginia Centinel No. 17 was reprinted in both the *New Hampshire Gazette*, April 15, 1757 (the text quoted), and the *New York Gazette*, May 2. The texts are essentially identical. Since the next number of the Centinel appeared in the *Virginia Gazette* on January 21, 1757, I suspect that this number appeared originally on December 31st or, more probably, January 7th. This essay, signed only "L." (like the ninth Centinel), continues the topic of the persecution of French Protestants, begun in the unnumbered Centinel essay reprinted in the *Maryland Gazette*. After a prefatory epigraph from John Oldham's "Satyrs upon the Jesuits," the Centinel opens: "COUNTRYMEN and Fellow Protestants! I have, in a former Alarm, given you some Specimens of the bloody Genius of Popery—of even *Frenchified* Popery;

which, notwithstanding the pretended Humanity and Politeness of
that Nation, is still found to be a bloody savage Harpy." Because
the Centinel has received "some new authentic Materials for
another Alarm" based upon the "Oppressions, Persecutions, Tortures and Death, under which the thin Remains of your Fellow
Protestants in *France* now groan," he will give "a Sketch of their
tragical History, founded upon very good Authorities." A footnote to the last statement reveals that the new source is "*two
Discourses on this Subject by the Reverend Mr. Gibbons, a worthy
Minister in London; Edit. 1755.*" (As I shall show below, this note
supplies a key clue in determining the authorship of the Virginia
Centinel essay series.) The Centinel quotes the "sanguinary Edict"
of Lewis XV of France, of May 14, 1724, "which has been carry-
ing into Execution in *France* above 30 Years, and is now in full
Force." To prove that the persecutions are still in effect in France,
he cites a series of letters written within the last five years—all of
them taken directly from Thomas Gibbons' work. The Centinel
breaks off, promising "some additional Articles of Intelligence for
my next, for Want of Room," and concludes with an exhortation:
"These may serve as a Specimen of the savage Genius of Popery
and a *French* Government. Can a Protestant, can a *Briton* or *Virginian*, read such Accounts as these without Indignation? Can we
behold the Incroachments of such a Government, with a *quantum
sufficit* of *Indian* Barbarity, without Horror? And must not our
Resentment fire us into Soldiers, to repel this dire *Apollyon* from
our Borders?"

The Virginia Centinel No. 18 was reprinted in the *New Hampshire Gazette*, April 29, 1757, from the *Virginia Gazette* of January 21. Although this number of the Centinel is unsigned, the last
sentence of the introduction asserts that it is by the same author
(i.e., "L.") as No. 17. Only the first paragraph and the concluding
verses are original; all the rest consists either of quotations of
letters from French Protestants (all quoted by Thomas Gibbons)
or (as the Centinel acknowledges) of quotations from Gibbons
himself. The Centinel's opening is extremely interesting, for it
directly defends freedom of religion, and implicitly justifies the
existence of dissenters in Anglican Virginia. After a prefatory epigraph from Virgil, the Centinel begins:

NOTHING can be more surprising and unaccountable, than that Men should be deemed bad subjects for being so honest as to follow their Conscience, and scorn all sneaking Compliances, in Opposition to the sacred Dictates of that *God within.* This Principle is the best Constituent of a good Subject, and the surest Source of steady uniform Loyalty. And tho' it may sometimes constrain a Man to dissent from some little Formalities in Church and State, it will render him, in the Main an useful Member of both, worthy of infinitely greater Confidence than the pliable Multitude, the *very many*, as old *Socrates* calls them, who are governed by mercenary and fashionable Principles. It is equally astonishing and unaccountable, that ever the mild, humane Religion of *Jesus*, that breathes a Spirit of universal Benevolence, should be perverted into a Pretence for unjust Oppression, Confiscations, Murders, and all the Tortures of the most bloody Persecution.

The Centinel then documents the existence of these persections in France. At the end of his quotations of letters by French Protestants, the Centinel exclaims: "See *Virginians!* see what must be your Doom, if this happy Country should become a conquered Province of *France.* And is there an apostate *Briton* among you, that can view the formidable Incroachments of this sanguinary Power upon your Brothers, with Indifference and Inaction?" He concludes the prose part of the essay by quoting "the Words of the animated Writer, who has favoured me with this Intelligence," thus suggesting that the author of the pamphlet, the Rev. Thomas Gibbons of London, is his correspondent. The Centinel ends the essay with a 26-line poem in blank verse urging Virginians to fight against "Black Persecution" and against the "Triumph" of Popery. It begins: "*Virginians!* rouse! and from your Borders drive / Black PERSECUTION, that enraptured views / Each bleeding Spectacle with ghastly Smiles, / And all the savage Luxury of Joy / That baleful Furies feel."

The last extant number of the Virginia Centinel essay series that I have found in the colonial newspapers is the nineteenth, reprinted in the *Boston Evening Post* of April 11, 1757. This essay pretends to be a letter addressed "To the Virginia-Centinel, No. XIX," and is unsigned in the reprint, but I suspect that it is by the author of the series. Like the infamous No. 10, this Centinel assails soldiers, but now the essayist widens the attack from particular, possibly cowardly soldiers, to one on the profession of the soldier.

The author's rhetorical strategy is the same as that in No. 10 (and, to a lesser degree, in No. 3), for the Centinel begins by praising the very group that he will assault. The ostensible letter to the Centinel opens:

> "SIR, IN the present State of Things, the Art of War is an useful and important Acquisition; the Profession of Soldiers is honourable, and even *benevolent*; and Valour is to be numbered among the *Virtues*. The Necessity and Justice of the present War casts a peculiar *amiable* Splendor upon all these; and I wish my Countrymen may acquire immortal Glory by them. But yet, it must be owned, this Honor carries in it something very *mortifying* [I suspect that the author meant the pun] to human Nature. The Excellency of these Things, like that of Medicines, supposes the present disordered State of the World; which requires such severe and desperate Remedies."

The essayist then turns to a "Manuscript Sermon" that "makes some new Reflections upon War." This sermon, happily, can be positively identified, for it appeared in the beginning of the nineteenth century in a volume of previously unpublished sermons by the Rev. Samuel Davies, originally "Preached at Henrico, January 1, 1757; being a day appointed by the Presbytery of Hanover to be observed as a religious fast, on account of the present state of public affairs."[23] The text of the sermon was James IV: 1: "From whence come wars and fightings among you? Come they not hence, even of your lusts that war in your members?" The Centinel quotes from his "Manuscript Sermon" an attack on the honor of the soldier: "Whence is it, that a great Warrior, that is, *a great Destroyer of Mankind*, should be an honorable and celebrated Character?" (*S*, p. 288). Later he returns to this theme: "What are Soldiers, but *Destroyers of Mankind by Profession*? What are Heroes and Conquerors, but the most *bold* and *successful* Destroyers of Mankind?" (*S*, p. 291). Reflecting upon the numbers of people killed throughout history, the Rev. Samuel Davies says

> A Thousand Swords are dividing this Atom Earth among a Thousand Lords; and yet, strange! they cannot agree after all. What exasperated Pride! what burning Resentment! what sullen Enmity! what invenomed Rancor! what Barbarities and Tortures, and eager Thirst for Blood! what public authorised Murders!—*Murders*, I say, for if the Man who *privately* takes away his Neighbor's Life unjustly, be guilty of Murder,

certainly, they who commence an unjust War, and thus take away the
Lives of *Thousands* unjustly, perhaps at a *Blow*, are still *more deeply*
guilty of Murder (*S*, p. 292).

The quotation from the sermon continues for another paragraph, maintaining that this condition of mankind exists because
man is fallen and because "the great fundamental Law of Morality,
is not now deeply impressed upon the Hearts of Men? viz. 'That
we should love the Lord our God with all our Hearts, and our
Neighbour as ourselves' " (*S*, p. 291). This last extant Virginia
Centinel concludes with the quotation of Davies' sermon. Davies,
like the person who supposedly sent in the letter to Virginia Centinel, says that the Virginians' cause is just and that this war is
"consequently our Duty." He adds, "But how corrupt must this
World be, when it is even our *Duty* to weaken and destroy our
Fellow-Men, as much as we can?" The quotation from Davies and
the last Centinel essay conclude on a somber and even disgusted
note: "The *brave BRITONS* are fallen Creatures." (*S*, p. 293).

Although only these ten of the nineteen known Virginia Centinel essays are extant, a number of generalizations may be made
about the characteristic style, content, and techniques of the series. The tone is commonly prophetic, frequently threatening (combining the two, the author often used diabole), often condemning,
almost always moral, sometimes factual, and usually exhorting.
The ideal audience is a group of young men, who are urged to join
the militia and fight against the French. The logic and reasoning
are loose, with little syllogistical reasoning; instead, the Centinel
usually attempts to prove his theses by citing comparisons from
classical authors, modern English poets, and the Bible. Indeed he
seems, to modern readers, overfond of such proofs: Douglas
Southall Freeman complained that the Centinel's "indignant paragraphs groaned with Latin quotations and frowned with historical
allusions" (II, 210). The Centinel sometimes adapts the work of
others and presents it as his own (a not uncommon eighteenth-
century practice). The diction is sometimes annoyingly imprecise.
The Centinel's favorite single technique is repetition, usually anaphora. The sentences are typically periodic, building up to the
conclusion; usually long and complex, suggesting a multitude of
reasons and causes and manifold relations between the parts of the

sentences and between the sentences comprising the paragraph. The diction is frequently heightened and the reporting exaggerated, suitable to the Centinel's propagandistic and persuasive purposes. In brief, the style is typically periodic, hieractic, hypotactic, Ciceronian and rhetorical: all in all, a fair example of the "sublime" style of the mid-eighteenth century.

The first paragraph of the first Virginia Centinel is a good example of the typical style:

> WHEN our Country, and all that is included in that important Word, is in the most threatning Danger; when our Enemies are busy and unwearied in planning and executing their Schemes of Incroachments and Barbarity, and our Countrymen are generally sunk in Sloth and Security; when the Regulations of our Legislature, so well formed for our Protection, cannot be carried into a speedy and vigorous Execution, for Want of a proper Spirit among the People; when such a Scene of Blood, Devastation and Terror opens before us in the approaching Summer; when in short our ALL is at stake, and the Die spins dreadfully doubtful; and the Patriot Passions must be roused in every Breast capable of such generous Sensations; and every Man that feels their Energy, must be pushed on by a resistless Impulse to do all in his Power for the public Safety.

We note the non-colloquial, highly literary, complex structure of the sentence-paragraph, complete only when it finally concludes. The characteristic use of anaphora (the repeated initial *when*s and *and*s); the piling-up of reasons and causes; the gradually cumulating effect of anxiety, brought about partially by the skillful holding-off of the conclusion of the sentence. We note too the curious syntactical uncertainty about the structure of the sentence itself: the reader is not quite certain that the sentence has actually been completed, for after "the Die spins dreadfully doubtful," the normal rhetoric demands a pause and a definite answer, "*—then* the Patriot Passions must be roused"; but instead the author continues his sentence as if this *and* is no different from the one introducing the clause "*and* the Die spins." Consequently the reader is left in syntactical and rhetorical anxiety whether the long-put-off conclusion of this highly periodic sentence is actually being given in the clause "and the Patriot Passions must be roused." I am not certain whether the Centinel meant the reader to experience this confusing *angst*, for it makes the meaning less clear. But, beyond a doubt, the Centinel did want to arouse anxiety with his repeated *ands* and *whens*, and he succeeded.

PART TWO: THE AUTHOR

No argued efforts to identify the Centinel have appeared. The most recent comment on the authorship states "The name of the writer is unknown." [24] Douglas Southall Freeman, in his monumental biography, wrote: "Nowhere did the anonymous author give a hint of his identity or of his grievance unless it was in a line that suggested as author some militia officer who had been to Winchester the previous spring and had not been treated acceptably there" (II, 209-10). (Despite re-reading the essay with this sentence in mind, I have been unable to find the basis for Freeman's suggestion, unless it was the general statement that the soldiers claimed all the credit when the militia deserved part of it— but what does this have to do with Winchester or with "the previous spring"?) Freeman did suggest the possibility that Richard Corbin may have been the author, but he made no effort to argue the case, and even cast doubt upon his own suggestion: "Washington's subsequent disfavor in the eyes of Richard Corbin inevitably raises the question whether Corbin may not have been the author, but there is no confirmatory evidence of any sort in his *MS Letter Book* and no indication that he was thinking particularly at the time of the subjects discussed by 'The Virginia Centinel' " (II, 210n). To Freeman's own dissent from this possible attribution, I might add that the aristocratic Anglican, Richard Corbin, does not at all fit the characteristics of the Centinel as they emerge from his extant essays.

When I started an analysis of the Virginia Centinel essay series, my hypothesis was that the Rev. James Maury wrote them. I had hurriedly read the essays while compiling an annotated bibliography of the American poetry in the colonial newspapers and magazines, and Maury seemed the logical author. [25] The Virginia Centinel was evidently a Virginia minister, especially concerned with conditions on the frontier (and Maury had a frontier parish); the Centinel not only had an extraordinary interest in the history of the Huguenots but also corresponded with French ministers during the previous years (of course it turned out that these essays were all borrowed; but Maury was, on both sides, a Huguenot descendant);[26] the author was obviously a person who loved literature and and knew contemporary English poetry, classical authors, and the Bible extraordinarily well (this brought to mind not only Maury's known writings but also his reputation among such judges as the Rev. Jonathan Boucher as an extraordinarily romantic writer);[27] and, most convincing, his suggestions for winning Indian friendship in the sixteenth Centinel were similar to the proposals made by Maury (shortly before that Centinel appeared) to Philip Ludwell.[28] But this hypothesis was demolished as soon as I began to read the Centinel essays painstakingly and to consider their implications, sources, and style. Although a few sentiments expressed by Maury are found in the Virginia Centinel essay series, I believe that either these opinions are borrowed from Maury or, more probably, they represent not uncommon sentiments among Virginia's frontier inhabitants. I am now certain that the primary—and perhaps the sole—author was the Rev. Samuel Davies.[29]

First, the style and techniques of the Virginia Centinel essays as characterized above are generally true of the "New Light" ministers [30] (though not all of them—and certainly not of the Rev. Jonathan Edwards) and particularly of the Rev. Samuel Davies. He frequently prophesies, condemns, and warns in his sermons. He uses emotionally heightened diction and exaggerated reporting in all his sermons on the French and Indian war—and in many of the others. His reasoning is loose, generally not syllogistic, and his favorite method of proof and of amplification is by piling up examples from classical authors, the Bible, and modern English poetry.[31] On one occasion, he apologizes and justifies these long quotations and allusions with the argument: "that which is common to all mankind, in all countries, in all ages, and of every religion, seems to be implanted in their nature by its author; and consequently, must be true" (S, p. 339).[32] He occasionally incorporated the works of others into his own sermons (he even borrows from such a famous contemporary sermon as Jonathan Edwards' *Sinners in the Hands of an Angry God*),[33] and he wrote poetry, including blank verse, prolifically and upon almost any occasion.[34] Perhaps his favorite technique for attaining emotional

appeal was anaphora. (For an example of anaphora used throughout an entire sermon, see S, II, 195-212.) His sentences are typically periodic, long, and complex. Above all, his style is rhetorical
and literary. Documentation for these various characteristics of
style will emerge in the quotations given below; but the identical
characteristics of style and techniques of both the Virginia Centinel and of Davies is only one of the kinds of evidence that I will
adduce to prove Davies' authorship.

The sources of the Centinel directly indicate the identity of the
writer. Benjamin Franklin's *Plain Truth* (Philadelphia, 1747),
which resulted in a voluntary military association of over one
hundred militia companies, evidently influenced the content and
arguments of the Virginia Centinel essay series. But, even though
Samuel Davies (as a young man of military age, 23, as a litterateur,
and especially as an itinerant minister of Pennsylvania, Delaware,
Maryland, Virginia, and New Jersey in 1747) was more likely to
have read the pamphlet than were Virginians, *Plain Truth* was so
widely circulated in America and so well-known that its influence
is not a telling argument for Davies' authorship.[35] The case is different for the other three sources. As I have shown, three essays
deal with the history of the persecutions of Protestants in France.
Two of these, Centinels Nos. 17 and 18, are based on the same
source and will be considered together. In No. 17, the Centinel
refers to "two Discourses . . . by the Rev. Mr. Gibbons, a worthy
Minister, in London." An examination of Thomas Gibbons'
*Sympathy with our Suffering Brethren . . . in two Discourses; oc-
casioned by the cruel oppressions of the Protestants in France*
(London, 1755) reveals that almost the entire seventeeth Centinel
is reprinted verbatim from Gibbons, pp. 13, 14, 15, and 17. Even
the prefatory verses from Oldham were found in Gibbons, p. 24.
The eighteenth Centinel is also almost entirely quoted from Gibbons, pp. 18, 19, 20, ii, and iii, respectively. Gibbons is well-
known to scholars of early Virginia literature because of his correspondence with the Rev. Samuel Davies, his funeral sermons on
Davies, and his edition of Davies' sermons. Gibbons was Davies'
major English correspondent and his literary executor.[36] Further, in
Sympathy, Gibbons quotes at length from a letter by Davies, pp.
ix-x (although the author is not indicated, the letter is dated from

"Hanover, Sept. 5, 1755," where Davies lived). And, as I pointed out above, the Centinel says in No. 18 that the "animated Writer" (Gibbons) himself "favored me with this Intelligence," thus claiming that Gibbons personally sent a copy of his *Sympathy* to the Virginia Centinel.

Of course Gibbons may well have corresponded with other people in Virginia besides Davies. But he is not known to have done so; it is certain that he corresponded frequently with Davies; and it is also certain that he would have sent Davies a copy of his pamphlet discussing the French encroachments on the Virginia Frontier and quoting a letter by Davies. Moreover, a careful reading of the introductory paragraph of the eighteenth Centinel reveals that the author was a dissenter (like, of course, the Rev. Thomas Gibbons), and Davies was not only the most famous dissenter of colonial Virginia, but also the one who most frequently fought for the rights of the dissenters and of the dissenting ministers. [37] This evidence strongly suggests that the Virginia Centinels No. 17 and and 18 were written by Davies.

The other Centinel essay concerned with the Huguenots was the unnumbered one, reprinted only in the *Maryland Gazette*. Although the Centinel makes no reference to the Rev. Aaron Burr's *A Discourse delivered at New Ark, in New Jersey, January 1, 1755 . . . On . . . the late Encroachments of the French* (New York, 1755; Evans 7373), the latter half (except for the brief concluding paragraph) of the Centinel essay is quoted from pp. 22-23 of Burr's *Discourse*. Further, most of the first half of the Centinel essay paraphrases Burr's *Discourse*. Burr writes of the St. Bartholomew Day Massacre:

> . . . *Paris*, where some of their Chief Men, being invited, under an Oath of Safety, to solemnize the Marriage of the King of Navarre, were, at a Signal, by the Toll of the Bell, fallen upon, and *inhumanly butchered* by the *Papists*, their being at the same Time an *Insurrection* against them in the other Parts of the Kingdom. By all Accounts, a great Number, and by some, not less than 100,000 were slain in this *perfidious* Manner. But detestable as their Custom was, the News of it was receiv'd with Joy, at *Rome* (p. 20).

A comparison of the Centinel's recounting of the same information shows that he merely paraphrased Burr:

> ... *Paris*, under the specious Pretence of solemnizing the Marriage of the King of *Navarre*, a Protestant Prince. They had the Security of an Oath for Safety; and received the warmest Professions of Friendship. But in an Instant, at a Signal given by the Toll of a Bell, they were most treacherously and inhumanly butchered, all thro' the City, while they dreamed of no Danger; and the Streets and Houses ran with their Blood. At the same Time there was an Insurrection against them in other Parts of the Kingdom; and they fell every where, like Sheep for the Slaughter. In this perfidious Manner, about 100,000 Innocents lost their Lives; ... And yet this News was received with public Rejoicings in *Rome*, and had the Approbation of the Conclave.

Significantly, Aaron Burr, then president of the College of New Jersey (present-day Princeton), was a friend of Davies; Davies had recently returned from collecting money for the College in England; Davies probably exchanged publications with Burr; and Davies, whether or not the two exchanged publications, no doubt read all of Burr's writings.[38] In view of the source of this unnumbered Virginia Centinel essay, it seems likely that Davies wrote it. To this evidence one may add that Davies, in a sermon preached on May 9, 1756 (nine days after the first Centinel appeared), said of France: "There the Protestants are still plundered, chained to the galleys, broken alive on the torturing wheel, denied the poor favour of abandoning their country and their all, and flying naked to beg their bread in other nations" (*S*, I, 305-306). The unnumbered Centinel used the same ideas and some of the identical words: "The miserable Sufferers were denied the poor Favour of flying naked into other Countries, to beg their Bread."

The one Centinel essay positively by Davies is the last, No. 19, for the quoted "Manuscript Sermon" on the nature of soldiers and on the causes of war is known to be by Davies. Entitled "Serious Reflections on War," the sermon was preached at Henrico on January 1, 1757, approximately a month before it appeared in the last extant Centinel. The first paragraph of this Centinel essay, supposedly written as a letter to the Centinel, also echoes sentiments expressed by Davies. Indeed, in this very sermon, he writes that "The present war, indeed, on our side, is just, is unavoidable; and consequently our duty" (*S*, p. 293). And the first paragraph of the nineteenth Centinel speaks of "The Necessity, and the Justice of the present War." Also, the concepts expressed in the Centinel's first paragraph may be paralleled in many of Davies' sermons (see, e.g., *S*, pp. 147-48).

If these four Centinel essays were the only ones extant, no one would doubt that the Rev. Samuel Davies wrote them. And his authorship of the Virginia Centinel essay series only becomes more apparent as we examine the style and content of the other essays.

Before turning to a comparison of the Virginia Centinel essays with the extant sermons of the Rev. Samuel Davies, it may be well to recapitulate Davies' role in the French and Indian war. Davies has long been famous as the "best recruiting officer in the province." [39] He preached a series of sermons giving "Alarms" [40] to the Virginians, urging the young men to join the militia, urging those who had joined to be brave, and asking the officers and men to behave differently from the notorious examples of the cowardly and luxury-loving militia so infamous to his auditors. The best known of these sermons were published contemporaneously. Chronologically first was: *Virginia's Danger and Remedy. Two Discourses occasioned by the severe Drought in sundry Parts of the Country; and the Defeat of General Braddock* (Williamsburg, 1756; Evans 7644). This tract consists of a morning and afternoon sermon preached in late July or the first few days of August, 1755 (the preface to the sermons, written after their delivery, is dated August 4, 1755). [41] Another recruiting sermon is: *Religion and Patriotism the Constituents of a Good Soldier. A Sermon Preached to Captain Overton's Independent Company of Volunteers raised in Hanover County, Virginia, August 17, 1755* (Philadelphia, 1755; Evans 7403). [42] A sermon first published by his correspondent Thomas Gibbons is *The Crisis: or, the Uncertain Doom of Particular Times, considered with Reference to Great Britain and her Colonies in their Present Circumstances. A Sermon preached in Hanover, Virginia, Oct. 28, 1756. . . . With a Preface by the Rev. Mr. Thomas Gibbons* (London, 1757). [43] And the final one dealing directly with the French and Indian war to achieve contemporary publication was: *The Curse of Cowardice: a Sermon preached to the Militia of Hanover County, in Virginia, at a general Muster, May 8, 1758. With a View to raise a Company for Captain Samuel Meredith* (London, 1758). [44]

In addition to those published contemporaneously, a number of

Davies' sermons on the French and Indian War appeared in Gibbons' collection of his sermons brought out after his death. More were added in the early nineteenth century, and all of these were thereafter printed with his collected sermons. In the chronological order of their delivery, the war sermons are: "God the Sovereign of all Kingdoms," preached on March 5, 1755 (S, pp. 329-54); "On the Defeat of General Braddock, going to Fort Duquesne," preached July 20, 1755 (S, pp. 307-28); "Practical Atheism, In Denying the Agency of Divine Providence, Exposed," preached April 4, 1756 (S, pp. 379-406); "The Mediatorial Kingdom and Glories of Jesus Christ," preached May 9, 1756 (S, I, 285-317); "The Signs of the Times," undated, but mentioning the Governor's proclamation of September 20, 1756, as recent (S, pp. 167-201; p. 195n for the proclamation); "Serious Reflections on War," preached January 1, 1757 (S, pp. 280-306; the sermon quoted in the nineteenth Centinel); "The Happy Effects of the Pouring Out of the Spirit," preached October 16, 1757 (S, pp. 202-27); and "A Thanksgiving Sermon for National Blessings," preached January 11, 1759 (S, pp. 355-78). All of these sermons, like those published contemporaneously, contain at least a few pages devoted to the war.

In the first Virginia Centinel, the striking reference to that "acceptable and popular Officer . . . Col. Washington" reveals an attitude similar to that expressed in Davies' famous praise and prophesy concerning Washington, first published as a note in *Religion and Patriotism*, preached August 17, 1755, where Washington is praised as "that heroic youth, Col. Washington, whom I cannot but hope Providence has hitherto preserved in so signal a manner, for some important service to his country" (S, p. 101). The paeon to courage concluding this Centinel is similar to the praise of courage found just before the prophecy concerning Washington (S, pp. 99-101). The general sentiment of the last paragraph of the first Centinel—that the superior numbers and situation of the English colonists do not necessarily mean that they will win the war— is the major topic of Davies' sermon of October 28, 1756, *The Crisis, or the Uncertain Doom of Kingdoms at Particular Times*. And the same notion, together with a prediction of "a Scene of Blood, Devastation and Terror . . . in the approaching Summer"

(VC #1), is part of the message of Samuel Davies' sermon preached in late July, 1755, on *Virginia's Danger and Remedy*, where Davies says:

> Our inhabitants are numerous, and some of them are resolute, and capable of making a good defence, and a considerable part of our forces have survived the fatal ninth of July [Braddock's Defeat], in which so many of them were slaughtered. These and sundry other things have an encouraging appearance; and we cannot overlook them without ingratitude, and excessive despondence. But notwithstanding these favourable circumstances, and notwithstanding such future turns of providence as may make for us, it is beyond all doubt, this will be the *most melancholy and calamitous year that* Virginia *has ever seen.*" (*VDR* p. 12; cf. *S*, p. 354 for the same sentiment.)

In some cases, the exact wording of this essay may be found in Davies' sermons. In the second paragraph of the Centinel, the author asks if Virginia "shall become a conquer'd enslav'd Province of France and the Range of Indian Savages." In Davies' *Religion and Patriotism*, the minister asks if he must look upon Virginia "as a conquered, enslaved province of France, and the range of Indian savages" (*S*, p. 96). In the Centinel's fourth paragraph, the author writes: "If Liberty, Property, Religion, Life, are Terms of any Significancy; if the tender Names of a Parent, a Child, an Husband, a Friend, have any Endearment; . . . Therefore, if you have any Thing of the Spirit of Men, of Britons, of Christians . . ." Compare Davies' exhortation: "If you a have a Drop of *British Blood* in your Veins, if you have any Thing of the Spirit of *Men*, or of *Christians*, exert yourselves on this Occasion. It now becomes you to be all *Patriots*, all *Soldiers*. Your Liberty, your Property, your Religion, your Lives, your All, are at Stake" (*VDR*, p. 44). In other cases, similar words express the same ideas. In the third paragraph, the Centinel refers to "The Tyranny, Perfidy and Cruelty of a mongrel Race of the French Papists and Indian Barbarities"; in *Religion and Patriotism*, Davies refers to "all the infernal horrors of popery, and the savage tyranny of a mongrel race of French and Indian conquerors" (*S*, p. 117). In the second paragraph, the Centinel contrasts "this favourable Spot of the Globe, this Land of Plenty and Liberty" with what it may degenerate to "owing to the Security or Cowardice of its present Inhabitants";

and in "On the Defeat of General Braddock," Davies contrasts the past condition of Virginia, "the region of Peace and tranquility; the land of ease, plenty, and liberty" with its present sad condition, when "in the midst of all these alarms, I see thy inhabitants generally asleep, and careless of thy fate" (S, p. 308; cf. S, p. 94 for similar sentiments). Further, the general ideas in this Centinel are found not only in the sermons by Davies on the French and Indian War, but also in some of his earlier and later sermons. The subject of this first Centinel is public spirit, and this anticipates Davies' address at Princeton, September 21, 1760, on *Religion and Public Spirit* (New York, 1760; Evans 8832; not in S).

The third Virginia Centinel, with its brief condemnation of the militia (which will be considered in the discussion of the tenth Centinel), its long attack on standing armies, and its radical note against the wealthy Virginia planters, has fewer echoes in Davies' sermons than any other Centinel essay, but even this one, having as its main purpose urging the men to join military associations voluntarily, asserts a thesis found almost pervasively throughout Davies' war sermons. And although I have not found a long passage on the composition of the Roman army in any of Davies' sermons, he must, as a classical scholar, have been familiar with the Roman military structure and seems to allude to the Roman soldiers as militia when he refers to them as "coloni" (S, p. 159). In addition, as I have suggested above, this Centinel essay expresses puritan and middle-class tendencies, typical of the Presbyterian Davies.

With the ninth Centinel, we are back on firm ground. Again the Centinel declares the uncertainty of the outcome of the war but finds reason "to hope, that these Commotions may terminate in our Favour." After Davies expresses the same uncertainty as to the outcome of the war, he says that "the cause may also encourage you to hope that the Lord of Hosts will espouse it" (S, p. 108; cf. "The Crisis," pp. 120-46). In the third paragraph, the Centinel says "Self-Confidence, and a presumptuous Assurance of Victory, is not a *Creature-like* Disposition: It does not become dependent Mortals, whose affairs are entirely under the Management of the supreme Ruler of the Universe. It is often the Source of that Security and Inaction, which brings on its own Mortification."

The thought, its sequence, and even the diction echo a passage from *Religion and Patriotism* where, after writing of the uncertainty of the result of the war, Davies says "Such language . . . sounds creature like, and God approves of such self-diffident humility. But to indulge sanguine and confident expectations of victory, to boast when we put on our armour, as though we were putting it off, and to derive our high hopes from our own power and good management, without any regard to the providence of God . . . such insolence is generally mortified" (*S*, pp. 108-109).

Paragraph five of the ninth Centinel, condemning the Virginians as a "guilty obnoxious People" and attributing the defeats in war to the sins of the Virginians, is a standard refrain in Davies' sermons (e.g., *VDR*, p. 11; *S*, pp. 112-13). On June 19, 1756, Davies anticipated the very words in judging the Virginians "a guilty obnoxious people" (*S*, p. 271). In the same paragraph the Centinel compares the "general Corruption" to a "Disease of a Body politic" which will "as naturally and necessarily ruin a State, as a Fever or a Consumption" will "destroy the human body." Then the Centinel condemns the soldiers: "Nothing is projected with Judgment and Unanimity, or executed with Courage and Expedition." The same metaphor and sequence of thought is found in Davies' *Virginia's Danger and Remedy*, where he compares the sum of the citizens to the "body politic. . . . And it is in the Body politic, as in the *natural Body*; when *one* Member suffers, *all* the Members suffer with it. To all this I may add, the poor State of our Militia, which has hitherto been a mere Farce" (*VDR*, p. 11). In his sermon of April 4, 1756, Davies also judged that the defeats and sufferings of the Virginians were "the chastisements . . . of an angry God . . . for the sins of the land" (*S*, p. 399). And he had claimed that former kingdoms fell as the result of the sins of luxury and sensuality: "The ruins of Egypt, Babylon, Rome, and many a flourishing city, country, and empire, proclaim this truth" (*S*, p. 399). And so the Centinel writes: "The Ruins of *Babylon, Jerusalem, Persia, Greece* and *Rome*, and many other flourishing Empires and Kingdoms, are tragical Monuments of this."

The long contrast in the ninth Centinel between England and France parallels a similar contrast in Davies' sermon of March 5, 1755 (*S*, pp. 351-53). The last paragraph urges that "every Man in his Station" do all he can to win the war. The particularization of different categories of the congregation is a favorite device of Davies, and he had specified the roles of various categories of Virginians in the war in his *Religion and Patriotism* (*S*, pp. 99-101). The Centinel's description of the clergy's role in the war fits Davies as well as or better than any other Virginia clergyman: "Let the Clergy especially, shock their Hearers with the Horrors of Popery; animate them with a publick Spirit, and the ardent Love of Liberty; and rouse them from their Lethargy with just Representations of their Danger," The Centinel's joining of religion and patriotism ("Let the Love of our Country be incorporated with our Religion") echoes all of Davies' sermons on the war (e.g., "Christians should be patriots," *S*, p. 321).

The long and infamous attack on the soldiers in the tenth Centinel was anticipated by one sentence in the third Centinel and by two in the ninth Centinel. Similar attacks on the soldiers may be found in three sermons by Davies before the appearance of the tenth Centinel, in one just after the tenth Centinel appeared, and in great detail in a sermon over nineteen months later. In his sermon "On the Defeat of General Braddock," July 20, 1755, Davies described the situation of frontier Virginia:

> slaughtered families, the hairy scalps clotted with gore; the horrid acts of Indian and popish torture. And, alas! in the midst of all these alarms, I see thy inhabitants generally asleep, and careless of thy fate. I see vice braving the skies; religion neglected and insulted [;] mirth and folly have still their places of rendezvous. Let our country, let religion, liberty, property, and all be lost: yet still they will have their diversions; luxury spreads her feast, and unmans her effeminate guests. In spite of laws, in spite of proclamations, in spite of the principle of self-preservation, thy officers are generally inactive, thy militia neglected and undisciplined, thy inhabitants unprovided with arms. . . . Our militia has hitherto been a mere farce, and most of the inhabitants know little or nothing of the art of war (*S*, pp. 308, 310).

Davies also, in this sermon, spelled out some of the duties of the officers and men: he implied that neither generally did their duty (S, pp. 320-21).

In *Virginia's Danger and Remedy*, evidently preached within two weeks of the former sermon, Davies again remarked on "the

poor State of our Militia, which has hitherto been a mere Farce"
and on "The stupid Carelessness, or sneaking Cowardice of not a
few of our Inhabitants" (p. 11). And in his sermon of April 4,
1756, Davies said of the Sandy Creek expedition under Major
Andrew Lewis to the Shawnee Indians:

> who would ever have suspected that the expedition should fail for want
> of provisions? that men, leaving a plentiful country, and about to
> march through a tedious and unknown wilderness, should not take a
> sufficient supply with them? Who would have thought that men in their
> senses would have been so stupid and improvident? To me, I must own,
> it looks like a judicial infatuation.

And after this incredibly blunt condemnation of the leaders of the
Sandy Creek expedition, he turned to the conduct of the soldiers
at the defeat of General Braddock: "Last summer, our men were
killed by one another, in the ever-melancholy engagement on the
banks of the Monongahela, and now a provoked God has let us see
once more, that he needs not the instrumentality of enemies and
arms to blast the expedition of a guilty people. By their own
mismanagement, they defeat themselves, and disconcert their own
schemes" (S, p. 399).

In *The Crisis*, preached on October 28, 1756, Davies echoes the
language used in the tenth Centinel the month before (September
3, 1756): "we have reason to fear from this disposition and conduct of many among ourselves, some in high places have been
suspected of treachery or cowardice, or at least bad conduct. A
spirit of security, sloth, and cowardice, evidently prevails; nothing
great is so much as attempted, much less executed" (S, p. 131).
The Centinel had written: "But when nothing brave is so much as
attempted, but very rarely, or by Accident, or for necessary Self-
defence." And in his "Serious reflections on war," preached January 1, 1757, Davies mentioned "the cowardice or mismanagement
of our own men" and chronicled the various defeats of the Americans (praising as an exception, the victory won by Col. John
Armstrong, a Presbyterian who found it objectionable that George
Washington gambled).[45]

Davies' most thorough condemnation of the Virginia soldiers is
found in *The Curse of Cowardice*, preached May 8, 1758—nine-

teen months after the tenth Centinel appeared. Here, Davies damns the Virginia soldiers in terms at least as strong as those in the tenth Centinel; he echoes the language of the Centinel; and he cites particular incidents and abuses that members of the audience must have recognized:

> If soldiers, instead of abandoning their ease and pleasure, and risking their lives in defence of their country, should unman themselves with sensual pleasure and debauchery; if, instead of searching out the enemy, they keep out of their way, lest they should search out and find them; if they lie sleeping or rioting in forts and places of safety, while their country is ravaged, perhaps in their very neighborhood: when they waste their courage in broils and duels among themselves, or in tyrannizing over those that are under their command: when they lay themselves open to false alarms, by being credulous to every account that magnifies the force of the enemy: when they are tedious or divided in their consultations, and slow and faint in the execution: when they consult rather what may be most safe for themselves than most beneficial for their country: when they keep skirmishing at a distance, instead of making a bold push, and bringing the war to a speedy issue by a decisive stroke: when they are fond of prolonging the war, that they may live and riot the longer at the public expense: when they sell themselves and their country to the enemy for a bribe: in short, when they do not conscientiously exert all their power to repel the enemy, and protect the state that employs them, but only seek to serve themselves, then they do the work of the Lord deceitfully; and his curse lights upon them as their heavy doom. I leave others to judge, whether the original of this ugly picture is to be found anywhere in the universe (S, pp. 160-61; cf. pp. 150, 157).

These quotations prove that Davies expressed the same attitudes as the tenth Centinel, that he anticipated the language and style of the assault before the tenth Centinel appeared, and that he reaffirmed these opinions in his later sermons. The quotations also demonstrate that Davies had the daring and the courage to avow these charges openly. Of course, the other aspect of the tenth Centinel, against the "Luxury and Sensuality" of the army, is a typical sentiment of the Presbyterian Davies (e.g., S, pp. 112ff, 313, 401).

The eleventh Centinel also echoes numerous passages in the sermons of Davies. Just as the Centinel celebrates the happy "mixt

Legislature" of English government, composed of "King, Lords, and Commons," so Davies celebrated its "proper mixture of monarchy, aristocracy, and democracy" (S, p. 351). And in a passage where liberty, property, and religion are celebrated, in that order, the Centinel echoes the language of Davies. Davies, on August 17, 1755, had preached that the militia were "to guard your religion, the pure religion of Jesus, streaming uncorrupted from the sacred fountain of the Scriptures" (S, p. 106). And so the Centinel, after praising liberty and property, writes: "We prize our Religion, the pure Religion of Jesus, streaming uncorrupted from the sacred Fountain of the Scriptures, as the richest Jewel in our Treasure." The Centinel continued on to say: "Instead of worshipping God, we must worship the Priest, and his consecrated Wafer; and instead of one Mediator, have an Hundred." This echoes the ideas of Davies, who, on July 20, 1755, had preached: "instead of worshipping God through Jesus Christ, you must worship images and pictures made of stone, wood, or canvas—you must pray to men and women that were once sinners like yourselves; and instead of taking bread and wine in remembrance of Christ, you must believe that the bread is the real body of Christ, a piece of true flesh, and that the wine is changed into the real blood of Christ, by a priest muttering a few words over it" (S, pp. 323-24).

Finally, the sixteenth Centinel also repeats the sentiments of Davies concerning what might happen if other Indian tribes joined the French. On October 28, 1756, Davies expressed his fear of the consequences "if the Indians that are now neuter [sic], or in the British interests, should join with them [the French], and with those tribes that are already so active upon their side" (S, p. 131; cf. S, p. 311). And the Centinel states his fear of the outcome if the French and Indians "should meet with a friendly Reception from many of our gloomy Domestics, which is not altogether an ungrounded Apprehension." This repeats the diction used by Davies in *Virginia's Danger and Remedy*, where he referred to "the Danger of Insurrection and Massacre from some of our own gloomy Domestics" (p. 11; cf. S, pp. 131, 327).

Let us summarize the argument for Davies' authorship of the Virginia Centinel essay series. The content and style are similar to those of Davies in his sermons written during the period, and sometimes the language is identical. The sources used in four of the essays are more likely to have been in the hands of Davies than of any other colonial Virginian. The author of the Virginia Centinel essays was a dissenter and possessed the typical puritan and middle-class attitudes of the day (as opposed to the aristocratic attitudes of, say George Washington or Richard Bland)—and so, of course, did Davies. And finally, quotations from one of Davies' manuscript sermons comprise almost the whole of one Centinel essay. I believe that the totality of these arguments indicates beyond any reasonable doubt that Davies was the author.

But was he the only author? Only four extant Centinel essays are signed. The ninth and seventeenth are signed "L." The tenth and sixteenth are signed "L. & V." I have shown above that the seventeenth and eighteenth Centinels are a continuation, and that the author of the seventeenth also refers to writing the unnumbered Centinel (besides, there is so little original writing in these three as to make it difficult to imagine a collaboration on the few sentences that are entirely original); therefore, we may assume that these two essays are also by "L." The last extant Centinel contains comparatively little original material in addition to the quotations from Davies' sermon. Thus, the overwhelming evidence indicates that, if the two initials stood for two different persons, the Davies was "L."; and "L." was the major author of the Virginia Centinel. But who was "V."?

It is tempting to speculate that Davies collaborated with Maury on the essay series, but the only evidence that I have seen concerning the relationship of the Presbyterian parson with the Anglican minister shows that, as we would expect, they were rivals, not friends.[46] If Davies had a collaborator, the most likely candidate is his friend and sometime assistant, the Rev. John Todd. Todd, who graduated from the College of New Jersey in 1749, took the oath prescribed for dissenting ministers in Williamsburg on April 12, 1752. Davies preached his ordination sermon on November 12, 1752. On September 10, 1755, Todd wrote a letter to the *Virginia Gazette* (published in the September 19th issue) on "the present *indolent*, tho' dangerous Condition of our Country." Todd describes the "Independent Company of Volunteers, under the Command of Captain Joseph Fox, consisting of Thirty odd in

Number" who had just marched off, well-equiped, to defend the frontier. Todd's letter concluded with an exhortation: "When the military Fire, which the God of Nature has put into the Breasts of *Virginians*, shall be kindled into a proper Flame, under those Regulations that Christianity inspires, and the Cause of Liberty and Protestantism require, at present; it is to be hoped, our Country will emerge from her Distress, occasioned by the Insults of *Rome* and its inhuman Accomplices." Too little evidence exists for one to argue that Todd was Davies' collaborator; but this patriotic and military Presbyterian parson, who became a militia Colonel in the Revolutionary War, and who served on the Louisa County Committee of Safety during the Revolution, is the logical choice.[47]

There are two other possibilities concerning the signatures. Perhaps Davies was the sole author, knew he would be recognized by some people as the author (indeed, the officers at Fort Cumberland who intended to submit their resignations if they did not receive an apology from Gov. Dinwiddie, said that they had their "goodly" countrymen to thank for making them the butt of ridicule outside Virginia—and this may have been a hit at the Presbyterian minister), and preferred to suggest that he collaborated with someone on the sensitive essays. Some possible evidence for this suggestion may be found in the Centinel's usual style of self-reference: in the tenth and sixteenth Centinels, signed "L. & V.," as in the ninth and seventeenth Centinels, signed just "L." (and in all the unsigned Centinels), the author refers to himself in the first person singular. Of course these references may be explained as the Centinel's portraying himself as a particular persona; but every time he refers to himself, the description perfectly fits the Rev. Samuel Davies. The other possibility is that the differing signatures "L." and "L. & V." were not meant to suggest two authors at all (although no other convincing explanation occurs to me). At any rate, the Rev. Samuel Davies was the major author of the Virginia Centinel essay series, and he may have been its sole author.

NOTES

1. Douglas Southall Freeman, *George Washington: A Biography* (New York: Scribner's, 1948), II, 208-31. Richard L. Morton, *Colonial Virginia* (Chapel Hill: University of North Carolina Press, 1960), II, 701. For a good brief overview of the situation, see ibid., 691-713.

2. Isaiah Thomas, *The History of Printing in America* (Albany: Joel Munsell, 1874; 1st ed., 1810), II, 164.

3. Martin Christadler, *Der Amerikanesche Essay 1720-1820* (Heidelberg: Carl Winter, 1968). Jay B. Hubbell, *The South in American Literature 1607-1900* (Durham, N.C.: Duke University Press, 1954).

4. Freeman, II, 209 and 221, located the Virginia Centinel, Nos. 9 and 16 in other newspapers, and Clinton Rossiter, "Richard Bland: The Whig in America," *William and Mary Quarterly*, 3rd ser., 10 (1953), 45, located the four reprintings of the tenth Virginia Centinel.

5. Leonard W. Labaree, et al., eds., *The Papers of Benjamin Franklin* (New Haven: Yale University Press, 1962), V, 272-75, 374-92. On the Virginia Frontier, the Rev. James Maury wrote, August 9, 1755, of the Albany Plan that "the great men on your side of the water [England] have not thought proper to apply [it], from a principle in politics [keep the colonies divided and thus weak], which we on this side of it think more obvious than wise or just." Ann Maury, ed., *Memoirs of a Huguenot Family* (New York: Putman's, 1874), 382.

6. James Maury expressed similar doubts, August 9, 1755:"were the race always to the swift, and the battle to the strong, our colonies would have little to apprehend from the exertion of all the power which France, especially in a general war, could spare to annoy us here on this continent. Her American strength, compared with ours, is quite contemptible in all respects but one, and that is, the wisdom and prudence with which it is directed." Maury, 381. The Centinel may echo Benjamin Franklin's argument in *Plain Truth* (1747) that a small number of French and Indians could conquer a large number of unorganized colonists. Labaree, III, 193.

7. See Freeman, II, 64-102, for a detailed account of Braddock's defeat and Washington's bravery. Franklin also used this technique in *Plain Truth* when he alluded to the New Englanders' victory at Cape Breton. Labaree, III, 202.

8. The *Boston Evening Post* follows the *New York Gazette* heading and its notice of Peyton Randolph's volunteers.

9. Franklin used the same quotation (in slightly different form) from Sallust on the title page of *Plain Truth*. Labaree, III, 189 and 204, n. 3.

10. Franklin mocked the same argument with the same anecdote in *Plain Truth*. Labaree, III, 201.

11. Morton, II, 681. Freeman, II, 115. Maury also objected to the fine; Maury, 404.

12. Although England declared war on May 17, 1756, the news did not reach Williamsburg until late July, and war was not proclaimed in Virginia until August 7. Washington read a proclamation of war to the Virginia Regiment at Winchester, Virginia, on August 15, 1756. Freeman, II, 204-205; Morton, II, 691.

13. Cf. Jack P. Greene, "Search for Identity: An Interpretation of the Meaning of Selected Patterns of Social Response in Eighteenth-Century

America," *Journal of Social History*, 3 (1970), 189-220, esp. 200-205. It seems to me that Greene does not sufficiently take into account the purposes of the speakers (ministers and judges supply his best examples) or the pervasiveness of these topics throughout the Western world of the eighteenth century. See also James Thomas Flexner, *George Washington: The Forge of Experience 1732-1775* (Boston: Little, Brown, 1965), 155, on the clash of "the lower middle class, which followed Puritan mores" and the "older code of behavior, the aristocratic."

14. Freeman, II, 212. If Washington's reply was published, it is, unfortunately, not extant. See below, n. 22.

15. The author [probably John Mercer] of the "Dinwiddianae," who reflected many of the same attitudes as the Centinel, also commented on the lack of freedom of the press in colonial Virginia. Speaking in the persona of Dinwiddie, he says: I hae the press, under my thumb, / to spak my pleasure, or be dumb, / so that nathing can be printed, / Until it hath by me been minted." Richard Beale Davis, ed., *The Colonial Virginia Satirist* (Philadelphia: Transactions of the American Philosophical Society, n.s., vol. 57, pt. 1, 1967), 25, ll. 305-308. See also J. A. Leo Lemay, "Robert Bolling and the Bailment of Col. Chiswell," *Early American Literature*, 6 (1971), 99-142, esp. 102, 115, 119-20, n. 7.

16. Worthington Chauncey Ford first printed Philo Patriae's defense of Washington and of the Virginia Regiment: "Washington and 'Centinel X,' " *Pennsylvania Magazine of History and Biography*, 20 (1898), 436-51. Rossiter (see above, n. 4) concurs that Bland was "Philo Patriae," 46.

17. Maury, pp. 404-405.

18. Davis, ed., *The Colonial Virginia Satirist*, 19, stanza 1 and note j.

19. Freeman, II, 174-75; cf. 184, 195-96, 382. Discontent always existed over the commission of Col. James Innes, who was generally regarded simply as a crony of Gov. Dinwiddie. See Jack P. Greene, ed., *The Diary of Colonel Landon Carter of Sabine Hall, 1752-1778* (Charlottesville: University Press of Virginia, 1965), I, 109; and Davis, ed., *Colonial Virginia Satirist*, 20, n. 1.

20. See, for example, Benjamin Franklin to Sir Everard Fawkener, July 27, 1756: "The Provincials . . . apprehend, that Regulars join'd with them, would claim all the Honour of any Success, and charge them with the Blame of every Miscarriage." Labaree, VI, 473. Cf. Franklin's long catalogue of the complaints of the American soldiers, published May 9, 1759; Labaree, VIII, 342-56. And for the colonists' own view of their supposedly heroic fighting at the defeat of Braddock, when the regulars turned coward, see Freeman, II, 141-42; and Gwenda Morgan, "Virginia and the French and Indian War: A Case Study of the War's Effects on Imperial Relations, " *Virginia Magazine of History and Biography*, 81 (1973), 23-48, esp. 30-33.

21. Cf. Maury's similar thoughts, and his statement, "Indians are the best match for Indians." Maury, 406. In *Plain Truth*, Franklin had also portrayed the terrible outcome if those Indians presently friendly would be converted to the French cause. Labaree, III, 194.

22. If the Centinel refers, as is most likely, to a published paper, it probably appeared in the *Virginia Gazette* and is no longer extant. I do not believe
that the Centinel has in mind Bland's Philo Patriae essay, for the Centinel
implies that the author, a "military Gentleman," wrote a strong attack on
him. It may be that he refers to George Washington's reply; see above, n. 14.

23. William B. Sprague, ed., *Sermons by the Rev. Samuel Davies* (Philadelphia: Presbyterian Board of Publications, 1864), III, 280n. Sprague notes, III,
167n, that the following sermons "were first published in London" in 1806.
Hereafter, references to this edition of Davies' sermons will be indicated in
the text by "*S*," and all references unless otherwise indicated will be to the
third volume.

24. Bernhard Knollenberg, *George Washington: The Virginia Period,
1732-1775* (Durham, N.C.: Duke University Press, 1964), 160, n. 64.

25. J. A. Leo Lemay, *A Calendar of American Poetry in the Colonial
Newspapers and Magazines and in the Major English Magazines Through 1765*
(Worcester: American Antiquarian Society, 1972), 183-84, no. 1324.

26. See the genealogy in Edward Porter Alexander, ed., *The Journal of
John Fontaine: An Irish Huguenot Son in Spain and Virginia, 1710-1719*
(Williamsburg: Colonial Williamsburg Foundation, 1972), 129-32, esp. 130.

27. *Maryland Historical Magazine*, 7 (1912), 163-64, 293-94. His obituary
in the *Virginia Gazette* (PD), August 24, 1769, 3, col. 2, comments "Abroad,
and in the world at large, he was every where esteemed and caressed as a man
of genius and letters."

28. "Letter of Rev. James Maury to Philip Ludwell, on the Defence of the
Frontiers of Virginia, 1756," *Virginia Magazine of History and Biography*, 19
(1911), 292-304; the letter is dated "Louisa, 10 February, 1756"; another
version, evidently a draft (with part missing and without the date), is in Ann
Maury, 431-42. James Maury mentions that, to carry out the proposals embodied in his letter to Ludwell, "I drew up, and, by means of my acquaintance, dispersed in the three frontier and five contiguous counties, petitions to
the General Assembly before its last session, praying, that such a line of forts
might be built, and such an Indian factory established." Maury, 404.

29. The fullest biography is George William Pilcher, *Samuel Davies: Apostle of Dissent in Colonial Virginia* (Knoxville: University of Tennessee Press,
1971).

30. For the general characteristics of the Calvinistic-revivalistic "sublime"
style of the mid-eighteenth century, see Alan Heimert, *Religion and the American Mind: From the Great Awakening to the Revolution* (Cambridge, Mas-
sachussets: Harvard University Press, 1966), 208-36; esp. 221ff. But, in characterizing all the Calvinists, Heimert produces an amalgam that does not
discriminate between the different styles of the ministers. Heimert, for example, says "The evangelical ministry avoided learned allusions, Latin (and
Latinate diction), and periphrasis." But Davies, whom Heimert frequently
cites, uses long learned allusions interminably. See also Richard Beale Davis,
"Samuel Davies: Poet of the Great Awakening," 133-48 in Davis, *Literature*

and Society in Early Virginia 1608-1840 (Baton Rouge: Louisiana State University Press, 1973).

31. For Davies' classical knowledge, see Richard Mott Gummere, "Samuel Davies: Classical Champion of Religious Freedom," *Journal of Presbyterian History*, 40 (1962), 67-74; reprinted in Gummere's *Seven Wise Men of Colonial America* (Cambridge, Massachusetts: Harvard University Press, 1967), 41-49. See also n. 27.

32. The appeal to the *consensus gentium* is a characteristic Enlightment motif. A. O. Lovejoy, "The Parallel of Deism and Classicism," *Essays in the History of Ideas* (New York: Putnam's, Capricorn Books, 1960), 33. See also *S*, I, 446.

33. See his sermon "A Time of Unusual Sickness and Mortality Improved," preached November 14, 1756; *S*, 244-46. See also *S*, I, 337.

34. Richard Beale Davis, ed., *Collected Poems of Samuel Davies* (Gainesville, Florida: Scholars' Facsimiles and Reprints, 1968). See especially "on the barbarities of the French, and their savage allies and proselytes, on the frontiers of Virginia," 170-72; and "Verses on Gen. Braddock's defeat," 219-21. Craig Gilborn lists contemporary English poets "in the approximate order of their importance to Davies: Alexander Pope, Edward Young, James Thomson, Isaac Watts, Elizabeth Rowe, Richard Blackmore, James Hervey, Phillip Doddridge, Joseph Addison, John Norris, and Matthew Prior"; "Samuel Davies' Sacred Muse," *Journal of Presbyterian History*, 41 (1963), 63-79, 65.

35. The total evidence of notes 6, 7, 9, 10, and 21, above, strongly suggests that *Plain Truth* was remembered and possibly consulted by the author of the Virginia Centinel essay series. In addition to the editors' notes on the popularity of the pamphlet (Labaree, III, 184), I can add that it was reprinted in the *Boston Evening Post*, January 11 and 18, 1748. For Davies' peregrinations during 1747, see Pilcher, 13-16. New Castle, Deleware, where Davies was initially granted a license to preach and where he was ordained (Pilcher, 12-13) is located on the Delaware River, just above the head of the Delaware Bay—an area directly affected by Franklin's proposals in *Plain Truth*. See the map "The Defenses of the Delaware, 1747-48," Labaree, III, 181. That *Plain Truth* was a model for the essay series suggests that the author hoped that he might have the success that Franklin achieved with his pamphlet and that the Centinel was one of Franklin's early imitators.

36. When Davies saw Gibbons in London on December 26, 1753, he referred to him in his diary as "my dear Correspondent." George William Pilcher, ed., *The Reverend Samuel Davies Abroad: The Diary of a Journey to England and Scotland, 1753-55* (Urbana: University of Illinois Press, 1967), 43. Hereafter cited as *Davies Abroad*. See Samuel Davies, *Sermons on the Most Useful and Important Subjects . . . In Three Volumes . . .* , ed. Thomas Gibbons (London: Printed for the Benefit of the Author's Widow, and sold by J. Buckland, 1766).

37. George Maclaren Brydon, *Virginia's Mother Church and the Political*

Conditions Under Which It Grew (Philadelphia: Church Historical Society, 1952), II, 154-77.

38. For reference to one letter from Burr, see *Davies Abroad,* 3.

39. William Henry Foote, *Sketches of Virginia* (Philadelphia: Martien, 1850), 296.

40. Just as the Centinel refers to his essays as "Alarms" (e.g., Nos. 17, 18, and 19), so Davies calls his war sermons "alarms," *S,* 310; *VDR* (see next note), 4, 43.

41. These two sermons are not included in Davies' collected works. They are hereafter referred to as *VDR.*

42. Reprinted in London in 1756. *S,* 94-119. Excerpts were reprinted under the title *The Good Soldier* (London, 1756).

43. In *S,* 120-46.

44. Reprinted in Boston and in Woodbridge, New Jersey, in 1759, Evans 8336 and 8333, respectively. In *S,* 147-66.

45. Flexner, p. 238.

46. On October 6, 1755, Maury complained to the Rev. William Dawson, Commissary of the Virginia Anglican clergy, that Davies and the Rev. John Todd had been in his parish preaching to the companies of Captain Overton and Captain Fox "at the Time of their Departur to range upon our Frontiers." Dawson Papers, Library of Congress.

47. For the Rev. John Todd (d. 1793), in addition to the account and the references in Pilcher's *Samuel Davies,* 96-99, see William B. Sprague, *Annals of the American Pulpit* (New York: R. Carter, 1859), III, 144n; Malcolm H. Harris, *History of Louisa County, Virginia* (Richmond: Dietz, 1936), 183-85; and Davies' ordination sermon for Todd: *The Duties, Difficulties and Reward of the faithful Minister. A Sermon, preached at the Installation of the Revd. Mr. John Todd . . . Nov. 12, 1752* (Glasgow: W. Duncan, Jr., 1754).

THE REVEREND JOHN CAMM: "TO RAISE A FLAME AND LIVE IN IT"

Homer D. Kemp

John Camm stands out as an epitome of those minor figures in American history who are relegated to footnotes and remembered only to be maligned for their opposition to the popular will.[1] English-born, English-educated, and fiercely jealous of the prerogatives of the Crown and the established Church, Camm struggled for over thirty years against those forces which eventually declared America independent of the Crown and disestablished the Church. He defied the authority of his local vestry, the Board of Visitors of William and Mary College, and the colonial legislature at great personal expense of both money and mental anguish. The many positions of responsibility to which Camm's peers elected him bespeak his capabilities and reputation among those who did not find themselves at the opposite end of his prolific pen or his litigious spirit.

Born in 1718, in Hornsea, Yorkshire, and educated in the school at nearby Beverley, Camm was admitted to Trinity College, Cambridge, as a sizar on June 16, 1738, and elected to a scholarship in April 1741. He took his B.A. in early 1741/2 and very shortly thereafter secured from the Bishop of Lincoln ordination as deacon on March 14, 1741/2, and priest on March 28, 1742. He would have received his £20 passage bounty from the Bishop of London and sailed for Virginia soon afterwards, for he was the minister of Newport Parish, Isle of Wight County, in 1745. His long and stormy career with the College of William and Mary and York-Hampton Parish, York County, began in 1749. [2]

Little is known of Camm's preaching or private life; however, he must have made a favorable impression on a great many persons, for his colleagues continually elected him their spokesman and even Governor Fauquier, who disliked Camm and alluded to his delight "to raise a Flame and live in it," grudgingly admitted that he was a man of abilities. [3] As early as the 1754 convention of the clergy at Williamsburg, Camm was chosen to serve as one of the first trustees of the widows and orphans fund and elected to most of the committees, including the one that drew up a report to the Bishop of London on the Church in Virginia. [4] He retained the rectorship of the prestigious York-Hampton Parish for more than twenty years and seems to have gotten along well with such powerful parishioners as the two Nelson brothers, one president and the other an important member of the Council.

We catch glimpses of him from time to time performing a wedding, or preaching a funeral sermon for a prominent parishioner. [5] One assuredly biased report of Camm's preaching has come down through the journal of a wealthy Lancaster County merchant of Presbyterian leanings: "Went with my wife to White Chapel Church, where we heard Mr. Cam preach a very indifferent discourse—nothing scarcely but external modes, much against Presbyterians—so that I was much disappointed by going to Church, for it was mispending the Lord's day." [6] And, of course, before the end of his life, Camm had rejoined the offices of Councillor, Commisary, and president of the college, no small feat for a man who had enraged so many of those who elected or recommended him to the offices.

The only anecdote about his private life which survives pictures the fiery parson in a far different light. According to tradition, he called on a young lady in his parish, Elizabeth Hansford, whom he had baptized as a child, to press the suit of a young man in the parish. When Camm cited the Bible as an authority in support of marriage, she refused the proxy offer and referred him to Samuel 12:7, which read "and Nathan said to David, thou art the man." The bachelor clergyman of fifty-one and his young parishioner were married July 8, 1769.[7] As with practically everything else he did, however, Camm's marriage embroiled him in another battle with the Virginia aristocracy. Professors were supposed to be bachelors living at the college, and the Visitors tried unsuccessfully to remove Camm and a colleague from their posts as a result of their marriages.[8]

If Camm's personal life is shadowy, there is no dearth of information about his public life. As early as 1752, Camm went to the defense of the rights of the clergy with a letter to the Bishop of London on behalf of his old Cambridge schoolmate William Kay.[9] Never one to back down from a good fight, Camm attacked the legislature over the first Two-Penny Act in 1755, defied the college Visitors in 1757, taunted Lieutenant-Governor Robert Dinwiddie's exercise of ecclesiastical authority in 1757 when he befriended the profligate John Brunskill, and carried his lawsuit against the second Two-Penny Act through the eight years of litigation to the Privy Council in England.[10] Although he was active in the attempt to establish an American episcopate and expressed his Tory sentiments to the very end of his life, Camm did not have to flee with Dunmore and never had to preach with pistols on his pulpit the way his friend Jonathan Boucher did.[11] It is a tribute to Camm's very great abilities and personal integrity that he was never molested even in the hottest part of the Revolutionary fervor in Virginia. The extent of his persecution for being a Tory was his removal as president of William and Mary when he refused to agree to the omission of the statement of loyalty to the King on the surveyors' licenses issued by the college.

Camm has never been seriously considered as a writer, but his essays and pamphlets compare favorably in quality with any written in his generation in Virginia. In addition to his copious letters and contributions to addresses to the King,[12] Camm penned three lengthly pamphlets, several dozen essays to the gazettes, and some scattered poetry. His pamphlets—*A Single and Distinct View* (Annapolis, 1763), *A Review of the Rector Detected* (Williamsburg, 1764), *Critical Remarks on a Letter Ascribed to Common Sense* (Williamsburg, 1765)—were highly competent answers to the Two-Penny Acts pamphlets of Landon Carter and Richard Bland.[13] Probably most significant among Camm's essays to the gazettes are those he contributed to the 1766 debates over separating the offices of Treasurer and Speaker and those he published during the 1770-1772 American episcopate controversy.[14]

The common attitude toward Camm's writing is voiced in Bernard Bailyn's cursory footnotes about two of the Two-Penny pamphlets. Bailyn skims over the "wild allegorical flight concerning the proper way to keep a pig from squealing" at the end of *A Review of the Rector Detected* and settles upon *Critical Remarks*:

> The pamphlet, though ineffective as a commentary on the constitutional problems, is remarkable at least for its frenzied effort to top Bland's raillery. It employs a bewildering array of devices, including doggerel verse, to denounce Bland's "scribendi cacoethes," his "haunted and hag-ridden imagination." At points the imagery is so elaborated, the conceits and name-calling so jumbled together, that it is almost impossible to follow the thought.[15]

This is really not a fair assessment of Camm's pamphlets. There is nothing wild about any of the writing; it is all carefully calculated for effect, and the mass of classical and contemporary literary allusions are controlled and effective. Throughout Camm's polemical writings, the reader sees a sharp, logical mind at work in the systematic refutation of his opponents' charges, and an author with a high degree of literary consciousness, fully aware of his classical and contemporary models. Camm's *Critical Remarks*, for example, has been considered only as a rather anti-climactic statement of Tory views on Crown prerogatives; however, the pamphlet is a highly effective piece of satire which generally reveals a more subtle use of the devices of irony than Richard Bland's *Colonel Dismounted* and exhibits a more thoroughly sustained satiric mask. From a mock dedication, through an elaborate Madame Drowsiness-Goddess of Dullness conceit, to the paraphernalia of the final ironic advertisements, Camm proves worthy of comparison to his models in Swift and Dryden.

All too many twentieth-century readers of eighteenth-century polemical literature forget the only true critical point of view—the author's intention. Persuasion was the chief aim of the eighteenth-century polemicist and John Camm was as well versed in suasory discourse as were his British models Dryden, Swift, and Pope.

These authors, as well as their intended audiences, were products of an education which was first and foremost classical in content and method; the chief element of this education was the study of rhetoric based upon the works of Aristotle, Cicero, Quintilian, and Hermogenes.[16] Camm's works reveal him to be a highly effective polemicist who employed the elements of classical rhetoric in the best tradition of the classical and contemporary writers whom he imitated and quoted.

It is impossible to separate completely the interrelated parts of suasory discourse, but it may be useful to point up some of the techniques Camm used in his battle with the two colonels.[17] Although the system of rhetoric which Camm inherited was somewhat rigid, the centuries of application and elaboration had allowed for adaptation to all conceivable circumstances. Camm was in the special position of having to debate against overwhelming odds; the arguments of his opponents Landon Carter and Richard Bland were extremely popular with Virginia readers. He met this challenge by changing slightly the five-part arrangement of classical oration. The ordinary arrangement was exordium, narration, confirmation, refutation, and peroration; however, the rhetor debating from an unpopular position often enhanced his arguments by placing refutation before confirmation.[18] Actually, there is very little confirmation at all in Camm's discourses; the facts were known, the chief arguments had been stated by his opponents, and he had to destroy their popularity. His use of all the rhetorical devices in his arsenal may be explained in light of this goal.

In his refutation of the assertions of Carter and Bland, Camm had to rely heavily upon the three modes of persuasion: ethical appeal (ethos), emotional appeal (pathos), and logical appeal (logos). The first concern in the defeat of his opponents was the establishing of his own ethos, an ethos which would be more creditable than those of the colonels. He appears in the pamphlets as a reasonable fact-finder who argues from a wealth of evidence, a man who has been falsely maligned but does not complain, and a modest man who admits his mistakes. Richard Bland ended his *Letter to the Clergy of Virginia* by challenging Camm to a debate in Virginia where "Facts can be known and Truth discovered" (p. 20) instead of misrepresenting matters to the Bishop of London.[19]

Camm answered in the beginning of *A Single and Distinct View* with an elaborate twelve-page (pp. 3-15) computation of his losses in salary as a result of the Two-Penny Act, supporting it with a detailed list of his parishioners and their tithables, and concluding that the law was totally unnecessary.[20] Although he has spent a great deal of money in defending his and fellow clergymen's rights in court, has lost tobacco at sea, and has been maligned for using his British rights of appeal to England (*S&DV*, pp. 20, 34), he has not complained. As a further proof of his persecution, Camm includes in *A Single and Distinct View* his and public printer Joseph Royle's correspondence concerning Royle's refusal to print the pamphlet (pp. 46-51). Frequently, he admits to some small error or omission as part of his ethos as a writer who concedes his weaknesses (i.e., *S&DV*, pp. 32-33, 37-38, 43).

Realizing that an integral part of the ethos in refutation is the destruction of the opponent's ethos, Camm gradually through the course of the debate builds "characters" for his two opponents. Bland is the "Syllogistical Colonel" ("Observations," p. xiv) who is a rather vain, imperious user of fierce language, as well as false logic and dishonest emotional appeals to prejudices. Carter, on the other hand, is an uncontrollable "Colonel Spitfire" (*Rev. Rec. Det.*, p. 20), whose incoherence and confusion may be exceeded only by his ill-temper and malevolent intent. Of the many devices Camm uses in diminishing his opponents, he seems most fond of what Charles A. Beaumont calls "refining" and Martin Price terms "redefining."[21] The colonels' favorite terms are redefined until they lose their effectiveness or prove their users ridiculous incompetents who unconsciously argue against their own side. Bland's famous *Salus Populi est Suprema Lex* (*S&DV*, p. 22-23) is shown to be a ruse for denying the power of the King, and his appeal to the "Necessity" of the Two—Penny Act is redefined throughout all three of Camm's pamphlets until it becomes anything but necessary. In his *Letter to the Bishop of London*, Carter used as a motto Paul's apostophe to charity in I Corinthians 13:2. "Charity" and its derivatives become a refrain throughout *A Single and Distinct View*; each time Camm shows another ill effect of the Two-Penny Act, he repeats Carter's call for charity. As a final crowning satiric touch, the Rector proves that the Colonel omitted part of the Biblical quotation because he himself is guilty of violating its admonition. Charity, according to Paul's account, "vaunteth not itself" (*S&DV*, p. 14); however, Carter not only gives away that which belongs to others, he boasts about his own contributions. Camm ends the pamphlet with an essay of Carter's which heatedly notifies the public that it was he, not his brother, who had financed a certain charity school (pp. 53-55). Even more damning is the use by the colonels of vague words and pathos to hide evil motives. Bland attempts to frighten colonials by comparing British monarchs to Turkish and Babylonian tyrants (*S&DV*, pp. 22-23, 36) and Carter whose motives "cannot be cover'd with too thick a Veil," wraps them up "Warm in a Cloudy Diction" (*S&DV*, p. 13) and hides behind "Clouds and thick Darkness" (*Rev. Rec. Det.*, pp. 9-10). Indeed, one of the most frequent images in Camm's pamphlets is that of dispelling fog and clouds.

In both enhancing his own ethos and diminishing those of his opponents, Camm makes ample use of pathos. His characteristic device is to appeal to traditional British prejudices. The Rector appears as a loyal Briton defending the prerogatives of the Crown against the imminent chaos of colonial legislatures defying established law; the colonels, on the other hand, are abusive, tyrannical radicals who would destroy the most sacred British freedom—the right of property. Bland, Carter, and the colonial legislature are depicted as those who would erect "an arbitrary Power over private Property" (*Rev. Rec. Det.*, p. 4), undermine "the known Principles of Commerce" (*Rev. Rec. Det.*, p. 13), and overturn "the Foundations of Justice and Property" (*Rev. Rec. Det.*, p. 13). In addition, the colonels dishonestly hide behind the approved abstractions of Right and Wrong, Reason, Truth, Common Sense, Charity, and Necessity (*Crit. Rem.*, pp. vi-vii). Camm, however, will "take Shelter in our Distress, under the Wings of the Prerogative; under the Protection of a most Gracious and Religious Monarch, eminently and illustriously attach'd to the true Interests and Felicity of his Subjects" (*S&DV*, p. 24).

Camm employs logos in much the same way as pathos to build his own ethos and discredit his opponents' arguments. He frequently imparts a sense of demonstration by weaving an airtight web of logic, much as a lawyer builds a case, stating both sides and then confidently answering the opponent's arguments. Because his chief concern is refutation, however, Camm usually relies upon an orderly charge and rebuttal procedure; he quotes his opponent's words and then refutes them one at a time by an elaborate syllogism, by a process of redefinition, or by a careful documentation from classical and contemporary authorities. In *A Review of the Rector Detected*, for instance, Camm answers Carter's charges that he writes in a "miscellaneous" manner by elaborately dividing the pamphlet into chapters and then heading the sections with page numbers from Carter's *Rector Detected*. Each page of Carter's pamphlet is answered one by one.

Of the multitude of schemes and tropes which constitute the elocution of the rhetor's arguments, Camm is especially fond of the schemes of repetition and the trope of erotema. He employs the schemes of alliteration and climax frequently, but he makes the greatest use of anaphora—the beginning of successive clauses with the same word or group of words. Anaphora recurs again and again throughout all his pamphlets. When he wishes to reinforce his assertion that Virginia is part of Great Britain, not an independent country, Camm builds up to a highly emotional, climactic statement which contains double anaphora:

> I am confirm'd in these Notions by considering, that the Natives, and those who reside here, have the Power and Riches of the Mother Country for their Defence against their Enemies; that they hold their Lands of the Crown; that they have the same Rights in the Mother Country as other *British* Subjects, that consequently other *British* Subjects have equal Rights here; that those Subjects, who Trade hither and have considerable Effects here, tho' residing in *Britain*, are properly a Part of the Colony, whose Interests must be attended to, as well as that of those who reside here; and that if those who reside here, could at pleasure suspend Laws confirm'd by the King, (which seems a Thing of the same Nature with a dispensing Power in the Crown) could dissolve all Contracts; could put every body in the State of Minors under Wardship; rendering them as little able to make Contracts as they are compellable to comply with them when made, could discharge Tenants from the Payment of their Rents and Arbitrarily dispose of every Man's Property: The Subjects residing in *Britain* would probably be as unwilling to Trust their Property here, as in any foreign Kingdom independent of the Crown of *Great-Britain* (*S&DV*, p. 38).

He lists his many persecutions in a series of preposition-participle
clauses (*S&DV*, p. 42) and he insinuates chaos in a repetition of
"No Wonder" sentences when he wishes to show that treasonable
radicals such as Patrick Henry and miscarriages of justice such as
the Two-Penny Act grow naturally out of loose statements by "so
old and deep a Politician as the Colonel" (*Rev. Rec. Det.*, p. 23).[22]

Erotema probably occupies more space in Camm's writings than
does any other single device. Almost every page has at least one
and occasionally a dozen or more rhetorical questions. When
Camm wishes to answer Carter's assertion that the Two-Penny Act
was passed for the good of the whole community, he combines
anaphora and erotema:

> For what very general and good Purpose could it answer to the Land-
> lord to have his Rents made liable to be disposed of by any Body but
> himself; to the Merchant to be deprived of the Benefit of his advanta-
> geous Bargains, and obliged to stand to the Detriment of such as turn
> out unfavourably; to the Parson to be stripped of two Thirds of [his]
> Salary for one Year, and have the Whole rendered precarious for ever;
> to the rest to be either damaged, or no Way benefited, by the Act?
> (*Rev. Rec. Det.*, p. 4)

The devices of anaphora and erotema are especially useful in establishing pathos, and that is how Camm most commonly employs
them. Perhaps he is merely revealing a preacher's fondness for the
devices which create great emotional intensity.

Nowhere is Camm's rhetorical training and skill or his kinship
with his British counterparts more evident than in the characteristic unit of thought in his essays. The primary unit is the rhetorical period, not the grammatical sentence. Morris Croll observes
that one or the other—either rhetorical or grammatical considera-
tions—is always foremost in a writer's mind, and that one or the
other is always foremost in every theory of literary education. [23]In
this last age before the advent of the grammars of the later eighteenth century, essayists in England and America were still predominantly rhetorical in their approach to composition. Many of
the rhetorical units in Camm's works are of paragraphic dimensions, consisting of an initial clause which states a proposition
followed by a succession of amplifying clauses:

All of which may be dexterously performed; provided the Superstition of the middling Frugal, and some of the poorer Ranks be quieted, by giving them a share in the Advantages of this profitable Doctrine, proportionable to their Circumstances: It being Hoped, that the boasted Respect of such for the Church and Clergy will not always amount to the value of Twenty Shillings; when that of their Superiors may be sometimes bragged of for Rising so high, as to gratify an Hungry and obliging Parson with a good Dinner; which is, what I must suppose Col. *Bland* chiefly means by *that general good Reception given to Clergymen of good Behaviour*; and is consonant to the printed Boast of Col. *Carter*, concerning the Encouragement bestow'd on the Learned in the Profession of Physick; when he tells us *the Labourers in that Vineyard have the Honour of being occasionally admitted to a share in the Delicacies of a plentiful Table (S&DV*, p. 14).

One sees the same rhetorical period in the polemical works of Dryden, Swift, and Steele.[24] Developing out of the extremes in prose style of the seventeenth century, this sentence has been called the "loose" period, the "Baroque" period,[25] and the "fluent Senecan" sentence.[26] Faced with a choice between the extremes of the curt sentence, consisting of a string of clauses joined by parataxis, and the "Ciceronian" sentence developed carefully by hypotaxis, most British and colonial essayists chose a middle ground. They chose what Ian Gordon and George Williamson call the conversational norm of the fluent Senecan style.[27] It is significant that Camm and his contemporaries "chose" their style. They wrote plain prose, but not because that was all they knew how to write. The plainness of the eighteenth-century stylist was the plainness of the learned man; some writers such as Dr. Johnson wrote in the grand "Ciceronian" manner. Each writer had to decide which form or combination of forms best suited his habits of thought and purpose in writing.

For the purposes of persuasion in controversy, both the British and colonial polemicist found the conversational norm of the loose, fluent Senecan sentence the most useful vehicle. This sentence has the merit of clarity and immediacy. It employs some hypotaxis, but only the loosest sort; generally it progresses by linear addition.[28] Each new thought is added by parataxis or simple co-ordination in clauses relatively free of each other. The reader can stop at almost any mark and the sense is complete. This practice reveals the natural order of a mind thinking—an exploratory, truth-seeking mind, the mind of a practical, busy man who wishes to get to the core of a problem quickly with a minimum of flourishes and to convince his reader of the validity of his findings at the very moment of discovery. When relative pronouns and subordinating conjunctions are used, they operate in only the most casual way, not to tighten structure, but as necessary keys to another stage in the straight-line advancement of an idea.[29] The reader is made to feel as if he is participating in the thought process as the case if built against an opponent—no insignificant accomplishment in persuasive writing.

Two examples from Camm will illustrate the effectiveness of this period. The first is one of his favorites—a tripartite construction with the main proposition putting out a logical branch and both being capped off by an absolute participle construction:

It is to be sure happy for us to have Laymen, who are not only infallible Judges of a Clergyman's Duty and Merit, but can perform such eminent Parts of his Office as well as himself; because, where this is the Case, there is the less Occasion to provide a good Maintainance for the Clergy, or for being punctual in paying their appointment whether it be great or little; the Office being by the same Means preserv'd from that Contempt, which justly falls upon the Person of the Minister (*S&DV*, p. 22).

Another period in the same pamphlet illustrates the characteristic growth by linear addition and use of connectives:

However, in the present Case this Measure was unavoidable: The late Commissary was desired to call the Clergy together; that they might meet at the same Time with the Assembly, who, according to Report, were going to pass an Act, in which the Clergy understood themselves to be very much concerned; but the Commissary, not being under the Influence of the Clergy, or in their true Interest, refused this Request: When the Assembly were met, the Speaker was applied to, that some of the Clergy might be heard before a Committee, upon the Bill depending, by themselves or their Counsel; which they imagined was agreeable to Parliamentary Proceedings; the Council were applied to for the same Purpose; the Governor for a Negative on the Bill; all this without any Kind of Success (*S&DV*, p. 34).

John Camm represents at its best that portion of Virginia society which looked at the same constitution and laws upon which

Bland and Carter wrote and saw there the "rights of Englishmen" in a quite different light. In his battles with the colonels and in his other works, Camm made a valuable contribution to American Revolutionary literature by stating cogently the minority viewpoint of Virginia loyalists. He would not rank with a contemporary writer such as Swift in depth of thought, but then his aims were narrowly polemical. If his works are compared to Swift's purely polemical essays, however, the Virginia Rector compares quite favorably in the mastery of a common tradition of rhetoric and prose style.

NOTES

1. Much of the material in this paper appears in the introductions to the author's edition of Virginia pamphlets and essays, "The Pre-Revolutionary Virginia Polemical Essay: The Pistole Fee and the Two-Penny Acts Controversies" (Diss. University of Tennessee, 1972). The basic research for that work was made possible by a Colonial Williamsburg Foundation grant-in-aid in 1971.

2. For biographical details, see Lyon G. Tyler, "Early Presidents of William and Mary," *WMQ*, 1st Ser., 1-3 (1892-1894), 71; Lyon G. Tyler, "Descendents of John Camm, President of William and Mary College," *WMQ*, 1st Ser., 4 (1895-1896), 61-62, 275-78; Edward Lewis Goodwin, *The Colonial Church in Virginia: With Biographical Sketches of the First Six Bishops of the Diocese of Virginia, And Other Historical Papers, Together with Brief Biographical Sketches of the Colonial Clergy of Virginia* (Milwaukee: Morehouse Publishing Co., 1927), 329, 340-41, 358. Several Virginians attended school at Beverly between 1745 and 1760; perhaps some of them were influenced by Camm to study at his alma mater.

3. Francis Fauquier to the Bishop of London, July 29, 1761, in William Wilson Manross, comp., *Fulham Papers in the Lambeth Palace Library: American Colonial Section Calendar and Indexes* (Oxford: Clarendon Press, 1965), 14:1-2, 205. All subsequent citations of Fulham Papers will refer to Manross's compilation and will appear, for example, as Manross, 13:3-4, 192 (Vol. 13, folios 3-4, Manross page number 192).

4. Manross, 13:132-61, 200.

5. See Colonel James Gordon's "Journal," June 9, 1759, quoted in William Henry Foote, *Sketches of Virginia, Historical and Biographical*, 1st Ser. (1850-1855; rpt. Richmond: John Knox Press, 1966), 362. A printed funeral sermon of Camm's is included in the Waller Papers, Colonial Williamsburg Foundation, Williamsburg, Virginia.

6. Foote, 364.

7. Tyler, 72. *Virginia Gazette* (Purdie & Dixon), July 13, 1769. Camm and his wife both died in 1779.

8. See Tyler, 72.

9. John Camm to the Bishop of London, June 4, 1752, Manross, 13:61-62, 196. This letter is the earliest extant example of the epistolary art of one of the most indefatigable letter writers in his generation. His career in letter writing culminates in a carefully penned sixty-five page letter to the Bishop of London in 1768 which in truth is an essay on the entire history of the Parsons' Cause and related problems of the clergy. For an account of Kay's struggle with his vestry, see Richard Lee Morton, *Colonial Virginia* (Chapel Hill: University of North Carolina Press, 1960), II, 759-62.

10. Camm led a small protest movement against the 1755 act, petitioning the home government; however, he had little success. See Clergy to the Bishop of London, November 29, 1755, Manross, 13:202-209, 201; Same, February 26, 1756, Manross, 13:212-19, 201; Thomas Dawson to the Bishop of London, Fegruary 25, 1756, Manross, 13:220-21, 202. Camm's many letters to successive Bishops of London are catalogued in Manross. Also, see John Camm to Mrs. Walter McClurg, *WMQ*, 1st Ser., 2 (1894), 238-39. For the details in the defiance of the Visitors by Professors John Camm, Richard Graham, and Emmanuel Jones, their subsequent dismissal, appeal to England, and reinstatement in 1763, see Morton, II, 772-76. See Morton, II, 763-65, for a discussion of the case of John Brunskill who was dismissed on charges of immorality from Hamilton Parish, Prince William County. Detailed accounts of the historical events of the Two-Penny Acts controversy may be found in: Richard Lee Morton, *Colonial Virginia* (Chapel Hill: University of North Carolina Press, 1960), I, chaps. xxvii-xxx; Clifford Dowdey, *The Golden Age: A Climate of Greatness, Virginia 1732-1775* (Boston: Little, Brown, and Co., 1970), 133-214; Glenn Curtiss Smith, "The Parsons' Cause," *Tyler's Magazine*, 21 (1939/40), 140-71, 291-306; Joseph Henry Smith, *Appeals to the Privy Council from the American Plantations* (New York: Columbia University Press, 1950), 607-26; Arthur P. Scott, "Constitutional Aspects of the Parsons' Cause," *Political Science Quarterly*, 31 (1916), 569; Robert Chester Daetweiler, "Richard Bland: Conservative of Self-Government in Eighteenth-Century Virginia," (Diss. University of Washington 1968), 123-60.

11. Jonathan Boucher, *Reminiscences of An American Loyalist*, 1738-1789, ed. Jonathan Bouchier (Boston: Houghton Mifflin Co., 1925), 113.

12. The most famous of his petitions, "The Humble Address of the Clergy to the Board of Trade," 1759, is extant in two versions: the Fulham Palace copy (Manross: 13:278-79, 204) and the one in the Board of Trade correspondence (P.R.O., C.O. 5/1329, ff. 119-20), the slightly altered text of which appears in Richard Bland's *Colonel Dismounted*, Appendix III, xxiv-xxvii.

13. Annotated texts of the extant pamphlets and essays growing out of the Two-Penny Acts controversy, as well as a discussion of the lost pieces, may be found in Kemp, "The Pre-Revolutionary Virginia Polemical Essay."

14. Camm published an essay, under the pseudonym "A Planter," advocating separation of the Chair and Treasury in Rind's *Virginia Gazette* on

August 8, 1766. When Landon Carter responded to his essay, Camm returned fire behind the mask of the ironic persona "R.R.," purportedly on Carter's side. A short note by the persona is followed by a poem by "A Planter," entitled "Advice to the Geniuses of the East and West, from the PLANTER proclaimed Mad by Buckskin NOT MAD"—a poem aimed especially at Carter ("Buckskin"). See J. A. Leo Lemay, "Robert Bolling and the Bailment of Colonel Chiswell," *Early American Literature*, 6 (1971), 116-17; 120, n. 9; 126, n. 43, for a discussion of the authorship of the pieces and the circumstances surrounding their publication. This poem and the satiric poems in *Critical Remarks* are the only clearly identified poems by Camm. He must have had a reputation as a versifier as early as 1751, however, for he was thought for awhile to have written the "Walter Dymocke" poems against Samuel Davies. Examples of Camm's essays in the Episcopate Controversy may be seen in *Virginia Gazette* (Purdie & Dixon), June 13, July 11, August 15, 22, 1771. There must surely be other essays and some poetry of Camm's published in this dispute under pseudonyms. For an account of the part Camm and others played in this highly significant quarrel, see: George Mac-Laren Brydon, *Virginia's Mother Church and the Political Conditions Under Which It Grew* (Richmond: Virginia Historical Society, 1947); Arthur Lyon Cross, *The Anglican Episcopate and the American Colonies* (1902; rpt. Hamden, Conn.: Archon Books, 1964); H. J. Eckenrode, *Separation of Church and State in Virginia: A Study in the Development of the Revolution* (1910; rpt. New York: Da Capo Press, 1971); Alan Kenneth Austin, "The Role of the Anglican Church and Its Clergy in the Political Life of Colonial Virginia," Diss. University of Georgia 1969; Goodwin, *The Colonial Church in Virginia*; William Wilson Manross, *A History of the American Episcopal Church* (Milwaukee: Morehouse Publishing Co., 1935); Norman Sykes, *From Sheldon to Secker: Aspects of English Church History, 1660-1768* (Cambridge, England: Cambridge University Press, 1959). Carl Bridenbaugh's *Mitre and Sceptre* (New York: Oxford University Press, 1962) gives an informative picture of the influence of the episcopate movement on the Revolution in New England but generally ignores the South.

15. Bernard Bailyn, ed., *Pamphlets of the American Revolution 1750-1776* (Cambridge, Mass.: Harvard University Press, 1965), I, 707n.

16. Among the many treatments of education in eighteenth-century England pertinent to the present study, see M. L. Clarke, *Classical Education in Britain, 1500-1900* (Cambridge, England: Cambridge University Press, 1959); William T. Costello, *The Scholastic Curriculum in Early Seventeenth-Century Cambridge* (Cambridge, Mass.: Harvard University Press, 1958); G. M. Trevelyan, *Trinity College: An Historical Sketch* (Cambridge, England: Cambridge University Press, 1943). It might be well to note that Camm was at Trinity College during the last years of the irascible Richard Bentley's turbulent mastership. Camm would have experienced firsthand the practical application of rhetoric.

17. For the discussion of rhetoric in the present paper, the author owes a

debt to the following works: Donald L. Clark, *Rhetoric in Greco-Roman Education* (New York: Columbia University Press, 1957); Richard E. Hughes and P. Albert Duhamel, *Principles of Rhetoric* (Englewood Cliffs, N.J.: Prentice-Hall, 1966); Edward P. J. Corbett, *Classical Rhetoric for the Modern Student* (New York: Oxford University Press, 1965); Charles Allen Beaumont, *Swift's Classical Rhetoric*, University of Georgia Monographs, No. 8 (Athens: University of Georgia Press, 1961); Richard I. Cook, *Jonathan Swift As a Tory Pamphleteer* (Seattle: University of Washington Press, 1967); Martin Price, *Swift's Rhetorical Art: A Study in Structure and Meaning*, Yale Studies in English, Vol. 123 (New Haven: Yale University Press, 1953).

18. Under arrangement, Cicero lists seven parts—exordium, narration, exposition, proposition, confirmation, refutation, and peroration. Some authorities call for six parts, dropping "exposition" and "proposition" and adding "division" between "narration" and "confirmation." Most practitioners of the art of written persuasion, however, regularly used only the five main parts, dropping "division."

19. On June 14, 1759, Thomas Sherlock, Bishop of London from 1748-1761, wrote a letter to the Board of Trade denouncing the 1758 Two-Penny Act. Camm was in London as agent for the Virginia clergy at the time, and Bland accused Camm of telling Sherlock what to write.

20. During their fall 1758 session, the Virginia House of Burgesses, faced with a short tobacco crop and general economic depression, passed a temporary act to commute one year's tobacco salaries into currency at the rate of two pence per pound of tobacco—thus the name "Two-Penny Act." Each clergyman was supposed to receive 16,000 pounds of tobacco per year plus cask and four percent for shrinkage, making his salary worth in ordinary times about £144, or two pence per pound. If they had received the entire amount of tobacco in the spring of 1759 from the 1758 crop, however, it would have been worth many times more than usual. Camm claimed in *A Single and Distinct View* that the law cost him £200. Subsequent references to Camm's works will appear in the text, with abbreviations as follows: *A Single and Distinct View* (*S&DV*), *A Review of the Rector Detected* (*Rev. Rec. Det.*), *Critical Remarks* (*Crit. Rem.*), and "Observations on Colonel Bland's Letter" ("Observations").

21. Beaumont, 29; Price, 22-31.

22. Camm is also quite fond of the catalogue. Although it technically is a scheme of balance, it is closely akin to anaphora in its emotional effect.

23. See Morris W. Croll, "The Baroque Style in Prose," in *Essays in Stylistic Analysis*, ed. Howard S. Babb (New York: Harcourt Brace Jovanovich, 1972), 116. Croll's article originally appeared in *Studies in English Philology*, ed. Kemp Malone and Martin Ruud (Minneapolis, Minn.: University of Minnesota Press, 1929), 427-56.

24. The present discussion of style owes a debt to the following works: Croll, "The Baroque Style in Prose"; Ian Gordon, *The Movement of English Prose* (London: Longmans, 1966); Brian Vickers, *Francis Bacon and Renais-*

sance Prose (Cambridge, England: Cambridge University Press, 1968). A special debt is owing to Louis T. Milic, "Against the Typology of Styles," in *Essays on the Language of Literature*, ed. Seymour Chatman and Samuel R. Levin (Boston: Houghton Mifflin Co., 1967), 442-50; George Williamson, *The Senecan Amble: A Study in Prose Form From Bacon to Collier* (Chicago: University of Chicago Press, 1951); K. G. Hamilton, *The Two Harmonies: Poetry and Prose in the Seventeenth Century* (Oxford: Clarendon Press, 1963); F. P. Wilson, *Seventeenth-Century Prose: Five Lectures* (Berkeley: University of California Press, 1960).

25. Croll, 107-17.

26. Williamson, 51; Hamilton, 24.

27. Gordon, 9; Williamson, 336-41. Gordon makes the point that this style appeals to the ear and that the essay as a form never loses touch with the ear. Both men agree that writers of the period made a purposeful choice of using as a norm the middle style of a cultured gentleman's conversation.

28. Williamson, 51.

29. Croll, 110-11. Cf. Williamson's discussion of limited hypotaxis, 51.

A MIRROR OF
VIRTUE FOR A DECLINING LAND:
JOHN CAMM'S FUNERAL SERMON
FOR WILLIAM NELSON

Jack P. Greene

In contrast to New England Puritans, Virginia Anglicans seem rarely to have published sermons preached at the funerals of leading citizens during the colonial period. There was, in fact, no known copy of such a sermon until the one reprinted below turned up among the Waller Family Papers when they were deposited with Colonial Williamsburg, Inc. just over two decades ago. Unlisted in any of the standard bibliographical indexes, the sermon appears to be doubly unique: it is the only known copy of the only known published colonial Virginia funeral sermon. For that reason alone, the sermon will be of more than common interest to the religious and literary historian. Certainly no less important, the sermon may—and should—also be read as an additional example of the anxious reactions displayed by many colonial Virginians to what they considered alarming social trends throughout the middle decades of the eighteenth century.

Because the title page is missing, identification of the author remains somewhat tentative. But a manuscript notation of undetermined date unequivocally identifies the publication as a "Sermon, preached by the Rev. John Camm, of William and Mary College, at the funeral of Mr. Nelson, Yorktown Va.," while a second note in another hand states briefly "Preached by the Rev. John Camm President of William & Mary College Mr. Nelson, of

York Town Va. Funeral Sermon." There is no reason to challenge this attribution. Camm (1718-1778), who is the subject of the previous essay in this volume,[1] had been a parish minister for the Nelson family for much of the 1750s and 1760s. Educated at Trinity College, Cambridge, he had emigrated in 1745 to Virginia, where he served first as minister of Newport Parish in Isle of Wight County; then, beginning in 1749, he assumed the position of Professor of Divinity at the College of William and Mary and minister of Yorke-Hampton Parish in York County until 1771, when he became president of the college, rector of Bruton Parish in Williamsburg, commissary of the Bishop of London in Virginia, and a member of the King's Council in the colony. He is remembered mainly for his conspicuous and vigorous role as the defender of the clergy in the famous Two-Penny Act Controversy during the early 1760s.[2]

There can be no doubt that the subject of the sermon was the Honorable William Nelson, one of the leading merchants of Virginia and a parishoner of Camm's during his service as minister of Yorke-Hampton. A member of the King's Council for over a quarter of a century beginning in 1745, longtime president of that body, and interim governor of Virginia in 1770-1771, William Nelson died on November 19, 1772.[3] The sermon, which is undated, was probably published in Williamsburg shortly thereafter.

The sermon was entirely conventional: it does not seem to have deviated in either tone or thrust from the common run of Anglican funeral sermons in contemporary England.[4] Considering the questions of what were the permissible limits of sorrow at the "loss of those wh[o are most] dear and valuable to us," Camm espoused adherence to the classic Anglican imperatives of indulgence, moderation, resignation, and faith. The grief of family and friends need not—indeed, should not—be entirely suppressed out of deference to God's will: "to be for some time inconsolable" in the face of such "an afflicting experience" was, Camm declared, "a pardonable weakness." What was not allowable was to permit one's grief to go unrestrained. To avoid the sin, condemned by St. Paul, of sorrowing *"like those who have no hope"* and, therefore, no faith in God required moderation. Sorrow was "blameable" when it was too "excessive . . . too violent in the expression," when it violated "that decency and good manners" required by one's obligation to maintain "regard or value" for the living and "respect and veneration" for God. Intemperate grief was "a sickly and unmanly passion." Self-control, which Camm implied distinguished the virtuous from "the bulk of mankind" who were unable to check their grosser tendencies toward "intemperence of excess," necessitated "fortitude of mind" and an acceptance, with equanimity, of "the changes incident to, and inseparable from, human condition." The impossibility of reversing God's actions favored a calm and magnanimous resignation in the face of His "sovereign pleasure" and left no rational alternative but an abiding faith "that the same good father who gave them life, who hath hitherto so kindly provided for them" would "take us up . . . wipe away our tears, protect and bless us on earth, and at length bring us to his everlasting kingdom and glory."

Such warm and indulgent counsel stands in sharp contrast to the pungent and firey polemics of Camm's earlier political pamphlets. No doubt, the differing conventions of these divergent literary genres, as well as the dissimilarity in the nature of the occasions on which they were employed account in large measure for the contrast. Yet a close reading of the sermon reveals that counterparts to the sharp indictments, found in the earlier pamphlets, of the behavior of Virginia's "decayed gentry" form a powerful secondary theme in the sermon.[5] For, in Camm's hands, Nelson's life becomes a counter-image for the behavior of Virginians as a whole, and his praise of Nelson's conduct must be read as a condemnation of that of many other Virginians of all classes. Indeed, the public importance of Nelson rather than any special distinction to be found in the sermon *qua* sermon provides the most plausible explanation for the unusual event of its publication; and Nelson's public importance, independent testimony strongly suggests, derived not alone—nor even most significantly— from his great wealth and long career in public life, but from his widely recognized exemplification of what, by the ideal standards of the society, a virtuous man was supposed to be. Having "grown old in all the well earned Honours which his Country could bestow," declared the editors of Rinds' *Virginia Gazette* in Nelson's obituary, he was "still more conspicuous for his Virtues than his exalted Station." "Justice, Humanity, and Impartiality," they continued,

> dictated all his Decisions [as a magistrate] ; and as a Man he was an
> Ornament to his Species. His Breast, animated by a general Philan
> thropy, each Day was counted lost, that was not marked by some Act
> of Benevolence. By his Death the Public are deprived of a useful Mem
> ber, his Family of an affectionate Husband, a tender Parent, and an
> indulgent Master, his Friends of the sensible and polite Companion, and
> the Poor of a Benefactor, whose Counsel assisted, and Liberality soft
> ened, all the Rigours of their Situation. [6]

In elaborating on Nelson's many virtues, Camm offered a fuller
and more explicit description of the personal values and social imperatives to which all Virginians were supposed to aspire. In his
personal relations, Nelson had seasoned "mirth, facetiousness, and
wit, with gravity, decorum, and wisdom." In his private life, he
had been equally temperate. Towards his wife, he had been "tender . . . without . . . being drawn by the most forcible of passions
into any impropriety of behaviour which could disgust the nicest
observer"; towards his children, he had been indulgent without
"taking off his eye" from their "true and best interests"; and
towards his servants and slaves, he had been "kind and generous"
without extending such freedom as was beyond the capabilities of
their station. A similar pattern of conduct characterized his public
life. As a public servant, he managed during the troubled times
after 1764 to discharge his duties to "his country" without forfeiting his "loyalty and fidelity to his soverign, to the interests of
the mother state, [and] to the general wealth of the grand aggregate of British dominions." His devotion to his religion and
church was "ardent" but without "bitterness or resentment
against those of a different persuasion." His charities were many
and munificent but always "disposed with choice and discretion."
His hospitality "in a country justly renowned for . . . that virtue"
was "extensive and liberal, yet judicious, and not set from the
restraints of reason and religion." Unlike that of many others,
Camm implied, Nelson's hospitality

> was not a blind propensity to profuseness, or a passion for a name to
> which he sacrificed the reasonable expectations of his family and de-

scendents, or by which he corrupted the morals of his friends and neighbours when his mind was most unbended, even in the hours of restivity, upon which vice or folly or impudence, are too apt to steal. He was no encourager of intemperance or riot, or lewd and profane discourse, or any practice tending to injure the health, the reputation, the fortunes, the manners, or the religious attainments of his company.

What underlay this pattern of virtuous behavior was an abiding commitment to the attainment of moderation in all areas of one's life. Those Virginians who most closely approached the idealized standards of conduct in the society were those who adhered most steadily to this commitment, those who were not oppressive of their servants and slaves, bigoted in their support of their religion, or, most important of all, imprudent in the use of their resources.

In this effusive praise of the extraordinary balance achieved by Nelson, Camm revealed what was troubling him as well as so many of his comtemporaries about the state of Virginia society. By the early 1770s, Virginians at all levels of society had become increasingly anxious about what seemed to be growing moral decay within Virginia society. A significant "increase of wealth" after 1730 had been accompanied by rising "extravagance, ostentation, and . . . disregard for economy," a mere "Deluge of Luxury and Pleasure." Anglican and Dissenting ministers alike denied the "great . . . Tendency amongst us to Extravagance and Luxury," warned of the "fatal Tendency" of the "prevailing Passion and Taste for Gaming . . . Racing, Cards, Dice and all other such Diversions," and admonished the gentry to eschew the "insignificant Pride of Dress, the empty Ambition of gaudy Furniture, or a splendid Equipage" and other similar examples of "expensive living." All of these manifestations of "Vice and Wickedness" in a country, they gloomily predicted, were "the certain Forerunners and Cause of its Disgrace and Destruction." [7]

Why Nelson's example was so significant for Virginia, an important reason why he had made so "deep an Impression upon his Countrymen," [8] was precisely because he had managed to resist these alarming trends. The secret of his achievement, Camm made clear, was his remarkable self-control. This "great man had, no doubt, his passions to contest with, as well as other men; but few," Camm lamented, had been so successful in keeping them under such good "regulation" or in finding them so "continually [such] virtuous and ample employment." Nelson, said Camm, was "an Instance, I wish," he hastily added in displaying the depth of his anxieties about the inner state of Virginia society, "he could not be reckoned a rare instance, of what abundance of good may be done by a prudent and conscientious man without impoverishing himself or his connections, nay while his fortunes are improving." Vice, indebtedness, and financial ruin, Camm made clear, were born companions: "Alas! generally speaking, they are not our virtues, but our vices . . . which are so costly and expensive as to devour our estates, and exhaust the fountain from which they derive their nourishment."

It was a commonplace of the day, as Charles Hansford, the blacksmith-turned-poet, put it in the early 1750s, that,

> A gentleman is placed so that he
> In his example cannot neuter be:
> He's always doing good or doing harm.[9]

By cultivating a "vivid Remembrance" of Nelson and all he exemplified, Camm thus hoped to encourage others "to tread in his steps." For as Camm as well as many of his contemporaries among the leaders of the Virginia gentry so firmly believed, only if men like Nelson did indeed become the "pattern to succeeding generations," only if his life became a mirror for those who remained behind and, as a result, those who managed to achieve his self-control—his virtue—became more rather than less numerous, could Virginians hope to stem the rush toward luxury, vice, dissipation, ruin and destruction.

Camm's sermon is reprinted in full below with the permission of the Research Department of the Colonial Williamsburg Foundation, the owner of the one known surviving copy.

A
SERMON, &c.
1st THESSALONIANS, IV. 13.

But I would not have you to be ignorant,
brethren, concerning them which are asleep,

that ye sorrow not,
even as others which have no hope.

It hath been the endeavours of the greatest and wisest Men, in all ages, to soften and take away the edge and smart of those afflictions which so frequently befal us in this life. But some, that have been thought to go the farthest in this matter, have really overshot the mark. They laboured, with much subtlety, to convince men that pain, diseases, and poverty, were no real evils; that the loss of friends, and power, and wealth, ought not to affect us, or give any sensible concern to a wise man. However finely spun such arguments might be, they had the disadvantage to contradict common experience and common sense: Men felt their pains, and no gloss or argument was able to convince them of the contrary. In spite of whatever reasonings, evil appeared in its natural horrours: Men were sure that losses, and thorns, and pressures, were what made them very uneasy; and, whether others would be pleased to call them evils or not, it signified little, they could not help wishing a deliverance from them, and groaning under their continuance.

[4] And among all the misfortunes wherewith human-condition is chequered there are few, perhaps none, that lie longer on o[ur hear]ts and sink deeper in our minds, than the loss of those wh[o are most] dear and valuable to us. When we are suddenly woun[ded in a] tender a part, it raises convulsions in our breasts, we with [care seek to] calm our tumultuous passions, the arrow sticks deep in our sides [and] the fretting pain often recoils upon us.

They know this who have ever lost an indulgent parent, lost him before he could be spared. They are sensible of it who have had a beloved husband or wife, or a hopeful child whom with much pains and charge they have brought up, immaturely snatched away. We have an afflicting experience of it when some circumstance or accident reminds us of the sudden fall of a sincere and generous friend, whom constant application and long services had made our own. These are blows which our nature hardly supports itself under, often is oppressed by. Philosophy fails us here, in its boasted assistances. It is, indeed, on these occasions, a pardonable weakness to be for some time inconsolable. It may be some time before we can listen to an exhortation even from the blessed mouth of an Apostle, *not to be sorry like men without hope.* And when we can conquer our rebellious passions and something soothe our sorrows, still, alas! we feel in our hearts grievous returns of affliction, many and piercing regrets, especially when we find the want of those whom we have lost.

But since the most valuable friends we possess are but mortal, since most of us have lost many, and soon may lose all, it may not be improper, towards lightening the evils that are past, towards arming us against those that are to come, to reflect on the holy counsel of Saint Paul, who bids us *not to be sorry as men without hope*.

[5] To this end I propose to point out what expressions of grief are allowable on the loss of our friends, and what are not so, but excessive blameable and unchristian, after which I shall touch on some of the principal arguments against the sorrowing in such an unallowable manner.

1. I have already intimated that their notions are big with absurdity, and full of impossibility, who would have us to be insensible, perfectly dispassionate, on these occasions. We are, the best and wisest of us, but men, we cannot always soar above mortal condition. We read of bitter lamentations made by the Patriarchs for their father Jacob, though he died in a very advanced age; and David breaks out into many passionate and almost imprudent lamentations for his ungracious but favourite son Absalom, *O my son Absalom* (says he) *my son, my son Absalom! would God I had died for thee. O Absalom! my son, my son!* (2d Samuel xiii. 23) so much may innocent nature struggle, even in the best. We read of the patience of Job; but what sort of patience was it? Not an insensible suffering of wo. He falls into great and many expostulations, even hard repinings, at the dispensations of Providence; and indeed shows us, with the saint, much of the man. It is his praise, and no little one it is, that he still submitted, and blessed his holy name who was pleased, out of his sovereign authority, to change the most prosperous condition for the most amazing affliction. For the rest, he demonstrates that there is but one copy perfectly fair, and worthy of our constant imitation; even his, who, after *strong crying and tears*, put up that never to be enough admired petition, *Father, if it be thy pleasure, let this cup pass from me; if not, thy will be done*. Tears, if they are a weakness, are a beautiful

one, and fit not ungracefully on our natures. [6] The all-perfect pattern whom we are to follow, the holy Jesus, not only wept for the miseries which he saw threatening the incorrigible Jerusalem but shed tears for what his beloved Lazarus had suffered in dying, though he was about to raise him again. This foible, as some would term it, or our constitution, deserves not blame or contempt, but love and pity. Sighs, regrets and complaints, must for some time be allowed to the unfortunate. A passion so deeply implanted in our nature can never, in itself, displease the great author of our being. He hath not here expressed his dislike of it. It is enough if we *sorrow not even as others who have no hope.*

Nor is it *to sorrow like those who have no hope* long to remember those whom we have loved and valued, and on some occasions to regret the loss of them; for this is pure nature, it cannot be otherwise among human creatures. It is not in our power to forget what we please, or not to be sorry at the remembrance of what we had reason to value. This then is not the grief condemned by the Apostle; what is so is next to be considered.

2. That sorrow is excessive and blameable which is too violent in the expression. One may violate that decency and good manners which are still due to the living by seeming to have no regard or value for those that remain, because we have lost those whom we most esteemed; but this is an indecorum more pardonable than when we forget the respect and veneration we owe to the holy majesty of God, the great king of the universe, in whose hands are the souls of every living creature, and the breath of all mankind. This is to reflect on his wisdon, as if it saw not what was best, for us and others, as if the punishment was more than we can bear, more than we have deserved. This is to be most ungrateful, as if we regarded not either how long [7] God has indulged us with the blessing which he has thought fit to take away, or how many other precious blessings he has still left us possessed of. And as sorrow may be thus faulty in the manner, so it may be equally blameable in the length and continuance of it: We may lose all the comforts of life that remain, by continually repining at what is gone; we may neglect all manly and social duties, out of sullen regrets and peevish reflections on our misfortunes. That grief is greatly to be condemned which endangers or ruins our health, unfits us for

conversation and the duties we owe to our friends, our families, our country, or mankind. This is to *sorrow like those who have no hope*; no hope in the divine goodness, which can, if it pleases, repair the greatest of losses; no hope of a resurrection, of that joyful time when those that sleep in Jesus (for of such the Apostle and we are now speaking) shall meet again with joy and abundant consolation. But this is one of the arguments, and the principal of them against sorrowing in an indecent, immoderate, and unchristian manner. Of this, and the rest, we will now treat.

3. And first, let us observe a very obvious truth, but yet such a one as those who indulge these excessive sorrows seem wholly to forget, or too little to consider; that is, that those whom they thus excessively lament were but mortal. If we consider the human body, of how nice a texture it is, how many thousand passages must be kept open, motions preserved, and decays repaired, that it may be retained in being, one would rather be amazed by what wonderful providence it is so long supported than why it declines so soon; especially if we add to this the many threatening dangers that surround us from the inclemency of seasons, badness of air and provisions, not to mention the hazards we expose ourselves to, for one end or other, from the sea, weather, or places to which the many occasions of life [8] entice us, to pass over the violences that the bulk of mankind, and almost all, one time or other, offer to nature, by intemperance or excess. Without any of these, we are made of brittle and perishing materials; and we may as well lament that the sun sets, the sea is tempestuous, or that spring and summer are so soon succeeded by harsh and unpleasant seasons, as that mortal and frail man should grow languid, sicken, die. It shows, then, a weak and inconsiderate mind too long to indulge a sickly and unmanly passion. Fortitude of mind is doubtless a virtue, and a graceful one too; but there is only a small share of it in that man who cannot bear up, with any equanimity, against the changes incident to, and inseparable from, human condition. But it may be said, and it must be owned for a truth, that all are not endued [sic] with magnanimity, and to those who are not should be made all due allowances; yet, that they may not indulge a hurtful weakness too long, let them consider that the thing is unalterable. They may as soon by tears recall them that died a

thousand years ago, or sigh them into being who never yet were, as stop the departing soul, or fetch up those whom the grave has just shut her mouth upon. As the tree falleth, so it lieth. Man lieth down in the dust, and shall not rise again till the heavens be no more. In vain do they break their spirits and their rest; their friends owe them no thanks that they impair their health, and neglect the duties and comforts of life. The dead are still the same as if neither tear, nor thought, nor lamentation, had been bestowed upon them. See 2d Samuel, xii. 22, 23.

If to this it should be replied, that the evils being without all possible remedy is the chief source of their affliction, let them then look up to the hand that strikes them. Was it not the will of your heavenly father? without which not a hair of your head, nor a sparrow, shall [9] fall to the ground. Did he not give life and being, not only to those whom you lament, but to yourself? And will you not suffer him to recall his favours, whenever he pleases? Dost thou well to be *angry*, or dissatisfied, if he command a *Gourd* to grow up and *overshadow thee*, and afterwards, out of the same his soverign pleasure, *bid a worm destroy it again*? But we need not recur to what, in supreme right, he might do. Can we say that we have not deserved the scourge that hath afflicted us? Doth not our conscience accuse us of not only general infirmities and failings, but of many wilful and gross transactions? These cry to Heaven against us, and force the Almighty to chastise us. We must all plead guilty before God: For, *behold! he putteth no trust in his angels, yea the Heavens are not pure in his sight; how much more abominable and filthy is man!* (Job, xv. 15). *Lay* then *thy hand upon thy mouth*, and keep silence before him. Humbly confess, *Righteous art thou, O Lord, and just are thy dispensations.* Bear his fatherly correction with meekness and patience; for *surely it is meet to say unto God, I have deservedly born chastisements, I will not offend any more. That which I see not, teach thou me. If I have done iniquity, I will do no more* (Job, xxxiv. 31, 32).

Let it be considered, farther, that he is not only just but good in his preceedings. If we bear these evils as we ought, he will turn them to our great advantage. If he did not see that we abused the good he took from us; that we valued it so much as to forget the donor; that it was necessary to take it from us, that he might wean us from the world, and turn our thoughts to himself; if, I say, he did not do this, however, it was the Lord, and it becomes us to say *let him do what seemeth him good.*

[10] And that we may the more readily do this, think we farther that our friends are gone from an evil world, from such who sometimes imbitter all that is joyous and desirable in life, by their follies and wickedness. No more shall evil tongues wound their ears, and disturb their peace. The injurious shall offer violence no more; they are out of the reach of injustice and oppression. The changes and chances of this world cannot now threaten them with poverty, want, and contempt. Death has set his seal on their actions; the power of the tempter is expired, and their defection from virtue and righteousness is no longer possible. And this is no small good, to have died in a good season; for it hath been the remark of some of the greatest Roman writers, that one of the most eminent of their countrymen was only unfortunate in not dying when a fever seized him in the height of his prosperity, that the publick vows and prayers unhappily prevailed for prolonging a life which was afterwards signalized by innumerable and almost incredible calamities. They that sleep in Christ are secure in peace. The follies and misfortunes of such as belonged to them shall afflict them no more; nor can they be corrupted by the contagious air which we breathe, or be led aside by ill example. Far distant from evil of all kinds, they sleep in Christ, incapable of having their own virtue and its rewards taken from them, and charitably hoping the best of others; adoring the wisdom and goodness of God who called them hence, and full of joyful expectation of a resurrection to life and glory immortal. It would then be a too selfish love, a love that might deserve the name of envy, to repine at their departure hence who are removed from the evils of life, rest in absolute peace, and expect a glorious resurrection.

This is the hope, the glorious hope, which the Apostle mentions in the text. We are fond of continuing ourselves, or friends, in a [11] calamitous and unpleasant state; because we would not leave the society of those we love, or because a desire of living is implanted in our nature. This, indeed, cannot always be gratified; but we have the next thing to be wished, an assured hope of living again. Let us then not act as if we were *ignorant concerning* the condition of *those which are asleep* in *sorrowing even as others who have no hope* in a resurrection. We will comfort ourselves that our brethren shall live again; that they now live through him who *is the resurrection and the life*, in whom whosoever *believeth though he die yet shall he live, and shall die again no more. Let go from thee* then *mortal thoughts that are most heavy upon thee, and haste thee to fly from these times* (Esdras, xiv. 14) prepare for leaving this mortal stage, and revisiting thy friends in a condition in which thou wilt find them greatly improved, and everlastingly safe from any future change or decay.

If you still urge that this removes only part of the evil you endure, your friends are, you doubt not, happy; but you yourselves are not the less miserable, in losing the kind assistance you wanted, the generous friendship which long acquaintance and infinite services, or the ties of nature, gave you. This is indeed what must bear hard, must be not a little insupportable. There is but one solid answer to be made to an objection of this sort, that the Lord who gave and took away is able to make it good again. *Here* then *is the trial of the faith and patience of the Saints*: They are to believe that the same good father who gave them life, who hath hitherto so kindly provided for them, will still do so if they do but continue objects of his loving kindness. We trust then willingly to his care and protection, who is the father to the fatherless and husband to the widow, the God of all mercies and boundless compassion, who comforts us by his prophet Jeremiah (xlix, 11) *Leave thy fatherless children to me, I [12] will preserve them alive, and let thy widows trust in me.* We will trust that when our father, or mother, or whomsoever else we have our friend on earth, is removed from us, the Lord will take us up, will wipe away our tears, protect and bless us on earth, and at length bring us to his everlasting kingdom and glory.

To the consideration of that glorious hope we willingly return. It is our firmest support, and most solid consolation. Life is very short, we are hastening apace after those whom we most lament; soon, very soon, we must follow them. We shall sleep together in the same dust, nor shall it in the least concern any of us which went first. But, to use those wonderful words which holy Job would have to be *written with an iron pen, and engraved on a rock for ever, we know that our Redeemer liveth, and that on the latter day he shall stand upon the earth; and though after my skin worms destroy this body, yet in my flesh shall I see God, whom I shall see for myself, and mine eyes shall behold, and not another* (Job, xix. 25, 26, 27). O happy and glorious day! when we shall meet not only with those whom we knew and loved, and obliged, but with our predecessors, with the greatest men which the first or best ages produced, with the saints and martyrs of whom we have heard and read, when we shall see the great Saint Paul, and, what is more, the great and dear redeemer of mankind. O blessed time, when we shall be added to that blessed assembly of the great and good, and shall leave the dregs and refuse of human nature on earth behind us! For we shall not only go to the great men we have been mentioning, but to our dear relations and particular friends, whose piety, virtue, and generosity, we could not but lament, could not bear the loss of, without much concern and repeated affliction.

[13] As we have hitherto been detained on such topicks as are necessary to break the force of the softer passions, and guard us against intemperate grief, on any the most melancholy occasion, it may be presumed, I hope, that we are the better prepared, you to hear, and I to make a few observations on, the conduct of that truly excellent person whose funeral we are at present attending, to pay him our last offices of respect. I mean not to present you with a flattering picture of him, I do not pretend to do him justice; that could not be done, I think, without trespassing on your patience, by passing the bounds allowed to the conclusion of a discourse of this nature. If it could be done, I am not the person to venture at more than drawing some of the outlines of a portraiture which deserves to be coloured and finished by the hand of a more skilful painter. What I have to say will, I suppose, be little more than what you will be able to go before me in; I shall be hardly more than an echo of what you must be saying to one another.

A rational and firm piety, an active and constant affection for the well-being and interests of mankind, a quick penetration, a solid judgment, an uncommon fortitude of mind, a native fund of ease, alacrity, and good humour, were some of the sources which united their powers to compose the gentle and bounteous stream of his life and conversation. If we could trace out, and follow, the course of this stream, from its origin to its entrance into the wide ocean of eternity, I am persuaded we should find it every where an engaging object of comtemplation, we should behold it every where beautifying and enriching the several soils through which it made its various and fertilizing windings and turnings. But some parts only of such a speculation, by way of sample, from which the whole may be judged of, can be pursued by us at present.

[14] If we call to our minds his behaviour in this place, either at the ordinary service of God or at the celebration of the blessed sacrament of the Lord's Supper (neither of which he ever failed of attendance at, when his health would permit him to be present) we can scarce help believing ourselves to be still witnesses of his unaffected and ardent devotion, a devotion that was sufficient to infect, if I may use the expression, all who needed such assistance with the like becoming disposition, and stood forth as an obvious though modest reproof, by its example, to the careless and negligent worshipper. He was a faithful member of the church, but harboured no bitterness or resentment against those of a different persuasion. His religion was indeed amiable: It had no tendency to sour his temper, or inspire his mind with gloominess, but had on him, as it ought to have on us all, a quite contrary and more consistent influence. Like most other things, for which he was remarkable, it sat easy upon him. It was not wordy or disputatious, but its effects went with him wherever he went, silently operating, and without ostentation, to render him fitter for the management of every transaction in which he thought it incumbent upon him to be engaged.

If we went along with him hence, and waited upon him home to his house, we there saw displayed to great advantage, and in a striking manner, the tender husband, without his being drawn by the most forcible of passions into any impropriety of behaviour which could disgust the nicest observer: The indulgent parent, without his suffering excess of fondness to take off his eye from the true and best interests of his children; the most affectionate and obliging brother; the useful and entertaining friend; the kind and generous master, not more revered than beloved by his lowest domesticks, even by his slaves, to whom he grudged not all the comforts and enjoyments, [15] let me say freedom, of which their situation is unhurtfully capable. What a vigorous exertion of these lovely affections shone in him during his last illness! How could they but be seized with unusual admiration who beheld such affections rise in him, to the greatest height, at a time when the mind is commonly too full of an approaching and awful change, to surrender itself to their impressions. He neglected no means likely to reserve him longer to his family. When all these visibly failed, he sought not comfort from others, as is ordinarily done on such an occasion, but he imparted and administered it all around him. He applied himself to his last and most arduous task, that of reconciling his distressed family to a disaster which it was manifest could not be avoided, and which it became them to submit to, if possible, without reluctance, as to the will of our Heavenly Father, who assuredly knows what is fittest for us. He laboured this point with earnestness, attention, and perseverance, and succeeded in it, at length, better than could be expected or imagined. After enjoying the peculiar delight of perceiving his pains, in an under-taking too singular, and too near his heart, not to be thrown away, shall I say he met the King of Terrours with composure and resignation? No, it was not the formidable spectre whom he saw advancing it was the gentle and smiling messenger of peace and good tidings. He gave his ready hand to the friendly conductor into everlasting glory; he bade him welcome, and embraced him, as well he might, with marks of high satisfaction in his countenance, and a degree of pleasantry and familiarity in his expressions. Here all was great, and noble, and natural, and of a piece with his preceding life; for, surely, he who can look back on his past labours with approbation has good cause to look forward on their reward with confidence. He who has made it his first care and study to lead the life of the righteous must be best entitled to that matchless and unrivalled ac[16]quisition, that crown of our fairest hopes and most laudable enterprises, THE DEATH OF THE RIGHTEOUS.

Betrayed by the amiableness, and sublimity of this last part of his conduct, I have got too forward in my account of it before I was aware. I must therefore turn back, but I shall take a very cursory view of what remains to pass under our inspection; for where there is so great a variety of matter many particulars cannot be so much as mentioned, and others cannot be commented upon so largely as their importance may demand.

In a country justly renowned for hospitality, he deserves to be held forth as a pattern to succeeding generations of that virtue. It was in him extensive and liberal, yet judicious, and not set free from the restraints of reason and religion. It was not a blind propensity to profuseness, or a passion for a name to which he sacrificed the reasonable expectations of his family and descendents, or by which he corrupted the morals of his friends and neighbours when his mind was most unbended, even in the hours of restivity, upon which vice or folly, or imprudence, are too apt to steal. He was no encourager of intemperance or riot, or lewd and profane discourse, or any practice tending to injure the health, the reputation, the fortunes, the manners, or the religious attainments of his company. He coupled freedom with innocence. His raillery was pleasant and entertaining, without being ill-naturedly poignant. He had the happy address to perform with ease perhaps the most difficult of tasks, that of seasoning mirth, facetiousness, and wit, with gravity, decorum, and wisdom.

As one of the first and most respectable merchants in this dominion, he had great opportunity of being acquainted with the circumstances [17] of many people whose cases would otherwise have escaped his knowledge. This knowledge was often turned to their advantage whose affairs fell under his consideration. I think I shall have the concurring voice of the publick with me when I say that his own gain by trade was not more sweet to him than the help which he hereby received towards becoming a general benefactor; and that he contrived at the same time, by a double or mixed effort, to lay up treasures on earth and treasures in heaven.

As he was a lover of justice, probity, and punctuality, with regard to those who had nothing more to ask at his hands, so he was most compassionate to the unfortunate and miserable. His charities were many, considerable, disposed with choice and discretion; studiously disposed too as to the manner, which he always wished to be such as might make his bounty the most serviceable to the receivers of it, and the least oppressive to their modesty. Had he been able, he would have made his munificence a secret to

all but his God and himself; but the attempt to have it as little
noticed as possible frequently proved unsuccessful, for either the
joy and gratitude of the person relieved would break out and make
a discovery, or the admiration of the person employed to convey
the benevolent gift could not bear to let it be concealed. This part
of his character became so well established, and so generally understood, that some time ago, when publick thanks for a charity
were returned to a person who desired to be unknown, universal
conjecture gave the credit of it to Mr. *Nelson*, while, in fact, the
charity, to my knowledge, was bestowed by other hands. The
publick seemed to be possessed of an opinion that in this equally
generous and religious part of his behavior he had no rivals or
imitators: God be thanked, that the common notion in this [18]
matter was somewhat erroneous. Setting this aside, for we cannot
dwell on such remarks, he is an instance, I wish he could not be
reckoned a rare instance, of what abundance of good may be done
by a prudent and conscientious man without impoverishing himself or his connections, nay while his fortunes are improving. Alas!
generally speaking, they are not our virtues, but our vices, or, to
say the least, our follies, which are so costly and expensive as to
devour our estates, and exhaust the fountain from which they
derive their nourishment. An estate raised with an unblemished
reputation, and diffused from humane and devout motives in the
service of multitudes, as well as the owners, it may reasonably be
expected will wear well, and have the blessing of Providence to
attend and protect it from generation to generation. After all, this
great man had, no doubt, his passions to contest with, as well as
other men; but few, I think, have been able, by the help of reason
and revelation, to keep them under better regulation, or to find
them continually more virtuous and ample enjoyment.

Thus far we have surveyed him only in his private walks. What
shall we say of the publick capacities and stations in which he
appeared? What, unless we had more time, can we say, but that he
here practised over again, on a larger scale, what he was hourly
performing on the smaller one; that his conduct, in each department, differed in nothing but in the materials which it had to
work upon; that he was every where in his element; that whatever
he did he was possessed by it, and filled it with assiduity and

ability; that he was a benefactor, a friend, a brother, a father, to his country; that in discharging these duties he found them perfectly consistent with loyalty and fidelity to his soverign, to the interests of the mother state, to the general wealth of the grand aggregate of British dominions; [19] and that, in humble imitation of him whom we ought all to aspire to the imitation of, he made it his business to go about doing good, stirred up and moved thereto by the delight which he took in that divine exercise and heavenly employment.

When a person thus adorned cheerfully obeys the summons of supreme power to remove into a world more commodious, more exalted, more stable and durable in its pleasures than this, into a world, in short, designed by Heaven for the reward of its servants and favourites, this event has another aspect with regard to us who are left behind, drooping and brooding over the loss which we have sustained. This event, though for some time expected, is apt to shock us at the first view. It seems to produce such a gap in society as would be made in the material frame of the world by some great alteration in the course of nature. Until we gain time to reflect, it startles us like the fall or disappearance of a mountain by which we had been long sheltered from threatening winds or overwhelming tempests; or rather, to return to the allusion with which I began this poor tribute to the memory of distinguished merit, it affects us like the failure and drying up of a river whose flux and reflux had been used to supply the poor on its banks with plenty of necessary sustenance, and the wealthy with a perpetual succession of variety of elegancies. When an incident so apparently fruitful of calamity first attacks us, why wonder if relations and friends, if neighbours and strangers, if the needy and the opulent, if the grave and the lively, if a whole country, burst into tears and remain for a while in a state of painful astonishment under the weight and oppression of unfeigned sorrow! However, if we have not done it already, let us now shake off the lethargy and stupefaction of grief, let us recollect ourselves, let us consider that both he and we are still in the hands of a kind Providence, [20] who careth for us. Since we cannot bring him back, nor ought to be desirous of making him so ill a return for past favours, if we had the power, let us cherish in our hearts a vivid remembrance of him, and keep his character alive and flourishing among us; which will be bringing him back in some degree, and to very good purpose, by putting it into his power still to do good offices among us, and much to promote our benefit: For hereby we may be encouraged to tread in his steps, and may in a little, perhaps a very little time, recover his most desirable society, and rejoice with him in the mansions of the blessed for ever and ever. AMEN.

F I N I S

NOTES

1. See Homer D. Kemp, "The Rev. John Camm," *infra.*

2. Camm wrote three pamphlets relating to this dispute: *A Single and Distinct view of the Act, Vulgarly Entitled, Three-Penny Act* ... (Annapolis, 1763); *A Review of The Rector Dectected: or The Colonel Reconnoitred* ... (Williamsburg, 1764); and *Critical Remarks on a Letter Ascribed to Common Sense* ... (Williamsburg, 1765). The dispute is discussed in Jack P. Greene, *The Quest for Power: The Lower Houses of Assembly in the Southern Royal Colonies 1689-1776* (Chapel Hill: University of North Carolina Press, 1963), 348-50.

3. See Emory G. Evans, "The Rise and Decline of the Virginia Aristocracy in the Eighteenth Century," in *The Old Dominion: Essays for Thomas Perkins Abernethy*, ed. Darrett B. Rutman (Charlottesville: University Press of Virginia, 1964), 62-78, and "Virginia Council Journals," *Virginia Magazine of History and Biography*, 33 (1925), 189-92.

4. See Horton Davies, *Worship and Theology in England from Watts and Wesley to Maurice, 1690-1850* (Princeton: Princeton University Press, 1961), 52-75.

5. Camm, *Review of the Rector Dectected*, 7, 10; *Critical Remarks*, 13-14.

6. *Virginia Gazette* (Rind, Williamsburg), November 19, 1772. Similarly, Purdie & Dixon's *Virginia Gazette* (Williamsburg), November 19, 1772, lamented "the loss of so benevolent a Member of Society, so firm a Patriot, and so upright a Judge" whose "Virtues have made too deep an Impression on his Countrymen to need the Assistance of Panegyrick."

7. See, for example, James Blair, *Our Savior's Divine Sermon on the Mount*, 2d. ed. (London, 1740), I, 58, 127, 132; William Stith, *A Sermon Preached before the General Assembly at Williamsburg* (Williamsburg, 1746), 31-34, *The Sinfulness and Pernicious Nature of Gaming* (Williamsburg, 1752), 11-12, and *The Nature and Extent of Christ's Redemption* (Williamsburg, 1753); James Horrocks, *Upon the Peace* (Williamsburg, 1763), 9-10, 14; Camm, *Review of the Rector Detected*, 20; and Samuel Davies, *Religion and Patriotism* (Philadelphia, 1755), 10-12, 27-35, *Virginia's Danger and Remedy* (Williamsburg, 1756), 12, 16, 20-21, 23, 25, 28, 48, *The Crisis: or, the*

Uncertain Doom of Kingdoms at particular Times, Considered (London, 1756), 28-35, and *The Curse of Cowardice* (Woodbridge, N.J., 1759), 8, 14-15, 40. Lay expressions of similar anxieties were widespread. See Francis Fauquier to Board of Trade, November 3, 1762, CO5/1330, ff. 339-40, Public Record Office (London); Landon Carter, *A Letter from a Gentleman in Virginia, to the Merchants in Great Britain, Trading to that Colony* (London, 1754), 28-29; and John Wayles to John T. Warre, August 30, 1766, American Loyalist Claims, Tr. 79/30, Public Record Office. The quotations are from Horrocks, *Upon the Peace*, 9-10, 14; Stith, *Sinfulness of Gaming*, 11-12; and the letter cited above from Wayles to Warre, Aug. 30, 1766. On the meaning of the widespread expression of decline throughout the colonies after 1730, see Jack P. Greene, "Search for Identity: An Interpretation of the Meaning of Selected Patterns of Social Response in Eighteenth-Century America," *Journal of Social History*, 3 (1970), 189-220. Continued manifestations of such fears in Virginia during the 1760s and 1770s are explored by Jack P. Greene, *Landon Carter: An Inquiry into the Personal Values and Social Imperatives of the Eighteenth-Century Virginia Gentry* (Charlottesville: University Press of Virginia, 1965), 40-90; Gordon S. Wood, "Rhetoric and Reality in the American Revolution," *William and Mary Quarterly*, 3d ser., 23 (1966), 20-32, and Edmund S. Morgan, "The Puritan Ethic and the American Revolution," *Ibid.*, 24 (1967), 3-41.

8. *Virginia Gazette* (Purdie & Dixon), Nov. 19, 1772.

9. "My Country's Worth," in *The Poems of Charles Hansford*, ed. James A. Servies and Carl R. Dolmetsch (Chapel Hill: University of North Carolina Press, 1961), 63.

PENMAN OF THE REVOLUTION:
A CASE FOR ARTHUR LEE

A. R. Riggs

... the American Party with Arthur Lee as a writer, have got possession of the [London] newspapers. This Lee was bred up to Physick, then turned Lawyer, and now finishes up a rebel. He is probably the Chief Incendiary of Virginia, and he is on this side of the Atlantick.

R. Falconer to Charles Gray, Member of Parliament,
August 9, 1775, RCHM,
Round MSS., p. 307

In 1767 a Philadelphia Quaker, Anthony Benezet, appended an essay by a young man who was then demonstrating what a fellow Virginian called an "itch of scribbling" in the gazettes of Williamsburg to a tract that he wrote on abolition.[1] Arthur Lee's essay, one of several that he signed "Philanthropos," found its way into the *Pennsylvania Chronicle,* May 4 to May 11. It included harsh criticism of the British for introducing and encouraging the slave trade to the American colonies. The next year, 1768, John Dickinson of Philadelphia sent a "song for American freedom" to James Otis of Boston with the explanation that his "worthy friend Arthur Lee"—familiar to Americans as the author of a recent series of newspaper essays, a diatribe against British taxes signed "Monitor"—had composed part of it.[2] And in 1771 the incomparable "Junius," a London journalist and ardent critic of the government, told John Wilkes, "my American namesake is plainly a man of abilities." William Samuel Johnson of Connecticut explained that "Junius Americanus," a writer who had challenged "Junius" to a newspaper debate on colonial policy, was "one Dr. Lee a Virginian, late a Physician, now a Lawyer, a sensible but very sanguine Man . . . who delights in the fire and fury of a Party, and is perfectly well adapted to please the Bostonians."[3]

Boston's Peter Oliver, Chief Justice of Massachusetts and a convenient target for the moral outrage of "Junius Americanus," agreed that his antagonist pleased a particular group in his town. He recalled in 1781 that "A certain *Dr. Lee* was another agent for the [Boston] Faction. Mr. *Samuel Adams* and some others wrote to him a long Catalogue of false Facts; and *Dr. Lee* published them in England, and doubtless made his Penny by the Sale. Numbers were sent to *Boston*, and *Adams* made Presents of some of them to the Inn Keepers in the Country, to furnish their Guests with a Stimulant to eating and drinking. Bitter indeed they were, for they were wrote with a Pen dipped in the Gall of Asps."[4]

Lee's polemical essays were not only handed around in Massachusetts, but also reprinted in all the other colonies. What's more, he added regularly to a growing list of newspaper pseudonyms. Writing to Samuel Adams in 1773, he told his friend that he was then addressing Lord Dartmouth, Secretary of State for the Colonies, as "Raleigh."[5] Also in 1773 an anonymous informant sent the harried Secretary a clipping of an essay signed "An American," one of a series that Lee was alleged to have written in collaboration with Sir John Temple, a former customs agent at Boston.[6] "He is the 'Bostonian,' . . . a pretty writer," wrote Lee's admirer Henry Laurens of South Carolina, who was a visitor in London in 1774.[7] The following year yet another newspaper series, signed "Vespucius," was brought to a sudden halt when a competitor identified the author as the "M__ch__tts A__t," a reference to Lee's official position in London as agent for the Massachusetts assembly.[8]

Arthur Lee probably wrote many additional essays before 1776 over signatures that will never be identified, and some material is unfortunately lost because newspaper files of the eighteenth century are far from complete. Each penname that can be attributed, however, points to a string of essays in British and American newspapers. When almost 200 known essays are combined with at least ten pamphlets—plus notices, petitions, and many letters inserted in colonial newspapers by friends—the entire collection may be accepted as evidence that the writer intended to influence public opinion on a grand scale.

"Advocacy journalism" is a less offensive expression than "propaganda" for Lee's deliberate attempt to mould public opinion. The word propaganda tacitly endorses Peter Oliver's unsubstantiated charge that patriots lied to the people in order to soften them up for a colonial rebellion. But whatever we call the remarkable avalanche of special pleading that preceded the Revolution, we know that those who disseminated their views in newspaper, pamphlet, and broadside were fully aware of the power of the press. Both in England and in the colonies, a compliant press, open to extraordinary fears of a massive conspiracy against American liberty, created government distrust that made a war of independence more acceptable.[9] In that light, this essay will proceed to examine the political writings of a single volunteer journalist of the "media war" that was waged by Americans against the British government between 1767 and 1776. While Arthur Lee never got possession of the London newspapers, he seems to have spread his attack more broadly and systematically, on both sides of the Atlantic, than anyone else.

The temperamental youngest son of Thomas and Hannah Lee of Stratford Hall, and the brother of two signers of the Declaration of Independence, Arthur Lee (1740-1792) spent most of his life engaged in one controversy or another. In 1768 he would have been delighted with the title "flaming patriot." That year Dr. Lee migrated from his comfortable home in Williamsburg, Virginia, with the professed desire to become the voice of America in London. He took with him an unqualified sense of the moral rectitude of his cause, matchless zeal, and a stock of political ideas and aphorisms that made him an excellent prospect for a foreign correspondent.

Lee's learning was truly impressive. An Etonian scholar, Fellow of the Royal Society, and holder of an M.D. degree (together with postgraduate study at both Edinburgh and Leyden), he committed himself in 1770 to four more years of schooling at the Inns of

Court, London. That action eventually won him admission to the English bar and capped twenty years of effort in the classroom. By 1775 Lee was practicing law in company with the ablest attorneys of the city. He could introduce as his closest friend the popular Lord Mayor; boasted of regular attendance at the opera, the playhouses, and at the concerts of J.S. Bach; claimed proficiency in Greek, Latin, French, Spanish, and Italian; was an honorary member of the Society of Arts and Architecture; and had read voraciously in everything from the classics to the English common law. "Much reading has produced in me the effect of age," he told his brother Richard Henry. [10] By 1775 Lee's prose style had also matured. Experts even attributed one of his pamphlets, signed with a pseudonym, to the eloquent Dr. Franklin, who provided Lee with some data from his files for that work. [11] While Lee's writing retained its emotional intensity, it could be, on command, both smooth and logical, a far cry from the shrill, undisciplined voice of dissent that characterized his earliest efforts on behalf of the patriotic cause.

Lee made his first foray into advocacy journalism while he was a student at the University of Edinburgh. As an exercise in logic, *An Essay in Vindication of the Continental Colonies of America* (London, 1764) was undistinguished, but the pamphlet, addressed to a single remark about Americans in Adam Smith's *Theory of Moral Sentiments,* exposed Lee's aggressive patriotism and offered some interesting ideas on slavery. Signed "By an American," the treatise expressed outrage at the Scottish economist's offhand reference to the slaveowners of America as "refuse of the gaols of Europe." The comment made Lee so angry that his personal hatred for the labor system in Virginia was momentarily subsumed in bitterness against the slaves themselves, and also against the British, who had brought the Africans to America in the first place. Before he was through, however, Lee left no doubt with the reader about how he viewed slavery. He called the bondage imposed upon Africans "absolutely repugnant to justice," dangerous to the morals of the community, "shocking to humanity," and "abhorrent utterly from the Christian religion." [12]

With the attack on slavery Lee introduced an unpleasant subject that was to provide him with a theme for further commentary. He believed that Britain, in encouraging the slave trade, sinned against humanity for the sake of her merchants, and he offered slavery in Virginia as an excuse for delaying his return from the University of Edinburgh until June 1766. Slavery was also the subject of an article he wrote for Rind's *Virginia Gazette*, March 19, 1767, and signed "Philanthropos." The essay, followed by another even more radical, a proposal for abolition that was suppressed in Virginia (but featured in the *Pennsylvania Chronicle*, August 31 to September 7, 1767), went through several editions as a pamphlet and was used to great advantage by Quaker abolitionists.[13]

No doubt Lee believed even then that any denial of established civil liberties was something akin to human bondage. He hinted in his famous "Monitor Letters" of 1768 that if Parliament looked with favor upon the enslavement of Africans, they might not hesitate to use the British Army, up to its full complement of 10,000 in America, to make "slaves" of the white colonists as well. The ten fiery installments of the "Monitor," which appeared weekly from February 25 to April 28, 1768 in Rind's *Virginia Gazette*, condemned the British for the Townshend taxes of 1767 and vehemently denied that Parliament could pass any act that was clearly unconstitutional.

Lee's "Monitor" was specifically designed to complement John Dickinson's more literate and reasoned essays on British tax policy as the "farmer" from Pennsylvania. Like the "Farmer's Letters," the "Monitor" essays, filled with stock quotations from Bolingbroke, Locke, Sidney, Camden, and numerous other authorities, both ancient and modern, asked Americans to unite to protest their loss of liberty with formal petitions and remonstrances to the British government. Ultimately Lee hoped for a colonial bill of rights, a *"Magna Charta Americana."*[14] Newspapers from Boston to Charleston, South Carolina reprinted essays in this series; a number appeared in England in the *American Gazette* (1768 and 1769), and the first ten were included in a pamphlet that sold extremely well in Virginia.[15] At least 31 additional "Monitor" essays were featured in British and American publications during the next eight years. In 1769 and 1770 Lee dispatched three reports from London over the penname, addressed to "My dear Countrymen." All of the major newspapers in the American colonies reprinted his "Monitor XI" and "Monitor XII."[16]

When the initial run of the series, the first ten, was complete,

Lee hurried to Philadelphia to visit John Dickinson. During the summer of 1768 the two men worked closely together on a public campaign designed to shame the merchants of the largest city in America into boycotting British goods. They also encouraged public meetings to force the government of Pennsylvania to draw up a petition against British policy. Lee contributed at least one essay to the newspapers signed with his initials, he edited some of Dickinson's writing for the press, and he presented his friend with his unfinished Liberty Song, which the Philadelphia lawyer completed and published. The rollicking ballad, set to the tune of *Hearts of Oak* and written to publicize a general nonimportation movement, became the most popular patriotic song of the Revolutionary era.[17]

By the fall of 1768 Lee had settled in London, where he aimed to influence a group of city radicals who shared his political beliefs and supported a notorious enemy of the administration, John Wilkes. Lee also drifted into a circle of colonial agents who were unofficial paid ambassadors, or lobbyists at Parliament and at the Board of Trade, for the assemblies of various colonies. Dennys DeBerdt, agent for the embattled assembly, or General Court of Massachusetts, was soon connected with Arthur's brother William Lee in the tobacco trade. DeBerdt and other agents were willing to supply Arthur with much of the material that he would need for political essays. Near the end of the year 1768 Lee informed his brother Richard Henry in Virginia that he had written two pieces on events at Boston for a London daily newspaper, the *Gazetteer*. One, he said, had been reprinted in the *Gentleman's Magazine* for November.[18] He signed the essays "C.L." and "C.O.," and he used the first pseudonym several more times during 1769 in the other leading daily of London, the *Public Advertiser*.[19]

Daily newspapers were not common in England, and none existed among the approximately forty newspapers in the colonies. During the eight years that Lee lived in London, the city and its environs supported eight to ten newspapers. Editors claimed to be impartial, but a majority seemed more tolerant to the foes than the friends of government. Within limits they invited any inspired amateur to try his hand, so success depended upon talent and industry. The successful columnist of the open forum newspaper

was rewarded with the place of honor and the *factotum*, or deco-
rated initial, on the lead column of the front page. Contributors
insisted on anonymity to protect themselves from the strictly enforced libel laws or from angry competitors who might wish to do
them physical harm. A wise essayist was careful to separate truth
from opinion, for the life of a signature depended on credibility. If
there seemed to be a good chance for extensive circulation, the
writer submitted his article, usually 800 to 1,000 words, to the
Advertiser or the *Gazetteer*, where he stood the best chance of
having his message broadcast throughout the empire.

Lee's first choice was the *Gazetteer,* but he wrote later for the
Advertiser and other newspapers. He was at last ready to undertake a periodical series in July 1769, and he deliberately patterned
his work after that of the most famous columnist of the century,
"Junius," a mysterious writer who attacked the Duke of Grafton,
head of the ministry. Lee posited as his arch-villain another member of the government, the choleric Earl of Hillsborough, Secretary of State for the American Department. The first "Junius
Americanus" attacking the Colonial Secretary appeared in the
London *Evening Post* as a preliminary exercise on July 17, 1769,
and it dominated the lead columns of the *Gazetteer* for the next
two days. The series, which promised to expose wrongdoing by
servants of the crown in England as well as in America, went
through seventy-six known installments by 1776.

By January 1770 most literate Americans, a majority of the
colonists, must have encountered Lee's new signature. Newspapers
in all the larger towns on the continent had reprinted his essays.
On April 6, 1772, the printers of the *Boston Gazette* referred to
"that able and stanch Advocate for the Rights of AMERICA and
Mankind, JUNIUS AMERICANUS, whose Name will be revered, as long
as hypocritical Sanctity, PERJURY and TREASON AGAINST THE PEOPLE,
are abhorred & execrated." The assembly of Massachusetts had
already elected Lee its assistant agent in London on the strength
of his essays and without knowing his real name.²⁰Evidence of Lee's
popularity in America may also be found in comments such as
that of Roger Atkinson of Petersburg, Virginia: "This gentleman
is, they tell me & I believe they say right, the famous Junius
Americanus who writes in the English papers under that signa-

ture—is a popular writer and the next best writer . . . to the real Junius, whoever or whatever the real Junius his name be." [21]

The notoriety of "Junius Americanus" lay both in its accusatory tone and in the daring of the revelations. While the essays may be traced through a network of reprintings, there is no yardstick for counting how many readers they attracted because newspapers were then passed from hand to hand and posted in every tavern and coffeehouse. Readers got a second look at the series when the agent Dennys DeBerdt charged the Massachusetts Assembly for the printing of 500 copies of a pamphlet containing twenty-four of the essays entitled *The Political Detection, or the Treachery and Tyranny of Administration, Both at Home and Abroad* (London, 1770). [22] The Boston *Evening Post* ran most of the contents in weekly installments.

The title of Lee's second compilation of essays is significant. People in the American colonies welcomed a simple explanation for British policy after 1763. They refused to believe the truth, that severe economic distress at home, attributable to the late war with France, could lead to a burden of taxation on the colonies that a majority in England considered fair and equitable. As Professor Bernard Bailyn and others have pointed out, Americans were then brought up on Whig history and hence conditioned to fear a return to the tyranny and corruption of England in the previous century. [23] "Junius Americanus," and others like him, did not set out to manufacture false charges against the ministry and the executive of Massachusetts. They merely fitted events into a plausible and consistent pattern of conspiracy that confirmed the suspicions of the people.

It took several years for "Junius Americanus" to perfect his indictment against the Colonial Secretary and his willing accomplice, the royal governor of Massachusetts. According to Lee, scheming advisers to the king had long since chosen America, and specifically Massachusetts, as a base camp for an experiment in the use of arbitrary power. The colonies were to be divided, one from another, and the preeminence of the executive department would eventually spread like a cancer out of New England to contaminate the whole British empire. Lee's attitude toward his native land made the alleged conspiracy even more horrifying. A blend of nationalism, manifest destiny, and mission, his idea of America spurred him to outrage against those who would corrupt and defile the new Eden, especially the native-born members of the "conspiracy" who resided in Massachusetts. "America," he wrote, "is like a mighty stone in motion. They who attempt to stop it may meet their fate, but will not impede its course. It is moved by the finger of God; and against that it is vain to resist." [24]

Who would attempt to disrupt God's plan for America? Who would presume to enslave the colonists by dividing them, would single out one province and export to it European corruption, European soldiers, and alien concepts of executive power? The answer, according to Lee, was Lord Hillsborough. Twice a member of the ministry in the 1760s, and after 1768 Secretary of State for the Colonies, Hillsborough had plotted in tandem with Governor Francis Bernard, first to subdue the democratic assembly of Massachusetts and to replace elected officials with a swarm of placemen, and then to establish a regime where unconstitutional taxes would be paid without protest.

Lee's first essay addressed to Governor Francis Bernard, which appeared initially in the *Middlesex Journal*, London, October 24, 1769, has been discovered in no less that thirteen American newspapers and in two from the city of London. Lee claimed in this piece that on a pretext of a need to maintain public order, Governor Bernard asked Lord Hillsborough for British troops in Boston. When the redcoats arrived they fomented the violence that the Governor desired. In other words, the disorder was contrived as a veiled excuse for the most brutal repression. According to Lee the fatal escalation of a quarrel between the people, represented in the Massachusetts General Court, and the Governor, representing arbitrary power, was set in motion already in 1768. Subsequent essays by "Junius Americanus" listed the highlights as: the Boston Massacre, the attempted "impeachment" of Governor Bernard by the Assembly, his replacement by Governor Thomas Hutchinson, the attempted "impeachment" of Governor Hutchinson, the Boston Tea Party, the Coercive or Intolerable Acts, and finally civil war, which was confidently asserted to be part of the plot.

The spreading of this detailed message of "a settled conspiracy" was facilitated by correspondence Lee set up with Samuel Adams,

Joseph Warren, John Dickinson, his brother Richard Henry Lee, and several other patriotic leaders in colonies both north and south. Lee's friends in America inserted his essays and many of his letters on politics in their local newspapers. Personal letters had an aura of truth about them that essays were unable to duplicate. Letters, however, were usually published anonymously and without their personal material, so they are even more difficult to ascribe than essays. One that Lee sent to Samuel Adams, a conduit for such material through the *Boston Gazette*, appeared in three Massachusetts papers, one in Connecticut, another in Rhode Island, and one each in New York and Pennsylvania.[25]

In 1772 Lee added at least two names to his growing list of newspaper aliases. Over a period of four years he submitted eighteen essays signed "A Bostonian," and fifteen signed "Raleigh." Lee explained that he adopted the signature "Raleigh" to address Lord Dartmouth, "with tenderness at first."[26] Dartmouth, a gentle man who disliked his job, replaced Lord Hillsborough as Colonial Secretary in August 1772. Massachusetts newspapers reprinted practically all of the "Bostonians," which were dispatched to Samuel Adams and invariably discussed matters of interest to the Bay Colony. Eight of them in the *Public Advertiser* described the humiliation of Benjamin Franklin, agent for the Massachusetts Assembly, before the Lords of the Privy Council on January 29, 1774. The incident came as a reaction to charges by the Assembly against Governor Hutchinson, and Lee regarded the hearing as prime evidence for his conspiracy case against the ministry. If an old man, recognized as the symbol of America in London and venerated by all the world as a philosopher, had to be humbled to satisfy the British government, what would be done to Boston in retaliation for its infamous Tea Party of December 1773? Arthur Lee had succeeded Franklin as agent for Massachusetts, and he would have to devise an answer for the incident in Boston harbor. Writing for the newspapers at a furious pace during the month of February 1774, he produced ten essays under various signatures in twenty-eight days.

After the Franklin hearing Lee was also preoccupied for a time with an attempt to raise a respectable opposition in Parliament against the Coercive Acts, which were passed in the spring of 1774 to punish Massachusetts. His petitions signed by native Americans residing in London against the punitive legislation received wide coverage in the papers and were introduced by Opposition leaders into the debates of the session. In the meantime, Lee had turned increasingly to the pamphlet as a vehicle for distributing his message. After 1774 he added two signatures to his roster of pen-names in order to address the Colonial Secretary, but only eighteen have been discovered—eleven by "Vespucius" and seven by "Memento"—these written over a period of two years. Except in response to an event of great importance, he seems to have neglected the papers.

Perhaps Lee considered it no longer important to submit essays to English newspapers that were directed as much to the press in America. The meeting of the First Continental Congress at Philadelphia in 1774 proved that the rest of the colonies would come to the aid of Massachusetts. The task in London after 1774, as Lee saw it, was primarily to influence public opinion in England. In February 1774 Lee agreed, however, to write a pamphlet for Henry Laurens of South Carolina. Too far removed in theme from the main concern at Boston, his *Answer to Considerations on Certain Political Transactions of the Province of South Carolina* was a financial disaster for its backer, but it dealt with the important issue of colonial sovereignty, a fundamental question of the era that was answered only by revolution.[27]

Lee sifted through agency files belonging to Benjamin Franklin for his next pamphlet, which was originally intended for English readers. *A True State of the Proceedings in the Parliament of Great Britain, and in the Province of Massachusetts Bay*, published by John Almon in May 1774 and reprinted the same year by Joseph Crukshank of Philadelphia, recapitulated familiar material from Lee's aggressive newspaper essays and closed on a rare note of supplication:

> Whoever will take the trouble of reading, in the history of this most meritorious and unhappy people, the unparalleled hardships with which they have purchased these liberties we have now torn from them, and view the deplorable, the desperate situation to which they are now reduced; however obdurate, however prejudiced he may be, he must think, at least, *one human tear may drop, and be forgiven.*[28]

Certainly this pamphlet shows evidence of a new tolerance, a new spirit of accommodation on the part of Arthur Lee. By 1774 the patriots he served in Massachusetts were no longer in a position to ask anything except sympathy from the people of Great Britain. In Lee's most popular pamphlet, written in Paris during the summer, the change in tone was even more striking. *An Appeal to the Justice and Interests of the People of Great Britain* opened with a glowing description of the harmony that existed throughout the empire during the last war, 1756-1763. The determination to tax the colonies after the war, Lee explained, had "given birth to a thousand calamities" that might end in "the dissolution of all American dependence on the parent state." [29] The pamphlet, circulated by the thousands on both sides of the Atlantic, was a huge success. It quickly went through four editions in England and one in America. The *Virginia Gazette* (Purdie) featured it as a serial between April 7 and April 21, 1775, it was spoken of with approval by Opposition leaders in Parliament, and it was translated into German in 1777.

Lee proposed to deal with two questions: whether Parliament had a right to tax the colonies, and whether such a policy was expedient. Citing numerous examples from English history that proved to his satisfaction that money or other property could not be transferred to the government except as a free gift by the people or their representatives, he set out to show that members of Parliament did not and could not represent Americans. As for expediency, Lee submitted data to show that the expense of collecting taxes in America since 1764 was almost as great as the revenue. And what would happen if, during the next inevitable European war, the injured colonies seized the occasion to rebel? British troops could not conquer the provinces without simultaneously laying waste to their productive capacity, which had enriched the mother country for almost two centuries. "The balance of trade is greatly against them," Lee argued; their deficits would aid France, who would surely fight the war in America on the side of the colonies. [30]

When Lee returned to London from a trip to the continent in late November 1774, he discovered that the First Continental Congress had met at Philadelphia and forwarded an "Address to the

King" and a "Declaration of Rights and Grievances." By January 1775 he had produced a lengthy pamphlet for Edward and Charles Dilly that was designed to "support a Petition from the General Congress in America to our Common Sovereign." *A Speech Intended to have been Delivered in the House of Commons*, another plea for conciliation, listed and illuminated each grievance of the Americans and was followed by a "short review of the rise and progress of this unhappy dispute." [31] A portion of the tract covered the entire front page of the *London Chronicle*, April 13-15, 1775; a second edition was printed by John Almon of London in 1775, and it was featured in the *Pennsylvania Gazette* for five installments between August 9 and September 6, 1775.

In late May 1775, two weeks before the government's version arrived in London, Lee received word of the Battles of Lexington and Concord. As agent for the Massachusetts Assembly, he again became active in a newspaper and pamphlet campaign to place the blame on the ministry and the forces of General Thomas Gage. In due form a hastily prepared tract on the war appeared that was part of Lee's extensive campaign in the press over the signatures "Raleigh," "A Bostonian," and "Memento." The anonymous pamphlet bore familiar expressions from Lee's other writings, and included the "Address to the King from the Continental Congress" as well as the affadavits Lee had received from Massachusetts in his capacity as agent, which were derived from soldier participants in the battles.

The Rise, Progress, and Present State of the Dispute Between the People of America and the Administration put a cap on a publishing event of some importance. No hint of moderation or conciliation was apparent in this tract, which was an appeal to the people of England to interpose against an abandoned ministry that had conspired to erect a system of arbitrary power upon the ruins of American liberty. "Every honest Englishman who loves his Liberty and his Country," the author concluded, "will support his Brethren in America and their cause, by every means in his power." [32] That sentiment was also the theme for an angry petition against the war, which Lee prepared for the Corporation of the City of London to present to the king on July 15, 1775.

Lee's final pamphlet during his eight-year sojourn in London appears to be his ninety-page *Second Appeal to the Justice and Interests of the People on the Measures Respecting America.* In keeping with the so-called Olive Branch Petition from the Continental Congress, which it was designed to support, the tract was reasonable and moderate in tone. But again the entire blame for developments in Massachusetts was placed upon the ministry. Again Lee warned in this pamphlet, published in 1775 by Almon, that victory was impossible if the French intervened, which they certainly would. Lee spent several pages refuting the charge that the colonies had long desired independence, but he was certain that the result of the war could be nothing less.[33]

About a year after the appearance of his last pamphlet, Lee left London for Paris at the request of the Continental Congress. Few of his writings during the year 1776 can be identified, although his letters, smuggled out of London, continued to appear in colonial newspapers.[34] There is no reason to believe that he had abandoned his newspaper campaign, but he had a more compelling reason than ever before for concealing his identity. He was then negotiating with an envoy from France for American aid while employed as a spy for Congress.

Until late in 1775 Lee vehemently denied any wish for the dissolution of the British empire, but he would have agreed with David Ramsay's comment in his *History of the American Revolution* (1789), that "In establishing American independence the pen and the press had merit equal to that of the sword." Ramsay went on to name twenty-two of the "most distinguished writers," who, in his judgment, contributed the most toward what he considered a glorious accomplishment.[35]

Perhaps the most prominent names on Ramsay's list, those who wrote enough between 1767 and 1776 so that they may be called journalists or columnists as opposed to occasional contributors, were Samuel Adams, Benjamin Franklin, Thomas Paine, and Arthur Lee. Of these four, only Adams and Lee wrote consistently and intensively for newspapers during the entire period. Paine wrote *Common Sense,* one of the most influential pamphlets of all time, but he did not turn up in the colonies until 1774. Franklin wrote important pieces of high quality for London and American newspapers, but he was not a pamphleteer, he discouraged his friends from inserting his personal letters in newspapers, and he never committed himself to a sustained periodical series.[36] For sheer volume Lee's contributions to the press exceeded that of anybody else on Ramsay's list, and Lee had the advantage of being able to reach out from London for a transatlantic following with both pamphlets and newspaper essays.

Researchers on the literature of the American Revolution have had few kind words for Lee's style, which has been judged mainly with reference to his youthful "Monitor Letters." Moses Coit Tyler, for example, noted that Lee's "high literary reputation among his contemporaries rests upon no material which can justify its revival at the hands of posterity."[37] Lee's style, however, had so changed by 1774 that one of his pamphlets was even published by Jared Sparks as a work by Franklin.[38] In any event, the issue here is not elegance of style but popularity. When the total impact of Lee's political writings is assessed in the light of how easily Americans accepted his charge that a conspiracy against their liberty had been hatched by the ministry—an accusation that helped drive them to rebellion—there is a strong case for calling him "the penman of the Revolution."

NOTES

1. Anthony Benezet, *A Caution and Warning to Great Britain, and Her Colonies* (Philadelphia, 1767). The remark about Lee, by John Mercer of Marlboro, may be found in Lois Mulkearn, ed., *George Mercer Papers Relating to the Ohio Company of Virginia* (Pittsburgh: University of Pittsburgh Press, 1954), 203-204. See also, Richard K. MacMaster, "Arthur Lee's Address on Slavery," *Virginia Magazine of History and Biography,* 80 (1972), 141-57.

2. Paul Leicester Ford, ed., *The Writings of John Dickinson* (Philadelphia, 1894), I, 421.

3. William Samuel Johnson to Jared Ingersoll, June 15, 1772, in F. B. Dexter, ed., "A Selection from the Correspondence and Miscellaneous Papers of Jared Ingersoll," *Papers of the New Haven Historical Society,* 9 (1918), 436; Junius to John Wilkes, November 6, 1771, in John Wade, ed., *Junius* (London, 1884), II, 102.

4. Douglas Adair and John A. Schutz, eds., *Peter Oliver's Origin and Progress of the American Rebellion* (San Marino, Calif.: Huntington Library, 1961), 77-78.

5. Lee to Adams, January 25, 1773, Bancroft TSS., Samuel Adams Papers, New York Public Library.

6. Letter signed "Fact," to Lord Dartmouth, August 2, 1773, Historical Manuscript Commission, *Fourteenth Report, Appendix, Part X, The Manuscripts of the Earl of Dartmouth, American Papers*, II (London, 1895), 164.

7. Henry Laurens to John Laurens, February 18, 1774, Henry Laurens Papers, South Carolina Historical Society.

8. *Public Advertiser* (London), February 15, 1775.

9. See, for example, Bernard Bailyn, *The Ideological Origins of the American Revolution* (Cambridge, Mass.: Harvard University Press, 1967), 157-58.

10. Arthur Lee to Richard Henry Lee, August 15, 1769, Correspondence of R. H. Lee and A. Lee, American Philosophical Society.

11. Lee resented the attribution. His comments are in the Arthur Lee Papers, VIII, 138, Houghton Library, Harvard University.

12. Adam Smith, *The Theory of Moral Sentiments* (New York: A. M. Kelley, 1966), 297; Arthur Lee, *An Essay in Vindication of the Continental Colonies of America* (London, 1764), 42-43.

13. Arthur Lee, *Extracts from an Address in the Virginia Gazette of March 19, 1767. By a Respectable Member of the Community* (Williamsburg, 1767). The short pamphlet was reprinted at Philadelphia in 1768.

14. "Monitor V," *Virginia Gazette* (Rind), March 24, 1768.

15. Arthur's brother Richard Henry Lee wrote a preface for *The Farmer's and Monitor's Letters to the Inhabitants of the British Colonies* (Williamsburg, 1769); rpt. in facsimilie with introduction by William J. Van Schreeven (Richmond, Va.: Whittet & Shepperson, 1969).

16. The essays appeared first in Rind's *Virginia Gazette*, June 1 and June 8, 1769. A third report over the signature was first published in Rind's *Virginia Gazette*, May 31, 1770.

17. Arthur M. Schlesinger, "A Note on Songs as Patriot Propaganda, 1765-1776," *William and Mary Quarterly*, 3rd ser., 11 (1954), 79.

18. Undated letter, Arthur to Richard Henry Lee, in R. H. Lee, *Life of Arthur Lee* (Boston, 1829), I, 190.

19. *Public Advertiser*, June 6 and October 21, 1769.

20. William Pepperrell to Arthur Lee, November 21, 1770, Miscellaneous Bound Manuscripts, Vol. xiii, Massachusetts Historical Society.

21. "Letters of Roger Atkinson, 1769-1776," *Virginia Magazine of History and Biography*, 15 (1908), 355.

22. Letters of Dennys DeBerdt, 1757-1770, Publications of the Colonial Society of Massachusetts, *Transactions* 13(1911), 302, n. 2.

23. Bailyn, *Ideological Origins*; See also H. Trevor Colbourn, *The Lamp of Experience; Whig History and the Intellectual Origins of the American Revolution* (Chapel Hill: University of North Carolina Press, 1965), and Pauline Maier, *From Resistance to Revolution* (New York, 1972).

24. Arthur Lee as "Raleigh," *Saint James Chronicle* (London), December 22-24, 1772.

25. Lee to Adams, January 25, 1773, Bancroft TSS., Samuel Adams Papers, New York Public Library.

26. Ibid.

27. The pamphlet has been reprinted by Jack P. Greene, ed., in *The Nature of Colony Constitutions, Two Pamphlets on the Wilkes Fund Controversy in South Carolina by Sir Egerton Leigh and Arthur Lee* (Columbia, S.C.: University of South Carolina Press, 1970), 125-205.

28. *A True State* (London, 1774), 24.

29. *An Appeal* (London, 1774), 2.

30. Ibid., 42, 44, 52.

31. *A Speech Intended* (London, 1775), 37.

32. *The Rise, Progress, and Present State of the Dispute* (London, 1775), 42.

33. *A Second Appeal* (London, 1775), 44, 70-78.

34. Some of the so-called "Colden Letters," written to Congress in 1776, have been reprinted by Peter Force, Ed., *American Archives*, IV-VI, 1775-1776.

35. David Ramsay, *The History of the American Revolution* (Philadelphia, 1789), II, 319-20.

36. Verner Crane, ed., *Benjamin Franklin's Letters to the Press, 1758-1775* (Chapel Hill: University of North Carolina Press, 1950), xi.

37. Moses Coit Tyler, *The Literary History of the American Revolution, 1763-1783* (New York: Ungar Publishing Co., 1966), I, 244.

38. Jared Sparks, ed., *The Works of Benjamin Franklin* (Boston, 1836-1840), IV, 486-515.

CHAOS AND IMAGINATIVE ORDER
IN THOMAS JEFFERSON'S
NOTES ON THE STATE OF VIRGINIA

William J. Scheick

Chaos threatened the young American nation during the years Thomas Jefferson composed his answer to the questionnaire of François Marbois, secretary of the French legation at Philadelphia. In 1780-1781, burgeoning America was harried by the upheaval of a war she seemed to be losing. The British, for instance, had invaded the state of Virginia, and Jefferson, its governor, had fled from the capital city at Richmond. Later even the governor's beloved estate at Monticello would fall into the hands of the enemy. Still more personal losses intensified the darkness of these years for Jefferson. On April 15, 1781, his two-year-old daughter, Lucy Elizabeth, died, followed by her mother in 1782. Moreover, not only had Jefferson sustained incapacitating injuries by falling from a horse, but he embarrassingly found his conduct as governor the subject of an investigation by the Virginia legislature. During these disquieting times, Jefferson, an instinctively methodical man, could not have escaped periodic reminiscences of an earlier pre-war period when a sense of order, permanence, and tranquility seemed to characterize his personal life as well as his nation.

His reply to Marbois, later published as *Notes on the State of Virginia,*[1] in several respects reflects his concern with chaos and order as the two most dangerous forces with which the new nation must cope. In a real sense, I think, this concern may be read as the theme of the book, unifying it in a way not immediately apparent in the question-and-answer format of the work. When we consider the *Notes* in the light of Jefferson's other writings, especially his letters, this theme subtly emerges. We can then discern the many ways in which Jefferson warns, throughout the book, of the threats arising from both rigid order and unlimited freedom. In the *Notes,* he recommends, as a *via media,* a concept he refers to as "temperate liberty," a notion which for him is synonymous with artistic or imaginative order. The aesthetic vision of "temperate liberty" represents, for Jefferson, a delicate balance between stringent order and unrestricted freedom.

Jefferson anticipated a new order which would eventually emerge from the disconcerting confusions spawned by the Revolutionary War. However, he had to exercise extreme caution in speaking of the need for order in America. The trouble was that the concept of order had traditionally been associated with monarchical rule. Later in fact, Federalists, politically antagonistic to the Jeffersonians, would see themselves as the advocates of order and would indict Jefferson and his followers for undermining cultural stability, at times resorting to apocalyptic imagery in order to portray the anarchistic influence of their liberal enemies. Speaking of the dangers and duties of the man of letters in 1809, for instance, Joseph Stevens Buckminster would typically lament: "It is our lot to have been born in an age of tremendous revolution; and the world is yet covered with the wrecks of its ancient glory." [2] Similarly, in another essay, Buckminster would depict federalist writers as the last defenders of order in an age when literature readily mirrored the disintegration of rational standards: "They are gentle knights who wish to guard the seats of taste and morals at home from the incursions of the 'paynim host'; happy if they should now and then rescue a fair captive from the giants of romance or dissolve the spell in which many a youthful genius is held by the enchantments of corrupt literature." [3]

Such was the image of chaos with which Jefferson had to reckon, not only in his later political career but at the time of the very foundation of the new nation. In Europe, during the years of the American Revolutionary War, adverse propaganda had given the impression that Americans were "a lawless banditti, in a state of

absolute anarchy."⁴ Jefferson realized that such a view was rein-
forced at some level by Count de Buffon's assessment of nature in
America. Buffon had maintained that since the new world had less
heat and more moisture than Europe, its animals were less perfect
than their European equivalents in that they tended to be smaller,
fewer in species, prone to degeneration if previously domesticated,
and frequently impotent. In short, "La nature vivante est beaucoup moins agissante, beaucoup moins forte" (*NSV*, p. 47). In
America, Buffon concluded, nature favored the reptile. Although
Buffon had not applied his arguments to human life in the new
world, it was an easy step to make, as Guillaume Raynal made
clear in his view of human degeneracy in America. At the level of
implication, both Buffon and Raynal were suggesting that America
possessed an inherent element of disorder. Particularly sensitive to
this implication, Jefferson painstakingly refuted these views in the
*Notes.*⁵ America, he argued, provided no evidence of "imbecility
or want of uniformity in the operations of nature" (*NSV*, p. 56).
All life in the new world conformed to the fundamental principles
of natural order.

Jefferson's reference to natural order, however, did not supplant his fear that politically America might well fall prey to destructive anarchy. Here, in fact, lay the hub of his dilemma. He
felt compelled to speak of the need for order and yet at the same
time to avoid addressing the problem in the traditional terms used
by the Tories and later by the Federalists.

Paradox provided one means whereby Jefferson treated the
idea of order. In the *Notes,* for example, he attacked all systems of
order which proved excessively rigid. Consequently, in one instance he focused on Virginia's coercion of uniform opinion regarding religion.⁶ Such a false sense of order, Jefferson warned,
supported "roguery and error all over the earth" (*NSV*, p. 160).
Unrelieved subservience to a similarly debilitating notion of order,
in his opinion, accounted for Europe's decline. Shackled to monarchical rule, Great Britain, for instance, no longer represented
"the legitimate offspring either of science or of civilization," for
she seemed to be undergoing an "awful dissolution, whose issue is
not given human foresight to scan" (*NSV*, p. 65). Symptomatic of
the actual collapse of order in Europe was the failure of the fami-

ly, that cornerstone of the social unit. To Jefferson, as he indicated to Lucy Ludwell Paradise in 1786, family life in America was "infinitely more replete with happiness than . . . in Europe" (*PTJ*, IX [1954], p. 592). A letter to John Banister, Jr. made this difference more specific; whereas in America one encounters "chaste affections," Jefferson explains, the traveller in Eruope "is led by the strongest of all human passions into a spirit for female intrigue destructive of his own and others happiness, or a passion for whores destructive to his health, and in both cases learns to consider fidelity to the marriage bed as an ungentlemanly practice" (*PTJ*, VIII [1953], pp. 636-37). As Jefferson remarked to Charles Bellini in 1785, the consequence of such an influence upon the Europeans themselves proves most detrimental: "Conjugal love having no existence among them, domestic happiness, of which that is the basis, is utterly unknown" in contrast "to the tranquil, permanent felicity with which domestic society in America blesses most of it's inhabitants" (*PTJ*, VIII [1953], p. 569). This destruction of the family unit belies the semblance of political order in Europe. Thus, in its rigid, artificial aspect, a principle of order could readily lead to discontent and, paradoxically, to upheaval.

That chaos was pernicious, all agreed. Jefferson, however, brought the argument full circle by indicating that political disorder became just as paradoxical as coercive order in that it tended to engender dictators. Indeed, the tumult of the Revolutionary War had nearly produced a dictator in Virginia (*NSV*, p. 126). Jefferson feared the excesses of unrestricted liberty as much as he fretted over enslaving despotism. On January 30, 1787, for instance, he noted in a letter to James Madison that liberty "has it's evils too: the principal of which is the turbulence to which it is subject" (*PTJ*, XI [1955], p. 93). Although "a little rebellion now and then is a good thing, and as necessary in the political world as storms in the physical" (*PTJ*, XI [1955], p. 93), the outcome of such upheavals could be as permanently disastrous as its opposite extreme; there was always the threat that the nation might not revive but "expire in a convulsion" (*NSV*, p. 161). Jefferson was certain that political anarchy and despotic control were merely opposite extremes of political chaos.

Nevertheless, this contention did not provide Jefferson with a solution to the problem he faced with regard to the order America would desperately need after the War. He had to formulate a positive definition as well. A clue to Jefferson's unique approach to this new order appears, I think, in his remarks on the relationship between reason and passion, frequently referred to by him as the head and the heart. As an eighteenth-century thinker, Jefferson respected man's rational capacities, recognizing the human mind as the chief attribute distinguishing mankind from other creatures in the chain of being. He maintained that "reason and free enquiry are the only effectual agents against error" (*NSV*, p. 159) because he was certain that reason and the truth evident in natural order were inseparable (*NSV*, p. 56). Reason, however, represented only one fundamental component of the human self; unchecked by the emotions of the heart, reason could give rise to an order, the rigidity of which might easily enslave men. As Jefferson explained in his famous letter to Maria Cosway (October 12, 1786), reason might usurp the whole man and, like a perverse monarch, "pretend authority to the sovereign controul of [human] conduct in all it's parts" (*PTJ*, X [1954], p. 450). Reason's tendency toward extreme governmental rigidity must be tempered by the feelings of the heart.

To be sure, in the light of eighteenth-century thought, Jefferson is cautious in his attitude toward the heart; for he knows that its passions tend toward chaos. He suggests this view, for example, in a letter dated August 18, 1785, in which he refers to the passions as forces "at sea without rudder or compass" (*PTJ*, VIII [1953], p. 404). Yet the heart, like the head, represents a crucial component in man's interaction with the world. Whereas the head responds to the natural order in a rational way, the heart responds to that same order in a moral way. "One generous spasm of the heart" in response to the "sunshine" of life, the heart explains to the head in Jefferson's letter to Maria Cosway, indicates that "when nature assigned us the same habitation, she gave us over it a divided empire. To you she allotted the field of science, to me that of morals" (*PTJ*, X [1954], p. 450). Thus, for Jefferson, the greatness of mankind must be measured with regard not only to reason but also to moral inclination. As he would later remark to

Thomas Law (June 13, 1814), "the general existence of a moral instinct" in the heart represents "the brightest gem with which the human character is studded." [7]

Neither the head nor the heart is more important than its counterpart. The heart should remind the head of "the proper limits of [its] office" and the head should prevent the heart from "imprudently engaging [its] affections" (*PTJ*, X [1954], pp. 450, 446). The moral sense of the heart, as Jefferson explains in a letter to Peter Carr (August 10, 1787), should submit "in some degree to the guidance of reason," even if it might, as a result, run the risk of being "led astray by artificial rules" (*PTJ*, XII [1955], p. 15). The alternative is chaos.

The heart possesses the power of imagination. Since the imagination is subject to many of the same excesses as is the heart, an unrestricted exercise of this faculty leads to the chaos of error. Thus, whereas Whateley's book of gardening demonstrates to Jefferson that its author's "fine imagination had never been able to seduce him from the truth" (*WTJ*, XVII, pp. 236-37), Buffon's study of America indicates that its author at times "cherished error . . . lending her for a moment his vivid imagination" (*NSV*, p. 64). The imagination is not inherently bad any more than is its seat, the heart. In fact, although most intimately related to the heart, the imagination in some way provides a liaison between the head and the heart, as, for instance, when "the spacious field of imagination is . . . laid open to our use, and lessons may be formed to illustrate and carry home to the mind every moral rule of life" (*PTJ*, I [1950], p. 77). In some sense, then, the imagination plays an important role in bringing about the necessary balance between the head and the heart.

Specifically, the imagination engenders art. Although in one instance Jefferson remarked that "no perfect *definition* of what is a fine art has ever yet been given," he apparently saw some validity in the argument that "those are *fine* arts which to manual operation join the exercise of the imagination or genius." [8] For Jefferson, genuine art is both beautiful and useful; it appeals simultaneously to the heart's sense of moral beauty and the head's sense of rational utility. Art bridges these two extremes. Likewise, the "art of life," as Jefferson refers to it, involves both the random, emotive response of the heart as well as the unyielding "calculation" of the head; the art of life requires one to "advance . . . with caution, the balance in . . . hand" (*PTJ*, X [1954], p. 448).

Of all the arts Jefferson admires,[9] architecture seems most, in his opinion, to embody this ideal union. Architecture represents an "elegant and useful art" (*NSV*, p. 153), one that appeals to the head through its utility as well as to the heart through its beauty. In America, Jefferson laments, imaginative vision has not yet sufficiently matured to give birth to true architectural art; "the genius of architecture seems to have shed its maledictions over this land," he explains, "the first principles of the art are unknown" (*NSV*, p. 153). "Every half century," Jefferson continues, "our country becomes a tabula rasa, whereon we have to set out anew, as in the first moment of seating it. Whereas when buildings are of durable materials, every new edifice is an actual and permanent acquisition to the state, adding to its value as well as to its ornament" (*NSV*, p. 154).

Before the American imagination can express itself through architecture, it must perfect the art of democracy. Jefferson sees that, like the self with regard to the head and the heart, America is currently torn between the strangling rigidities of aristocratic tyranny and the draining liberties of mob-inspired anarchy. The balance between these extremes, which Jefferson presents in the *Notes*, lies in an aesthetic vision of democracy, in what he calls "temperate liberty." A passage concerning the problems caused by emigrants provides the most explicit statement of this vision: "They will bring with them the principles of the governments they leave, imbibed in their early youth; or, if able to throw them off, it will be in exchange for an unbounded licentiousness, passing, as is usual, from one extreme to another. It would be a miracle were they to stop precisely at the point of temperate liberty" (*NSV*, pp. 84-85). Later in the work he defines "temperate liberty" further when he writes of the ideal government as "one which should not only be founded on free principles, but in which the powers of government should be so divided and balanced among several bodies of magistracy, as that no one could transcend their legal limits, without being effectually checked and restrained by the others" (*NSV*, p. 120). This notion of "temperate liberty," a concept to which Jefferson refers elsewhere as the exercise of "a wholesome control" (*WTJ*, XV, p. 234) and as the "establishment of a free and well-ordered republic" (*WTJ*, X, p. 78), is an imaginative order stemming from the art of democracy.

Law embodies a beautiful and useful expression of this art of democracy and, like architecture, it eventually will contribute to balance and stability in America.[10] Establishing law in the new nation, however, is not any easier than developing the fine art of architecture. Thus, Jefferson makes clear in the *Notes*, law in America has not yet brought about the ideal balance between tyranny and anarchy. Concerning the defects of the Virginia constitution of 1776, for instance, he explains that "this constitution was formed when we were new and unexperienced in the science of government" (*NSV*, p. 118). The imperfection of legal artistry in America also becomes apparent in a humorous passage in which Jefferson speaks of places where "the *laws* have said there shall be towns; but *Nature* has said there shall not" (*NSV*, p. 109).

The importance of law to Jefferson's aesthetic vision of "temperate liberty" is similarly evident in his discussion of the Indians of Virginia. The Indians, he writes, "never submitted themselves to any laws, any coercive power, any shadow of government. Their only controuls are their manners, and that moral sense of right and wrong" (*NSV*, p. 93). In Jefferson's view, such an arrangement is imperfect; liberty requires limits, for "great societies cannot exist without government" (*NSV*, p. 93). In the absence of a proper balance, the free condition of the Indians is, of course, preferable to tyrannical order: "were it made a question, whether no law, as among the savage Americans, or too much law, as among the civilized Europeans, submits man to the greatest evil, one who has seen both conditions of existence would pronounce it to be the last: and that the sheep are happier of themselves, than under care of the wolves" (*NSV*, p. 93). The Indians, moreover, may not have achieved an ideal government, but they do possess all the rudiments for establishing, within themselves as well as within their society, an imaginative order or balance between the head and the heart. Whereas, in Jefferson's opinion, the blacks seem more inclined toward "sensation than reflection" and seem "dull, tasteless, and anomalous" with regard to the imagination (*NSV*, p.

139),[11] the Indians occasionally, in "strokes of the most sublime oratory . . . prove their reason and sentiment strong, their imagination glowing and elevated"; in short, there exists "a germ in their minds which only wants cultivation" (*NSV*, p. 140).

The image of cultivation contributes significantly to Jefferson's theme in the *Notes*. What the Indians require is precisely what young America requires, cultivation or education.[12] Cultivation and education are synonymous to Jefferson, as the following passage indicates: "By that part of our plan which prescribes the selection of the youths of genius from among the classes of the poor, we hope to avail the state of those talents which nature has sown as liberally among the poor as the rich, but which perish without use, if not sought for and cultivated" (*NSV*, p. 148). Education will impress upon Americans both "useful facts and good principles"—that is, both the head and the heart will be instructed—rendering them the "guardians of their own liberty" (*NSV*, p. 148). From an educated people derive good laws, and such laws contribute to the realization of the democratic art of imaginative order or "temperate liberty." Indeed, education furnishes "the principal foundations of future order" (*NSV*, p. 147).

In Jefferson's view, formal institutions, albeit important in themselves, do not provide all the cultivation Americans need. A large number of citizens must turn to the land itself for lessons on moral principles and useful facts. America possesses "an immensity of land courting the industry of the husbandman," and "those who labour in the earth are the chosen people of God, if ever he had a chosen people" (*NSV*, pp. 164-65).[13] Jefferson's agrarian notions are well known;[14] but it is important to place them within the context of the theme of the *Notes*. In a letter to James Madison (December 20, 1787), Jefferson writes: "I think our governments will remain virtuous for many centuries; as long as they are chiefly agricultural; and this will be as long as there shall be vacant lands in any part of America. When they get piled upon one another in large cities, as in Europe, they will become corrupt as in Europe" (*PTJ*, XII [1955], p. 442; cf. *NSV*, p. 165). As a "chosen people," American farmers regain paradise, as Jefferson intimates in a letter to Angelica Schuyler Church (February 17, 1788): "The learned say it is a new creation; and I believe them. . . . Europe is a first idea, and crude production, before the maker knew his trade, or had made up his mind as to what he wanted" (*PTJ*, XII [1955], p. 601). In this paradise nature and the farmer can exist in mutual harmony. Consequently, in contrast to exploitative tobacco farming, the cultivation of wheat in Virginia not only covers "the earth with herbage" and preserves the fertility of the land but also "feeds the labourers plentifully, requires from them only a moderate toil, except in the season of harvest, raises great numbers of animals for food and service, and diffuses plenty and happiness among the whole" (*NSV*, p. 168).

Thus, what the student learns at the formal institutions of education, the farmer learns from the land. Both require useful facts and moral principles instructive to the head and the heart, respectively. "Dependance begets subservience and venality, suffocates the germ of virtue, and prepares fit tools for the designs of ambition" (*NSV*, p. 165), a point Jefferson particularly stresses in his polemic against slavery (*NSV*, pp. 162-63). The farmer, like the student, learns self-reliance; in his breast or heart the Creator "has made [a] peculiar deposit for substantial and genuine virtue" (*NSV*, p. 165): the "cultivators of the earth are the most virtuous and independant citizens" (*NSV*, p. 175). Education, both in school and in the field, cultivates this germ of virtue. With the flowering of virtue comes good government; virtue, in conjunction with law, yields the fruitful art of "temperate liberty." At the very foundation of this art is America herself, especially as manifested in Virginia, a place where each individual may fully develop his own head and heart: "It is a country where a rational and studious man may follow his inclinations with less interruption, and where a warm heart will meet with more genuine returns of friendship than in Europe" (*PTJ*, IX [1954], p. 592).

Jefferson knew, of course, that the realization of his ideal of imaginative order lay within the future.[15] Still embroiled in the Revolutionary War, America was very young, a mere "child of yesterday" (*NSV*, p. 65). Yet, like her Indians, America possessed the rudiments of rationality, moral sentiment, and imagination; she simply needed cultivation, which would eventually, together with the "ripening" of her citizens (*NSV*, p. 87), give rise to the art of democracy. Just as "what is called style in writing or speak-

ing is formed very early in life while the imagination is warm,"
(*PTJ*, VIII [1953], p. 637) so too the art of democracy was being
perfected as the youthful, vital American imagination strove for a
balance between enslaving order and dissipating liberty.

Apparently even the American landscape seemed to suggest to
Jefferson the future imaginative order which would emerge from
the current discord of war and internal strife. The American landscape, especially as typified in Virginia, demands only "a moderate
toil," as we already noted, and provides as well instructive images
of an aesthetic order: "It is worthy of notice, that our mountains
are not solitary and scattered *confusedly* over the face of the
country" (*NSV*, p. 18; italics added). Moreover, even climatic extremes are becoming more temperate: "A change in our climate ... is taking place very sensibly. Both heats and colds are
become much more moderate" (*NSV*, p. 80). As the land slowly
achieves a balance between extremes, so will its people; "for man
is an imitative animal. This quality is the germ of all education in
him" (*NSV*, p. 162).

Jefferson's remarkable portrait of the confluence of the Shenan-
doah and the Potomac Rivers represents the best instance of how
the American landscape adumbrates the ideal of imaginative order.
The passage is worth citing at length:

> In the moment of their junction they rush together against the moun-
> tain, rend it asunder, and pass off to the sea. The first glance of this
> scene hurries our senses into the opinion, that this earth has been
> created in time, that the mountains were formed first, that the rivers
> began to flow afterwards, that in this place particularly they have been
> dammed up by the Blue ridge of mountains, and have formed an ocean
> which filled the whole valley; that continuing to rise they have at length
> broken over at this spot, and have torn the mountain down from its
> summit to its base. The piles of rock on each hand, but particularly on
> the Shenandoah, the evident marks of their disrupture and avulsion
> from their beds by the most powerful agents of nature, corroborate the
> impression. But the distant finishing which nature has given to the
> picture is of a very different character. It is a true contrast to the
> fore-ground. It is as placid and delightful, as that is wild and tremen-
> dous. For the mountains being cloven asunder, she presents to your
> eye, through the cleft, a small catch of smooth blue horizon, at an
> infinite distance in the plain country, inviting you, as it were, from the
> riot and tumult roaring around, to pass through the breach and partici-

pate of the calm below. Here the eye ultimately composes itself; and
that way too the road happens actually to lead (*NSV*, p. 19).

Charles Sanford properly observes that Jefferson's "concern here
was not with nature as a logical concept or even as a substantive
reality demonstrating logical concepts, but with nature as an object of human feeling."[16] More on target is Howard Mumford
Jones' focus on Jefferson's fascination with the "vastness and . . .
the allure of the distant."[17] We should note further, in the light of
our preceding comments, that the "placid and delightful" distance
symbolized for Jefferson the future of America; the "small catch
of smooth blue horizon, at an infinite distance in the plain country" expresses his vision of a future imaginative order, his hope for
the realization of a "temperate liberty" eventually redeeming men
from the chaotic "riot and tumult" in which they presently find
themselves. This hopeful catch of blue conveys "the distant finishing which nature has given to the picture,". and Americans, who
are attuned to nature through an attachment to their land, will
cultivate the germ of this vision both within themselves and within
their government. The future augers well, in Jefferson's opinion;
for already Americans have instinctively responded to nature's instruction: "that way too the road happens actually to lead."

Jefferson believed that in America animals and humans did not
degenerate; nature, in all its forms, achieved its most beautiful
expression in the new world. He was equally sure that by means of
cultivation or education—and in this regard the very book he had
written would play a significant role—Americans would supplant
the chaos inherent in enslaving tyranny and in razing anarchy.
Cultivation would balance these extremes, both in the individual
(in whom virtue would harmonize the head and the heart) and in
government (in which democratic law would mediate between
political extremes). This beautiful and useful equilibrium, this art
of democracy (an imaginative order or a "temperate liberty") constitutes the underlying aesthetic vision informing Jefferson's *Notes
on the State of Virginia.*

NOTES

1. For a good discussion of the complicated history of the various editions
of this work, see William Peden's introduction to *Notes on the State of*

Virginia (Chapel Hill: University of North Carolina Press, 1954). This edition is the source of my quotations from the *Notes* and will be identified parenthetically in the text as *NSV.*

2. *The Federalist Literary Mind,* ed. Lewis P. Simpson (Baton Rouge: Louisiana State University Press, 1962), 95.

3. *The Federalist Literary Mind,* 83-84. See also Josiah Quincy's apocalyptic portrait of the God-defying forces of liberty in "Climenole, No. 7" (*Port Folio,* March 17, 1804), quoted by Linda K. Kerber, *Federalists in Dissent: Imagery and Ideology in Jeffersonian America* (Ithaca: Cornell University Press, 1970), 177.

4. *The Papers of Thomas Jefferson,* ed. Julian P. Boyd, X (Princeton: Princeton University Press, 1954), 447. Hereinafter this series will be cited parenthetically in the text as *PTJ,* with volume, year, and page numbers.

5. Edwin T. Martin discusses the specific details of the argument in *Thomas Jefferson: Scientist* (New York: Schuman, 1952). See also Ruth Henline, "A Study of *Notes on the State of Virginia* as an Evidence of Jefferson's Reaction against the Theories of the French Naturalists," *Virginia Magazine of History and Bibliography,* 55 (July 1947), 233-46; and Dwight Boehm and Edward Schwartz, "Jefferson and the Theory of Degeneracy," *American Quarterly,* 9 (Winter 1957), 448-53.

6. On Jefferson's entry on religion, see Bernhard Fabian, "Jefferson's *Notes on Virginia*: The Genesis of Query xvii, *The different religions received into that State,*" *William and Mary Quarterly,* 12 (October 1955), 124-38.

7. *The Writings of Thomas Jefferson,* ed. Andrew A. Lipscomb and Albert Bergh, XIV (Washington, D.C.: Thomas Jefferson Memorial Association, 1907), 143. Hereinafter cited parenthetically in the text as *WTJ.*

8. In a letter to Ellen Randolph (July 10, 1805), printed in *Thomas Jefferson's Garden Book* (Philadelphia: American Philosophical Society, 1944), 304.

9. See Eleanor Davidson Berman's useful *Thomas Jefferson among the Arts* (New York: Philosophical Library, 1947). See also Richard Beale Davis, *Intellectual Life in Jefferson's Virginia, 1790-1830* (Chapel Hill: University of North Carolina Press, 1964), 210-11.

10. Jefferson's "major concern was for freedom . . . and he would not leave freedom to chance but would buttress it by law" (Dumas Malone, *Jefferson the Virginian* [Boston: Little Brown & Company, 1948], 380).

11. To be fair, it should be noted that later in the *Notes* Jefferson confesses that "the opinion, that they [the blacks] are inferior in the faculties of reason and imagination, must be hazarded with great diffidence" (*NSV,* 143). See Milton Cantor's interesting essay, "The Image of the Negro in Colonial America," *New England Quarterly,* 36 (December 1963), 452-77.

12. James B. Conant discusses some of Jefferson's attitudes toward education in *Thomas Jefferson and the Development of American Public Education* (Berkeley: University of California Press, 1962).

13. Jefferson speaks similarly in the Inauguration Address of March 4,

1801. See also Bernard W. Sheehan's interesting essay, "Paradise and the Noble Savage in Jeffersonian Thought," *William and Mary Quarterly*, 26 (July 1969), 327-59.

14. See, for instance, Daniel J. Boorstin, *The Lost World of Thomas Jefferson* (New York: Henry Holt & Company, 1948), 227-28. For a discussion of the importance of environment, among other factors, to the central theme of Southern history, see David L. Smiley, "The Quest for the Central Theme in Southern History," *South Atlantic Quarterly*, 71 (Summer 1972), 307-25.

15. Boorstin observes, in a more general context, that "since the hope and the fact were not yet one, the Jeffersonians had a sense of living at the beginning of history" (p. 238).

16. *The Quest for Paradise: Europe and the American Moral Imagination* (Urbana: University of Illinois Press, 1961), 137.

17. *O Strange New World* (New York: Viking Press, 1964), 359.

THE LITERARY AESTHETIC
OF THOMAS JEFFERSON

Stephen D. Cox

It is not easy to identify the basis of Jefferson's literary ideas. No single, dominant theory emerges from the fragments of criticism scattered through his works. In the absence of such a theory, some of Jefferson's commentators have suggested that he was preoccupied with the didactic value of literature. Gilbert Chinard, for instance, denies him an emotively "romantic" taste and asserts that "his was not a poetical mind. Even as a student he read more for profit than for pleasure."[1] Yet there is good reason to believe that Jefferson valued literature as much for its subjective appeal as for its ability to advance the rationalistic principles he admired. In fact, both his critical remarks and his own literary productions suggest that he often viewed rationality and emotive force as related principles. In this essay, I will not attempt to prove that Jefferson's aesthetic was either free from contradictions or particularly ingenious. Rather, I will explore the variety of his responses to literature and illustrate the means he employed—often rather hesitantly, it is true—in attempting to unify his diverse patterns of thought. Finally, I will investigate the manner in which Jefferson's taste in literature manifests itself in his own writings.

As Chinard suggests, some of Jefferson's remarks on literature do not betray an acute sensitivity to purely aesthetic questions. In a well-known letter of 1785, he subordinates *belles-lettres* to less

creative forms of literature by advising Peter Carr, his young correspondent, to spend more time studying history than poetry. He
suggests that Carr read certain modern poets, but only "in order to
form your style in your own language."² This advice suggests that
literature is merely a polite or, at most, a useful accomplishment.
Yet Jefferson's list of recommended poets strongly implies that
the "style" he admires is not merely perspicuous, but imaginative
as well. Along with Pope and Swift, the list includes Milton and
Ossian. It is quite possible that the example of Milton's elevated
manner might be helpful in developing an effective style; but if
this were Jefferson's only purpose in recommending him, he could
easily have suggested more directly useful and contemporary models. Further, it is difficult to believe that Ossian would be useful in
forming anything but highly-wrought sentiments.³

While it may puzzle modern readers, Jefferson's admiration for
Ossian provides a definite indication of his sensibility for emotive
literature. On February 25, 1773, he wrote his acquaintance
Charles McPherson, a relative of Ossian's supposed "translator"
James Macpherson, asking for help in obtaining a Celtic version of
the "bard's" poems. Although Jefferson seems never to have advanced any clear stylistic or didactic reasons for his partiality to
Ossian, in this letter he calls him "the greatest Poet that has ever
existed" because of his "sublime" emotionality: "These peices
[sic] have been, and will I think during my life continue to be to
me, the source of daily and exalted pleasure. The tender, and the
sublime emotions of the mind were never before so finely wrought
up by human hand." After requesting McPherson to disregard expense in procuring a richly bound copy of the manuscript for him,
Jefferson proclaims that "the glow of one warm thought is to me
worth more than money" (*Papers,* I, pp. 96-97). This interest in
Ossian was not temporary. In 1782, the Marquis de Chastellux
found that when Jefferson discussed Ossian the conversation soon
became "a spark of electricity which passed rapidly from one to
the other [as] we recalled the passages of those sublime poems
which had particularly struck us."⁴ Later, Jefferson seems to have
suspected the fraudulent element in Ossianic literature, but he
persisted in admiring it. On November 4, 1823, less than three
years before his death, he wrote to La Fayette that "Ossian, if not
ancient . . . is equal to the best morsels of antiquity."⁵

In valuing Ossian for the "sublime emotions" and "exalted pleasure" which his poems engendered, Jefferson participated in an
important critical phenomenon. As Samuel H. Monk has demonstrated,⁶ the concept of sublimity became more and more influential in English criticism throughout the eighteenth century. By
Jefferson's time, a succession of prominent theorists, including
Richard Hurd, Edmund Burke, and Lord Kames, had adopted sublimity as a major aesthetic principle. Despite their differences on
certain points, such critics agreed that a primary purpose of literature was the encouragement of exalted subjective states. It was
thought that the mind best attains such states when con-
fronted with images that force it beyond its usual conceptions;
and the sources of the sublime were often discovered in descriptions of vast scenes, overpowering forces, or unsearchable mysteries. Theorists of the sublime increasingly concerned themselves
with literature's effects rather than its formal values. Hurd, for
example, exalting poetry's subjective power over its audience, declares that *"rules, art, decorum,* all fall before it. It goes directly to
the *heart,* and gains all purposes at once."⁷

By Jefferson's day, therefore, the concept of sublimity was al-
lied with a subjectivist view of art. In this climate, a literary en-
thusiast like Jefferson might easily believe he had discovered the
sublime in any work which highly pleased him. "Sublimity" is
perhaps the most frequent term in his critical vocabulary. He uses
it so automatically, in fact, that it sometimes loses all critical
meaning. In one of his letters, for example, he calls the whole
exercise of reading classical literature a "sublime luxury."⁸ Even
when he uses the concept in evaluating specific works of literature,
Jefferson usually employs it as an indefinite approbation of whatever he finds affecting. He considered Patrick Henry's oratory sublime, yet he once wryly observed to Daniel Webster that Henry's
speeches had neither a polished delivery nor a particularly memorable content: "His eloquence was peculiar, if indeed it should be
called eloquence; for it was impressive and sublime, beyond what
can be imagined. Although it was difficult when he had spoken to
tell what he had said, yet, while he was speaking, it always seemed
directly to the point. When he had spoken in opposition to my
opinion, had produced a great effect, and I myself been highly
delighted and moved, I have asked myself when he ceased: 'What

the d---l has he said?' I could never answer the inquiry. . . . His pronunciation was vulgar and vicious, but it was forgotten while he was speaking."⁹ Jefferson's idea of the sublimity of Henry's orations probably did not exclude a latent appreciation of their content. He listened to these speeches when revolutionary fervor was steadily increasing, and when both he and Henry were in the vanguard of revolt; despite their differences, it may be supposed that Jefferson was in sympathy with Henry's spirit. His evaluation of Henry does, however, emphasize his own tendency to assert the presence of emotive force in literary works while neglecting to define the qualities that produce it. In his *Autobiography,* Jefferson praises Henry as the greatest orator he ever heard: "He appeared to me to speak as Homer wrote" (Lipscomb, I, p. 5). It would be interesting to discover what similarities Jefferson was able to find between Henry and the ancient poet; yet he immediately drops the comparison, and it is not until fifty pages later that he offers a sketchy outline of Henry's positive characteristics—a "poetical fancy," a "lofty and overwhelming diction," and, of course, a "sublime imagination" (Lipscomb, I, p. 55).

Even Jefferson's technical descriptions of poetry in his *Thoughts on English Prosody* suffer from his tendency to indulge in vaguely impressionistic judgments. In this essay he attempts to classify and define a number of basic literary devices, yet he sometimes loses precision by grounding his opinions on purely individual, subjective experience. He alleges, for instance, that "what proves the excellence of blank verse is that the taste lasts longer than that for rhyme" (Lipscomb, XVIII, p. 447). Since the "taste" he appeals to may differ with every reader, such analysis could hardly culminate in any definitive aesthetic statement. At one point, Jefferson's critical emotionalism forcefully emerges as he denounces an inability to scan one passage of Greek verse properly as if it were a highly serious failure of the human spirit: "Though it is written in the manner of prose, yet he who can read it without pausing at every sixth foot, like him who is insensible to the charm of music, who is insensible of love or of gratitude, is an unfavored son of nature to whom she has given a faculty fewer than to others of her children, one source of pleasure the less in a world where there are none to spare" (Lipscomb, XVIII, p. 442). It is, perhaps, some further indication of the character of Jefferson's literary taste that in choosing examples of poetry for this essay he shows a marked preference for emotive verses from such poets as Collins and Shenstone.

Of course, Jefferson's letters make it obvious that his first allegiance was to ancient authors. Yet when he makes evaluative distinctions between them, he sometimes bases his judgments less on the "classical" principles of balance, economy, and order than on his personal desire for heightened emotions. Sometimes he pointedly contrasts emotive force with the less affecting virtue of correctness. In an exchange with John Adams in 1813, he is forced to allow a measure of sublimity to Cleanthes' hymn to Jupiter: "It is as highly sublime as a chaste and correct imagination can permit itself to go." He insists, however, that a higher form of sublimity exists: "Yet in the contemplation of a being so superlative, the hyperbolic flights of the Psalmist may often be followed with approbation, even with rapture; and I have no hesitation in giving him the palm over all the Hymnists of every language, and of every time. . . . Even [the translator] Sternhold, the leaden Sternhold, kindles, in a single instance, with the sublimity of his original."[10] Jefferson's image of sublimity as a kindling fire and his references to rapture and hyperbole enforce his preference for literature that is expressively emotional rather than decorously correct.

It is clear, then, that a tendency to evaluate literature by its effect on the individual imagination is fundamental to Jefferson's criticism. Yet he was frequently sceptical of literary excess. As Louis B. Wright has suggested,[11] this tendency probably explains his hesitance in commenting on the patriotic fervor of his friend Joel Barlow's *Columbiad.* On receiving a copy in 1801, Jefferson explained to John D. Burke that he considered himself "the last who should undertake to decide as to the merits of poetry. In earlier life I was fond of it, and easily pleased. But as age and cares advanced the powers of fancy have declined."[12] Yet, as Wright observes, Jefferson continued to discuss poetry in his correspondence. Further, it is apparent that he maintained an active interest in the great British reviews.[13] However, he was far from enjoying to the same degree all the literature which he might have recognized as profitable. Some of it he could not appreciate at all. He was capable of sarcastically condemning even patriotic writers when he discovered defects in their style. Writing to Adams on August 22, 1813, Jefferson dissents from John Marshall's attribution of the Petition to the King of 1774 to Richard Henry Lee; he rates Lee's style as "loose, vague, frothy, rhetorical. He was a poorer writer than his brother Arthur; and Arthur's standing may be seen in his Monitor's letters, to ensure the sale of which they took the precaution of tacking to them a new edition of the Farmer's letters; like Mezentius who 'mortua jungebat corpora vivis ["bound dead bodies to the living"]' " (Letters, II, pp. 369-70). On the other hand, in a letter to Adams on October 14, 1816, Jefferson commends Destutt de Tracy's Treatise on Political Economy because "all it's principles are demonstrated with the severity of Euclid, and, like him, without ever using a superfluous word. I have procured this to be translated, and have been 4 years endeavoring to get it printed" (Letters, II, p. 491). Despite his Ossianic enthusiasm, Jefferson maintained a respect for rational clarity of expression which comports well with his interest in the classics.

Additionally, of course, Jefferson's taste for emotive literature was moderated by concern for philosophic and moral truth. As Richard Beale Davis has remarked, he was not "a thoroughgoing impressionist, either in criticism or creation. . . . Jefferson many times emphasized the utilitarian moral quality of good literature."[14] Jefferson was capable, on occasion, of overlooking stylistic defects when he was satisfied that an author had correctly fulfilled his didactic function; and, as might be expected, he was particularly concerned about the effect of literature on political ideology. For instance, writing to Madison on February 17, 1826, he states that he considers the "black-letter text, and uncouth but cunning learning" of Coke's seventeenth-century legal commentary far superior to "the honied Mansfieldism of Blackstone"; Coke, unlike Blackstone, possesses the correct "political principles" (Lipscomb, XVI, p. 156). Although he enjoyed David Hume's stylistic excellence, Jefferson maintained that this virtue makes Hume's reactionary principles even more dangerous, because he "has consecrated, in his fascinating style, all the arbitrary proceedings of the English kings."[15]

Jefferson's interest in didacticism emerges in a particularly crude form in a letter written on March 14, 1818, to Nathaniel Burwell, who had solicited his advice on the education of girls. Here Jefferson denounces modern novels; they are "poison" because they are useless and unrealistic. They lead their readers to reject anything that is not "dressed in all the figments of fancy. . . . The result is a bloated imagination, sickly judgment, and disgust towards all the real businesses of life." Only if novels are firmly founded "on the incidents of real life" can they be "interesting and useful vehicles of a sound morality." He recommends the works of the novelists Maria Edgeworth and Madame de Genlis and the sentimental *Moral Tales* of Jean François Marmontel ("but not his old ones, which are really immoral"). On the same ground of practical morality, he advises that "much poetry should not be indulged. Some is useful for forming style and taste. Pope, Dryden, Thompson, Shakspeare [sic], and of the French, Molière, Racine, the Corneilles, may be read with pleasure and improvement" (Lipscomb, XV, p. 166).

If nothing else, the Burwell letter is emphatic. Yet its importance in the total context of Jefferson's thought should probably not be over-emphasized. His endorsement of didacticism was usually not so simplistic. The taste of his age could, no doubt, extract a useful moral from most of the literature Jefferson enjoyed; yet his letters do not show that he was much more assiduous in deriving specific moral judgments than specific aesthetic principles from literature. The steady vituperation of the Burwell letter seems to be unique among Jefferson's remarks on literature's moral utility. Nowhere else does he discourse so violently on literary threats to virtue, or so determinedly disparage the imagination. In fact, in a letter written to Adams on April 20, 1812, he refers to the "display of imagination" as that which "constitutes excellence in Belles lettres" (*Letters,* II, p. 298). It seems likely that Jefferson intended his advice to Burwell to be applied only to the then-limited scope of female education, a topic which he admits at the start "has never been a subject of systematic contemplation with me" (Lipscomb, XV, p. 165).

On August 3, 1771, Jefferson had addressed a more detailed discussion of literary didacticism to his correspondent Robert Skipwith. In this letter, he firmly allies moral utility with imaginative power. He argues that fiction is more useful than history in exciting men to virtuous action, because the imagination can construct a wider variety of affecting images than the study of history can discover: "Considering history as a moral exercise, her lessons would be too infrequent if confined to real life. Of those recorded by historians few incidents have been attended with such circumstances as to excite in any high degree [a] sympathetic emotion of virtue. We are therefore wisely framed to be as warmly interested for a fictitious as for a real personage. The spacious field of imagination is thus laid open to our use, and lessons may be formed to illustrate . . . every moral rule of life." It should be noted that Jefferson proceeds to this particular justification of fiction only after recording what he considers the obvious assumption that "the entertainments of fiction . . . are pleasant when well written, [as] every person feels who reads," and after mildly satirizing the torpid "gravity" which cannot be aroused by these "entertainments" (*Papers,* I, pp. 76-77). This is the ardent letter of a young man; yet its defense of imaginative pleasures is integrated with both the major impulses we have found in Jefferson's later criticism—the quest for moral efficacy and the desire for powerful feeling.

As might be expected, however, sometimes when he attempts to evaluate artists whose style he admires but whose ideas offend him, he must struggle hard to define a standard of emotionally effective yet useful literature. Unfortunately, his critical remarks contain few of these crucial struggles. His susceptibility to enthusiasm sometimes betrayed him into uncritical admirations. He lacked the passionate scepticism of his correspondent John Adams, who railed at Homer for making his gods a "Rabble of the Classic Skies" and in a burst of indignation denounced the philosophy of all the great figures of the Enlightenment, from Voltaire to Gibbon, as "insideous, fraudulent hypocritical and cruel." [16] Jefferson neglected even to respond to these opinions. His taste was broad and genial, and he seldom insisted that literary works conform completely to his own moral and political philosophy in order to merit his approval.

Yet at times Jefferson attempted to define his critical attitude somewhat more precisely than usual and to recognize and balance his contrary impulses toward literature. An interesting example is furnished by two similar letters—one written to Adams on July 5, 1814, and the other to William Short on October 31, 1819. In both letters, Jefferson expresses an opinion of Plato and of Cicero, whom he considers Plato's ideological ally. Although he was never fond of Plato, his reaction to Cicero wavered between admiration and boredom.[17] These letters, however, attempt a more judicious judgment of both men. In the first, Jefferson decides that Cicero was "the first master in the world" of style, but regrets his "eulogies" of Plato. He admits that Plato attained an elegant diction, but he suggests that the mysticism of his philosophy destroyed much of his literary, as well as ideological, merit by corrupting his diction with "unintelligible jargon." Further, Jefferson alleges that this combination of philosophical and verbal confusion has been highly useful to the aggressive enemies of reason: "The Christian priesthood, finding the doctrines of Christ levelled to every understanding and too plain to need explanation, saw, in the mysticisms of Plato, materials with which they might build up an artificial system which might, from it's indistinctness, admit everlasting controversy, give employment for their order, and introduce it to profit, power and pre-eminence" (*Letters*, II, pp. 432-33). In the letter to Short, Jefferson resumes his attack against the "mysticisms incomprehensible to the human mind" with which the admittedly "eloquent" Plato defiled his works. Although he refers to Cicero as "enchanting," in the same breath he juxtaposes him with "his prototype Plato" and judges the Roman's style also as partially corrupt—"diffuse, vapid, rhetorical." He vigorously recommends Jesus' teachings as a salutary contrast to the complexities of Platonism and, implying the style and ideology are somehow corollaries, boldly asserts that Jesus' "innocent" philosophy can be recognized amid the "rubbish" of the crudely mystical Gospel writers by "the stamp of [his] eloquence and fine imagination" (Lipscomb, XV, pp. 219-21). It would be difficult to advance a more forthright claim that some crucial relationship exists between truth and imagination! Jefferson's judgments of Plato, Cicero, and Jesus indicate that, although he was quite capable of judging form and content separately, he was edging toward a literary attitude which attempts to discover a relationship between them.

Further, it is evident that Jefferson tended to reserve his highest praise for literature which expresses rational truth in a lucid but affecting manner. Unlike many of his contemporaries, he usually did not associate the sublime with Gothic obscurity but with a kind of sensitive rationality. He believed that Jesus, whom he did not consider divine, had achieved both truth and imaginative eloquence by returning to a state of benevolent reasonableness. Writing to Adams on October 12, 1813, Jefferson advances an analogous opinion about the rational origin of Socrates' teachings: "What did Socrates mean by his Daemon? he was too wise to believe, and too honest to pretend that he had real and familiar converse with a superior and invisible being. He probably considered the suggestions of his conscience, or reason, as revelations, or inspirations from the Supreme mind."[18] In the same letter, Jefferson relates his own project of cutting verse after "unintelligible" verse out of the mystic "dunghill" of the Gospels in order to preserve only the actual teachings of Jesus, which are both clear and "sublime." In the case of both Jesus and Socrates, therefore, Jefferson considers that sublimity proceeds from nothing more than a rational conscience; all else, in his word, is artificial "Nonsense" (*Letters,* II, pp. 384-85).

Unfortunately, although Jefferson is usually a vigorous critic of philosophy, his stylistic judgments are characteristically imperfect. Yet this is no sign that he was disposed to make aesthetics entirely dependent on ethics and metaphysics. Just as he claims to distinguish Jesus' true philosophy by his eloquence, so Jefferson sometimes withholds the laurels of sublimity from philosophically admirable authors whose style lacks either lucidity or high emotional effect. Even Seneca, whom he applauds as "a fine Moralist," misses the sublime by "affecting too much of antithesis and point."[19] Writing to Francis Eppes on January 19, 1821, Jefferson makes an interesting comparison between the achievements of Thomas Paine and Lord Bolingbroke. He judges their ideas with almost equal favor: "Both were honest men: both advocates for human liberty." Yet after praising Paine's "simple" but admirable style, he turns with apparently greater enthusiasm to Bolingbroke's sonorous eloquence. He characterizes Bolingbroke as "sublime"; then he introduces a list of his most agreeable qualities: "Lord Bolingbroke's . . . is a style of the highest order. The lofty, rhythmical, full-flowing eloquence of Cicero. Periods of just measure, their members proportioned, their close full and round. His conceptions, too, are bold and strong, his diction copious, polished and commanding as his subject. His writings are certainly the finest samples in the English language, of the eloquence proper for the Senate" (Lipscomb, XV, pp. 305-306).

Of course, these judgments hardly constitute incisive criticism. Jefferson again employs some of the indefinite terms he habitually uses; although even in his enthusiasm he might shrink from directly asserting the similarity of two figures as diverse as Jesus and Bolingbroke, his criticism does not hesitate to apply the same label of sublimity to both. The label shows that Jefferson found in each the eloquence and rationality he admired. But although such judgments cannot very well be molded into a complete and coherent aesthetic, they are implicitly grounded on what might be called a standard of rationalistic sublimity—on the idea that the products of man's reason should arouse his most sublime emotions.

There is, of course, a close alliance between Jefferson's aesthetic ideals and his belief in liberty and rational social progress. He believed that the freest societies tend to produce the most eloquent men. In *Notes on the State of Virginia,* he favorably compares an American Indian oration, Logan's Speech, with "the whole orations of Demosthenes and Cicero," and explains that the power of Indian oratory is encouraged by what he regards as the liberty of Indian society: "The principles of their society forbidding all compulsion, they are to be led to duty and to enterprize by personal influence and persuasion. Hence eloquence in council, bravery and address in war, become the foundations of all consequence with them."[20] In a letter to John Bannister, Jr. (October 15, 1785), Jefferson exalts the reasonable simplicity and liberty of American society above the decadence of Europe, and represents imaginative eloquence as both the natural product of a free society and also the quality which that society rewards most readily:

> Let us view the disadvantages of sending a youth to Europe. . . . He returns to his own country, a foreigner . . . speaking and writing his native tongue as a foreigner, and therefore unqualified to obtain those distinctions which eloquence of the pen and tongue ensures in a free country; for I would observe to you that what is called style in writing

or speaking is formed very early in life while the imagination is warm, and impressions are permanent. . . . Cast your eye over America: who are the men of most learning, of most eloquence, most beloved by their country[men] and most trusted and promoted by them? They are those who have been educated among them, and whose manners, morals and habits are perfectly homogeneous with those of the country (*Papers,* VIII, p. 637).

Jefferson additionally believed that in a revolutionary age all men might progress to the sublimity of reason. Writing to Adams on May 5, 1817, for example, he hails the "advances of the mind" which can be made by abandoning the "Monkish darkness" of irrational tradition in favor of "the moral precepts, innate in man" and "the sublime doctrines of philanthropism, and deism taught us by Jesus of Nazareth" (*Letters,* II, p. 512).

Jefferson's concern for a rationalistic sublimity achieves some interesting expressions in his own literary works about the history and politics of his time. Sometimes, it must be admitted, his prose is merely routine—correct, but unexciting. Yet often it is exalted by his aspiration for the sublime. Jefferson's descriptions of nature in *Notes on Virginia* are probably his best-known attempts at lyric emotionality. In one instance, delighting in the "wild and tremendous" mountain scenery which he describes at some length, and speculating on its geologic origins, he offers the following reflection: "This scene is worth a voyage across the Atlantic. Yet here, as in the neighbourhood of the natural bridge, are people who have passed their lives within half a dozen miles, and have never been to survey these monuments of a war between rivers and mountains, which must have shaken the earth itself to its center" (*Notes,* pp. 19-20). A curious but, I think, significant analogy exists between this passage and certain others in Jefferson's works. Just as he here discovers the sublime in geological forces, so at other times he evokes the sublimity of tumultuous historical processes, particularly of revolutionary struggles for reason and liberty.

One would expect to find emotional effect in his writings on the American Revolution, especially the Declaration of Independence. In writing the Declaration, Jefferson acted somewhat like a lawyer preparing a brief, justifying action taken against the offending monarch by citing a series of particular violations of funda-

mental law. Yet he was successful in placing rational proof in an
emotive context. He deeply regretted the editing that Congress
perfomed on his original draft,[21]and a glance at the portions removed shows that they contained some of his most emotional
passages. In summarizing the grievances of America against the
English nation, Jefferson becomes almost maudlin: "These facts
have given the last stab to agonizing affection, and manly spirit
bids us to renounce for ever these unfeeling brethren. we must
endeavor to forget our former love for them, and to [hold them as
we hold the rest of mankind enemies in war, in peace friends] . we
might have been a free and a great people together; but a communication of grandeur & of freedom it seems is below their dignity. be it so, since they will have it. the road to happiness & to
glory is open to us too." [22] Jefferson would have concluded this
sententiously emotional passage with a declaration not only of
"separation," but of "eternal separation." In another passage ultimately deleted, he challenges the reader's imagination to con-
ceive the British monarch's villainy: "Future ages will scarcely
believe that the hardiness of one man adventured, within the short
compass of twelve years only, to lay a foundation so broad & so
undisguised for tyranny over a people fostered & fixed in principles of freedom" (*Papers,* I, pp. 318-19). If, according to late eighteenth-century ideas, the sublime can be suggested by depicting
extreme actions, states, or qualities, then this polemic clearly as-
pires to a type of sublimity.

Jefferson's other works also frequently contain highly-wrought
passages; and, although he is seldom very original in creating them,
he at least employs them forcefully. He often represents revolutionary progress by vivid images of fire and light, as when, writing
to Adams on July 9, 1819, he recalls Henry's resolutions of 1775
as "lightning" that "kindled both sides of the Atlantic" (*Letters,*
II, p. 543). Sometimes he images the drama of progress as a battle
between the natural, freely-spreading fire of liberty and the tight-
ly-controlled, artificial "engines" of tyranny. On September 12,
1821, he proclaims to Adams that "the flames kindled on the 4th.
of July 1776. have spread over too much of the globe to be
extinguished by the feeble engines of despotism. On the contrary
they will consume those engines, and all who work them" (*Let-*

ters, II, p. 575). The idea of weakness incorporated in this image is an attribute Jefferson typically associates with tyranny. He frequently contrasts the essential impotence of states governed by irrational authority with the might of free men. Writing Adams on August 1, 1816, he prophesies that America will become a titanic champion of reason and liberty: "We are destined to be a barrier against the returns of ignorance and barbarism. Old Europe will have to lean on our shoulders, and to hobble along by our side, under the monkish trammels of priests and kings, as she can. What a Colossus shall we be when the Southern continent comes up to our mark! What a stand will it secure as a ralliance for the reason and freedom of the globe. I like the dreams of the future better than the history of the past" (*Letters,* II, pp. 484-85).

In his desire to find the proper emotional pitch, Jefferson sometimes produces rather ambitious arrays of imagery. In another letter written to Adams (January 11, 1816), a characteristic assertion that the "light from our West seems to have spread and illuminated the very engines employed to extinguish it" is one of a variety of exclamatory images representing scenes in the battle for liberty in Europe. In Jefferson's imagination, "rivers of blood" gush forth; "oppressors . . . cut off heads after heads, but like those of the Hydra, they multiply at every stroke"; captive peoples rise in insurrection; armies march back and forth across Europe; and the continent degenerates into "an Arena of gladiators" (*Letters,* II, pp. 459-60). Jefferson leaves no device untried in depicting the arduous ascent toward rational liberty as a drama of sublime violence.

Late eighteenth-century taste was far from confining the sublime to images which are gratifying in themselves. On the contrary, sublimity was often derived directly from terror. As Samuel Monk has remarked, Edmund Burke's *Philosophical Enquiry into the Origin of Our Ideas of the Sublime and Beautiful* (1756), which gives special critical approbation to the terrible, "provided the age with an idea of sublimity that suited nicely its increasingly sensational tastes" (*The Sublime,* p. 99).[23] Jefferson certainly conforms to this sensibility by using images of terror to heighten the emotional tone of his descriptions of political and historical events. He typically employs hyperbolic expressions in reference to reactionary forces, denouncing them as "Incendiaries," or noting with disgust that "the Cannibals of Europe are going to eating [sic] one another again." [24] The essential humorlessness that Richard Beale Davis has remarked in Jefferson [25] reveals itself in grimly unfunny sarcasms. Through the years, Jefferson poured a torrent of transcendent abuse on his great enemy Napoleon. He represented the dictator as "the Attila of the age . . . the ruthless destroyer of 10. millions of the human race"; as "a moral monster" possessed of "a ravenous thirst for human blood"; and, after the Emperor's final defeat, as an "exorcised demon." [26] Jefferson's ability to magnify the wickedness of his adversaries significantly aids his attempt to portray contemporary history as a tale fraught with sublime importance.

But although Jefferson's flashes of invective are entertaining, he shows his skill as a writer to greater advantage when he develops more extended literary effects. The latter part of his *Autobiography* in particular, shows Jefferson at his best at integrating "sublime" effects into a narrative structure. Jefferson began shaping old letters, documents, and observations into a story of his life in 1821; he eventually completed recording events up to 1790. The *Autobiography* is almost entirely occupied with his public life, and makes only passing references to his marriage and the deaths of his wife and one of his daughters. Unfortunately, its first sections, which recount Jefferson's role in Congress and in the Virginia legislature, can hardly be considered as emotive, or even very well-structured narrative. With a lawyerly interest in detail, Jefferson descends to minute descriptions of the legislative procedures he witnessed and the documents he wrote or reviewed; in this case, the fact that these proceedings were revolutionary and that one of these documents was the Declaration of Independence seldom awakens his eloquence. Although he includes several lively descriptions of men and events, he generally limits himself in these early sections to fulfilling the pragmatic intention he states at the beginning: "At the age of 77, I begin to make some memoranda, and state some recollections of dates and facts concerning myself, for my own more ready reference, and for the information of my family" (Lipscomb, I, p. 1). [27] But Jefferson's description of the opening days of the French Revolution, which fills most of the second half of his *Autobiography,* shows much more conscious art. Following his characteristic method of drawing extreme contrasts between progressive and reactionary forces, Jefferson repeatedly strives to reveal sublimity in the events he describes.

Beginning his account with a discussion of the "remote causes" of the Revolution (p. 102), he distinguishes the rational and libertarian proceedings of American statesmen from the degraded maneuvers of European courts. He describes the farcical politics surrounding France's abortive intervention in Holland in 1786 and 1787, revealing the feeble stupidity of almost all the European leaders involved (pp. 108-16). Beside these emblems of wretched failure Jefferson tellingly inserts a discussion of the successful formation of the American Constitution. He emphasizes the fact that American "good sense" has avoided the irrational violence to which France was destined, and represents the success of rational politics as "a happy augury of the future march of our Confederacy" (p. 117). Jefferson later uses this metaphor of orderly progression—the "march" of free men—to great effect. When he describes the beginning of the French Assembly's deliberations on the Declaration of the Rights of Man, he states that "the quiet of their march was soon disturbed by information that troops, and particularly the foreign troops, were advancing on Paris from various quarters. The King had probably been advised to this, on the pretext of preserving peace in Paris" (p. 143). By repeating his metaphor, Jefferson thus establishes a poignant contrast between the rational advance of freedom and the false order which the marching troops of tyranny would impose upon society.

Yet before he depicts the actual outbreak of violent revolution, Jefferson's imagery effectively expresses the violent political polarization that caused it. He sharply contrasts the French people's growing pressure against a multitude of lurid abuses with the cool indolence of the French ministry in enacting reforms, and he invokes his characteristic imagery of inhumanly savage oppression by declaring that "this people were ground to powder" by "monstrous abuses of power" (p. 127). This image is particularly apt, because it suggests not merely the atomized subjection of the French people, but also the fact that they were numerous and therefore potentially dangerous.

Having indicated the people's condition, Jefferson gradually describes the other leading forces involved in the Revolution, sometimes succinctly characterizing them by forceful images of weakness or strength, artifice or candor. For example, Louis XVI, while at heart a good man, is easily controlled by those who surround him, whether they happen to be "high-flying" aristocrats "noted . . . for the Turkish despotism of their characters" (pp. 143, 144), or the moderate leaders of the National Assembly under whose control Louis eventually becomes "a passive machine" (p. 150). Jefferson draws an emblem of deceptive beauty in his character of Marie Antoinette. Though she is adorned by Burke's false eloquence, her decadence and irrationality belie her pretensions to grandeur and fix on her the responsibility for the greatest crimes:

> This angel, as gaudily painted in the rhapsodies of Burke, with some smartness of fancy, but no sound sense, was proud, disdainful of restraint, indignant at all obstacles to her will, eager in the pursuit of pleasure, and firm enough to hold to her desires, or perish in their wreck. Her inordinate gambling and dissipations, . . . her inflexible perverseness, and dauntless spirit, led herself to the Guillotine, drew the King on with her, and plunged the world into crimes and calamities which will forever stain the pages of modern history (pp. 150-51).

On the other hand, Jefferson invariably represents the friends of liberty as rational, strong in moral force, and candid. They are "of honest but differing opinions, sensible of the necessity of effecting a coalition by mutual sacrifices, knowing each other, and not afraid, therefore, to unbosom themselves mutually." Their leader, La Fayette, is strength incarnate, an "Atlas, who had no secrets from me" (pp. 155-56, 158).

Having drawn two highly opposed sets of characters, Jefferson does not merely summarize the effects of their actions, but strives for dramatic impact by allowing them to display their natures in a number of vividly realized scenes. He shows a considerable ability to isolate salient details in the events he describes. Several lengthy passages could be cited which exemplify his effectiveness in narrating violent action; but instead of quoting these, it might be more interesting to illustrate his facility for maximizing the impact of comparatively unimportant scenes. In the following passage, Jefferson uses simple syntax and diction and records only a few details, yet he manages to suggest a comprehensive view of the state of French affairs at the beginning of revolt: "The Queen sent for M. Necker. He was conducted, amidst the shouts and acclamations of the multitude, who filled all the apartments of the palace. He was a few minutes only with the Queen, and what passed between them did not transpire. The King went out to ride. He passed through the crowd to his carriage, and into it, without being in the least noticed. As M. Necker followed him, universal acclamations were raised of 'vive Monsieur Necker, vive le sauveur de la France opprimée' " (p. 141). The Queen's uncommunicative isolation in her palace is a detail which finely suggests her nature as Jefferson wished to portray it—that of a plotting, luxurious éminence grise. The crowd's reactions not only represent the excited state of the public mind and the good opinion generally held about Necker's benevolence in attempting to reform the state; they also validate Jefferson's judgment of the King's weak, inconsequential character.

Jefferson does not, however, confine himself to vivid descriptions of revolutionary events; he also explicitly tries to exalt their importance. In order to do so, he surrounds the contrasting extremes of "monstrous" oppression and calmly rational liberation with highly emotive imagery. He speaks of the desired success of the Revolution under the metaphor of rebirth: "I considered a successful reformation of government in France, as insuring a general reformation through Europe, and the resurrection, to a new life, of their people, now ground to dust by the abuses of governing powers" (p. 139). Having secularized this leading metaphor of religion to express the sublimity of the universal struggle for liberty, he later employs contrasting extremes of negative imagery to depict the Satanic results of that struggle's temporary failure. Lamenting the course of European history after 1789, he attacks "the atrocious conspiracy of Kings against their people; . . . their unholy and homicide alliance to make common cause among themselves and to crush, by the power of the whole, the efforts of any part to moderate their abuses and opressions" (p. 140). Later, he regrets that the Revolution's failure led to the "usurpation of a military adventurer," Napoleon, and to "those enormities which demoralized the nations of the world, and destroyed, and is [sic] yet to destroy, millions and millions of its inhabitants." This is the prologue to a universal survey of human wickedness:

> There are three epochs in history, signalized by the total extinction of national morality. The first was of the successors of Alexander, not omitting himself: The next, the successors of the first Caesar: The third, our own age. This was begun by the partition of Poland, followed by that of the treaty of Pilnitz; next the conflagration of Copenhagen; then the enormities of Bonaparte, partitioning the earth at his will, and devastating it with fire and sword; now the conspiracy of Kings, the successors of Bonaparte, blasphemously calling themselves the Holy Alliance, and treading in the footsteps of their incarcerated leader (p. 152).

Of course, the *Autobiography* as a whole patently constitutes a recommendation of rationalistic progress; yet it gains its considerable emotive force from Jefferson's contrastive method, his ability to portray contemporary events as part of a crucial struggle between two transcendent principles—the heroic desire to recreate the world, and the demonic impulse to tyrannize over its ruins. This work can therefore be viewed as a notable attempt on Jefferson's part to realize his critical insistence on both rationalism and sublimity.

It is interesting to note that the *Autobiography* employs aesthetic as well as political principles to distinguish positive from negative historical figures. Jefferson's sarcastic allusion to Burke's role in disguising Marie Antoinette as a gaudy "angel" recalls his disgust for Plato's habit of concealing falshood beneath a superficially eloquent style. By contrast, Jefferson praises the French liberals who met with him in Paris as statesmen of an exalted order who had achieved the highest eloquence through their devotion to reason: "I was a silent witness to a coolness and candor of argument, unusual in the conflicts of political opinion; to a logical reasoning, and chaste eloquence, disfigured by no gaudy tinsel of rhetoric or declamation, and truly worthy of being placed in parallel with the finest dialogues of antiquity, as handed to us by Xenophon, by Plato and Cicero" (p. 156).

These remarks give us evidence once again, of course, that Jefferson's enthusiastic critical judgments may frequently sound simplistic or naive. Had he analyzed literature more systematically, he might have refined his ideas on the connection between reason and artistic excellence into more incisive observations. His criticism suffers from his tendency casually to suggest, from time to time, some new and rather imperfect relation between rational philosophy and effective art. Yet the same tendency likely helped him to enliven his own writing by converting political ideas into strongly emotional effects. Whether he is depicting the sublimity of revolutionary history or describing the libertarian genesis of artistic creation, he struggles to exalt his subject to a level of transcendent importance. No account of his critical ideas should neglect the fact that for Jefferson the act of reason can be the ally, rather than the enemy, of the aesthetic impulse.

NOTES

1. *The Literary Bible of Thomas Jefferson* (Baltimore: Johns Hopkins Press, 1928), 32. Susan Ford, in "Thomas Jefferson and John Adams on the Classics," *Arion*, VI (Spring 1967), 122, also concludes that Jefferson was not "particularly poetic by nature" and emphasizes his interest in didacticism. Although he qualifies Chinard's judgment, Merrill D. Peterson in *The Jefferson Image in the American Mind* (New York: Oxford University Press, 1960), 408, considers Jefferson's esthetic interest clearly less important than his taste for literary moralism.

2. August 19, 1785, in *The Papers of Thomas Jefferson*, ed. Julian P. Boyd (Princeton: Princeton University Press, 1950-), VIII, 407-408. This edition cited hereafter as *Papers*.

3. In her valuable *Thomas Jefferson among the Arts* (New York: Philosophical Library, 1947), Eleanor Berman, arguing against Chinard, clearly establishes the presence of considerable emotionality in Jefferson's taste. Yet she concludes that "profit was pleasure" for Jefferson, and that "his touchstone was always the social uses of expression and communication" (232, 201). Her account over-emphasizes the degree to which his literary pleasure was habitually identified with, and simply included within, his "utilitarian" concern for instructive reading and authorial technique. As a result, she seems to imply that didactic interest might even explain Jefferson's great enthusiasm for Ossian (201-202).

4. *Travels in North America in the Years 1780, 1781, and 1782*, revised trans. by Howard C. Rice, Jr. (Chapel Hill: Univerisity of North Carolina Press, 1963), II, 392.

5. *The Writings of Thomas Jefferson*, ed. Andrew A. Lipscomb and Albert

Ellery Bergh (Washington: Jefferson Memorial Association, 1905), XV, 493. This edition cited hereafter as Lipscomb.

6. *The Sublime: A Study of Critical Theories in XVIII-Century England* (1935; rpt. Ann Arbor: University of Michigan Press, 1960). My discussion of the concept of sublimity follows Monk's general conclusions.

7. "Notes on the Epistle to Augustus," in *Q. Horatii Flacci, Epistolae ad Pisones et Augustum* (London: Bowyer, 1776), II, 116.

8. To Joseph Priestley, January 27, 1800, Lipscomb, X, 146-147.

9. *The Private Correspondence of Daniel Webster*, ed. Fletcher Webster (Boston: Little, Brown, 1857), I, 367.

10. October 12, 1813, in *The Adams-Jefferson Letters*, ed. Lester J. Cappon (Chapel Hill: University of North Carolina Press, 1959), II, 385. This edition hereafter cited as *Letters*.

11. "Thomas Jefferson and the Classics," *Proceedings of the American Philosophical Society*, LXXXVII (July, 1943), 229.

12. June 21, 1801, in *The Writings of Thomas Jefferson*, Federal Edition, ed. Paul Leicester Ford (New York: Putnam, 1905), IX, 267. See also Jefferson's less than enthusiastic response to Barlow himself on January 24, 1808, in Lipscomb, XI, 430.

13. Letters to John Waldo, August 16, 1813, and to John F. Watson, May 17, 1814, in Lipscomb, XIII, 340, 346; XIV, 134-36.

14. *Intellectual Life in Jefferson's Virginia, 1790-1830* (Chapel Hill: University of North Carolina Press, 1964), 256.

15. To Adams, November 25, 1816, *Letters*, II, 498.

16. December 16, 1816, and June 20, 1815, *Letters*, II, 503, 445-46.

17. To George W. Summers and John B. Garland, February 27, 1822; to John Wayles Eppes, January 17, 1810; in Lipscomb, XV, 353; XII, 343.

18. It should be noted that just as Jefferson distinguished Jesus' own teachings from those of his disciples, so he also distinguished "the superlative wisdom of Socrates" from Plato's representation of it. See letters to William Short, October 31, 1819, and August 4, 1820, in Lipscomb, XV, 220, 258.

19. To William Short, October 31, 1819, in Lipscomb, XV, 220.

20. Ed. William Peden (Chapel Hill: University of North Carolina Press, 1955), 62. Hereafter cited as *Notes*.

21. "Anecdotes of Benjamin Franklin," from letter of December 4, 1818, to Robert Walsh, Lipscomb, XVIII, 169.

22. Quotation follows the text from Jefferson's "Notes of Proceedings in the Continental Congress." Brackets enclose words retained by Congress.

23. See *Philosophical Enquiry*, 3rd ed. (London: Dodsley, 1761), 96-98.

24. To Adams, November 25, 1816, and June 1, 1822, *Letters*, II, 496, 578.

25. *Intellectual Life in Jefferson's Virginia, 1790-1830*, 292.

26. To Adams, July 5, 1814, February 25, 1823, and June 10, 1815, in *Letters*, II, 431, 589, and 442; to Benjamin Austin, February 9, 1816, in Lipscomb, XIV, 436.

27. Henceforth all references are to page numbers in the first volume of the Lipscomb edition.

TUCKER'S
"HERMIT OF THE MOUNTAIN" ESSAY:
PROLEGOMENON FOR A COLLECTED EDITION

Carl Dolmetsch

Although St. George Tucker quite probably engaged in belletristic efforts at sporadic intervals from his student days at the College of William and Mary before the Revolutionary War until sometime near the end of his life, in 1827, only those of his compositions written before 1800 have been known to historians of our early literature. The reason for this, quite simply, is that all but a small fraction of what Tucker wrote after *The Probationary Odes of Jonathan Pindar* (Philadelphia, 1796) remains as yet unpublished and has been known only to such scholars as Jay B. Hubbell, Richard Beale Davis, Lewis Leary and a handful of others. Fortunately, a large body of Tucker's post-1796 literary manuscripts—including four plays and a considerable amount of poetical and prose writings—together with a large quantity of his correspondence and the major portion of his personal library survives in the Tucker-Coleman Collection of the Swem Library at the College of William and Mary. All of these manuscripts, it is to be hoped, will soon be published and, when they are at long last made accessible, St. George Tucker will be seen to have been a far more important writer than has previously been supposed and a literary figure of national, not merely regional significance.

Among Tucker's extant manuscripts are twenty holograph essays (two of which exist in more than one version) written mainly in August and September 1811 and headed, on each composition, "FOR THE OLD BACHELLOR" [sic] and two later essays (plus a fragment of a third) written September 1813 in a holograph notebook and bearing the title NUGA: THE HERMIT OF THE MOUNTAIN. It is clear from the extant correspondence between Tucker and his friend and fellow-jurist, William Wirt, that, although the "old Batchellor" and "Hermit" works were composed under differing circumstances and for different purposes, it was their author's ultimate but unfulfilled intention to integrate all of these essays into a single collection to be published under the latter title.

The history of the composition of these "Hermit of the Mountain" essays, as I believe they must properly be designated, as well as their author's intention concerning them cannot be understood without some detailed discussion of the series of Addisonian essays, entitled *The Old Bachelor,* which began appearing on December 22, 1810 in Thomas Ritchie's Richmond *Enquirer;* they continued through twenty-eight numbers at irregular intervals until December 24, 1811 and were gathered, together with five other essays, into book form by Ritchie in 1814.[1] *The Old Bachelor* was a collaborative effort, presided over by its chief contributor and guiding spirit, William Wirt, and enlisting the pens of a circle of Wirt's and Tucker's Virginian friends that included the brothers Frank and Dabney Carr, Richard E. Parker, Dr. Louis Girardin, George Tucker (cousin of St. George's and possibly the most illustrious writer of the group, saving only Wirt himself), and Major David Watson. It is possible but, as we shall see, by no means certain that St. George Tucker may have contributed one essay to the series himself. Both Davis and Hubbell have, before now, assumed that he did so and Wirt's biographer, John Pendelton Kennedy, listed "Judge Tucker" (as distinct from Professor George Tucker) among the asserted contributors to *The Old Bachelor* without linking any specific contribution to him.[2]

This series, which Richard Beale Davis has called, perhaps a bit too enthusiastically, "the high watermark of the familiar essay in the early nineteenth century in Virginia and in some respects in the whole nation," was the successor to a similar series of *Enquirer* essays, entitled *The Rainbow,* to which Wirt and most of the members of the "Old Bachelor" circle (plus two or three others) had contributed in 1804.[3] The immediate predecessor to the series, however, was *The Sylph,* an abortive series of essays conceived by Wirt in November 1810 and quickly dropped because he thought it displayed "too palpable fiction, want of community of character and interests, and unmanageability. . . ."[4] Unlike *The Sylph,* which seems to have been suggested without much forethought, *The Old Bachelor* was carefully conceived, planned, and directed by Wirt to carry out a thoroughly didactic function in an entertaining way. As Wirt made clear in the twelfth number, its purpose was to

> endeavor to awake the taste of the body of the people for literary attainments; to make them sensible of the fallen state of intellect in our country; to excite the emulation of the rising race, and see whether a groupe [sic] of statesmen, scholars, orators, and patriots, as enlightened and illustrious as their fathers, cannot be produced without the aid of such another bloody and fatal stimulant.[5]

There is an ominous note in the phrase "such another bloody and fatal stimulant" here which reminds one that these essays were written in troubled times leading up to the War of 1812. Indeed, the series may best be read against the background of the immediate pre-war disturbances in the social and political climate of Virginia and the nation.

The "Old Bachelor" of the title was the fictitious "Dr. Robert Cecil," the principal pseudonym of William Wirt himself in the series. The good doctor introduced himself and gave something of his personal history in the opening number. He was, he claimed, of good family, well-educated and widely travelled in his country and abroad, and a bit melancholic, having given up the active practice of medicine after his first patient, his own mother, died in his arms. Nevertheless, he added, "Enthusiasm is the promient feature of my character," and he did not hesitate to arrogate to himself the role of a "teacher" of the young.[6] In subsequent numbers he added autobiographical details and introduced the members of his "family," consisting of two nephews, "Galen" and "Alfred"—who later contibuted letters to the series—and a pretty, harp-playing niece, "Rosalie," who (as befitted proper young ladies of good family in that period) did not. The "nephews" were, in fact, the pseudonyms of two other contributors: Frank Carr, of Richmond, and Judge Richard E. Parker (later a United States Senator), respectively. The other pseudonyms that have been identified by Kennedy, Hubbell, or Davis were: "Arthur O'Flannegan" (Wirt himself), "Obadiah Squaretoes" (Dabney Carr), "Edward Melmoth" (Dr. Louis Girardin, sometime professor at William and Mary and, later, at both Georgetown and Baltimore colleges), "Tim Lovetruth" (also Girardin), "John Truename" (Major David Watson, of Louisa County), "Richard Vamper," and "Peter Schryphel" (both names used by George Tucker). The only contributions that have thus far not been putatively identified are two letters in the twentieth number by "Stephen Micklewise" and "Romeo" and two more in the twenty-seventh by "Diogenes" and "Susannah Thankful."[7] If, indeed, St. George Tucker contributed anything at all to the published "Old Bachelor" essays, it was probably these last two letters.

Wirt, as prime mover of both the "Rainbow Association" and the "Old Bachelor" coterie, invited contributions from his friends in and around Richmond (that is, within a sixty-mile radius of the capital), constantly soliciting their collaborations and their confidential advice in the conduct of both series. The coterie consisted almost entirely of professional men (most of them lawyers) of stature in their communities who shared Wirt's resolutely Jeffersonian political convictions. Richmond at the time was a hotbed of Federalist adherents and, in the correspondence that passed between William Wirt and his "Old Bachelor" cronies, there are hints of an exciting, almost conspiratorial atmosphere that surrounded this undertaking. Certainly there was something quite heuristic in the essays' dual purpose set forth by Wirt in his eleventh number—"virtuously to instruct, or innocently to amuse"—with emphases falling unremittingly upon the first of these aims. In essay after essay on education, oratory, manners, patriotism (and factionalism—its putative opposite), gambling, intemperance and avarice, the sentimental tone of the "O.B." sometimes gave way to gentle satire but, whether sentimental or satiric, it was always hortatory.

Whether or not the true identities of the pseudonymous contributors to *The Old Bachelor* were known beyond the writers' circle itself is conjectural, but something of the popular response the series evoked may be discerned from the fact that Wirt was bombarded with unsolicited (and unwanted) contributions. In his sixteenth number, "Dr. Cecil" was thus constrained to reply:

> The O.B. intended ere this to give Theodore Hopewell a place in his papers. But, as Hopewell's letter would in some measure break the unity and consistency of his plan, he persuades himself that he shall be readily pardoned for the omission, by that polite and benevolent writer. The O.B. has received several communications which have much individual merit, but not forming, by their nature, an integral part of this scheme, he has been obliged to deny himself the pleasure of using them. As, however, it is a pity they should be lost to the public, the O.B. repeats his engagement that he will, on application by their authors, return them by the same channel through which he received them. [8]

Notwithstanding this kind of response, Wirt felt "dispirited" when the series was finished "by the little effect such things produce." As he explained in a letter to Dabney Carr:

> I wrote in the hope of doing good—but my essays dropped, dropped [sic] into the world like stones pitched into a Mill pond—a little report from the first plunge—a ring or two rolling off from the spot—then in a moment all smooth & silent as before and no visible change in the waters to mark that such things had ever been. [9]

To the same correspondent (in December 1814), Wirt commented ironically on the fifth reprinting of his most popular work, *The Letters of a British Spy* (1803), "while the O.B., an infinitely better thing, slumbers comparatively unheeded & unknown." In that very month, however, Thomas Ritchie, the editor-publisher of the Richmond *Enquirer* and one of three book printers then in the city, brought out his long-promised collected edition of *The Old Bachelor*. Both this edition and that printed in Baltimore four years later are quite rare today and it is to be regretted that no one has yet seen fit to reprint *The Old Bachelor* in our own time.

St. George Tucker was very likely among those Wirt invited to contribute to "the O.B." (as he and Tucker customarily referred to the series) and the extant Tucker manuscripts headed "For the old Batchellor" represent the major part of Tucker's efforts to respond to that opportunity. In the Tucker-Wirt correspondence are passing references to several more such pieces by Tucker—perhaps as many as eight—and there are gaps in the series of arabic numerals (1-28) that Tucker wrote in the upper left margin of each essay, apparently indicating thereby their order of composition, which make it obvious that eight pieces (possibly more if Tucker's numbering went beyond 28) are now missing. One of these may very well be the twenty-seventh number of the published *Old Bachelor* series, containing two letters signed, respectively, "Diogenes" and "Susannah Thankful." There are four bits of external evidence that would seem to indicate this rather conclusively: Tucker refers twice in his letters to Wirt to his employment of the pseudonym, "Diogenes", (August 8 and 19, 1811), the second of these references being to one of the missing manuscripts (presumably No. 10 in Tucker's scheme); in the end papers of Tucker's personal copy of the 1814 edition (now in Swem Library) are pencilled notations, quite probably in Tucker's own hand, identifying the pseudonyms of several of the *Old Bachelor* contributors and including, at the end of this listing, "Diogenes, p. 72." without other identification or explanation; and, finally, at the bottom of the first page of the notebook containing the "Hermit of the Mountain" essays, Tucker has drawn a hand with pointing finger and written "Memo: NB Diogenes—O:B: No. 27, printed Dec, 27, 1811" for no particularly discernible reason. There is no such evidence to connect Tucker with the "Susannah Thankful" signature except the circumstances that both signatures (i.e., "Diogenes," and "Susannah Thankful") are contained in the same essay and that Tucker's own "old Batchellor" manuscript essay number 27 is a similar letter from "Susannah Trifle" to "Dr. Cecil" (and supposedly answered by him) which begins with direct references to the "Susannah Thankful" letter. It would take close comparative stylistic analyses of all of the published *Old Bachelor* essays and Tucker's "old Batchellor" manuscripts to prove the point (if it could ever be proven) but, in the absence of such evidence, I think it more than likely that Tucker did contribute the "Diogenes/ Susannah Thankful" number. If so, it was unquestionably his only contribution to the published series. This fact raises the key question of these manuscripts: why, having stimulated his friend to what may without exaggeration be called feverish literary activity, did Wirt not publish more of Tucker's "old Batchellor" essays?

There are several plausible answers to this question or, if one prefers, the question has a complex answer in several parts. The evidence for arriving at an answer (whether one or more) may be found in the frequent letters exchanged by Tucker and Wirt during August and early September 1811 and at less frequent intervals in 1812 and 1813. The picture that emerges from this evidence is one of what might fairly be called a *collaboration manqué*.

In March 1811, Tucker resigned his judgeship on the Virginia Court of Appeals and returned to private life in Williamsburg, determined "never again to engage in any Business or Office."[10] It was a determination he could keep for only a little over two years, accepting (in November 1813) President Madison's appointment as Federal Judge of the District of Virginia—a position he retained until shortly before his death some fourteen years later. But, in his brief respite from judical duties, Tucker had leisure to cultivate his avocations, the chief of which was always literary composition. At what point after his "retirement" he was first solicited for contributions to *The Old Bachelor* cannot be ascertained from the extant correspondence, but on August 7, 1811, William Wirt acknowledged receiving some essays from him, as follows:

> I have received your elegant communications for The O.B. for which I beg you to receive my thanks. They shall all have a place, except the last letter from Mitis the Federalist, which they will all think too true a joke to be a joke at all—at least so I fear—and I, therefore, beg leave to retain it a few days, *ad referendum.* I am very glad your spirits have taken this turn, and in so fine a walk, which, indeed seems natural to them. I hope they will not weary. The allegory on memory is beautiful. . . .
>
> In your first communication you salute me by the name of "Old Squaretoes"—this, I know, is waggery—but it will be necessary to change the address, because a number has already appeared from a correspondent who assumed *that* as *his real name.*
>
> What say you to a character of Walter Scott as a writer generally or a *critique* on either of his poems?
>
> Or what say you to a set of strictures on the public speaking of this country—whether of the pulpit, senate or bar, and a notation of the prevailing defects. . . .
>
> Ritchie says that he will not bind up more than thirty numbers in the first volume which is to come out by the winter. He has already five

and twenty in hand, and I have two or three others prepared for him: so that you see I am bespeaking materials for the second volume, as it becomes a good provider to do. I shall be not a little proud to be bound up with you in the same volume and I cannot help flattering myself that we may be of some service in this country.[11]

Wirt continues in this letter to describe the subject of a play "on our rancor in politics," suggesting it as a proper theme for "a sentimental comedy" about two families "hating each other, like the Capulets & Montagues, for politics' sake" and being ultimately reconciled through personal tribulations stemming from common danger in the land. He concludes this paragraph with an appeal to Tucker to undertake the writing of this play: "How much more could you make of this than it would be possible for me to do!"

This suggestion was clearly the impetus for Tucker's writing within the next few months (by December 7, 1811, according to his manuscript) an extremely interesting melodrama, *The Times: or, The Patriot Rous'd,* containing precisely the theme and plot proposed by Wirt. It is one of two plays Tucker composed about the coming and the conclusion of the War of 1812 (the other being a sequel, *The Patriot Cool'd,* in 1815) which remain unpublished and unperformed. Although *The Patriot Rous'd* would probably have reached the stage in Richmond but for the catastrophic burning of the theatre there, with tremendous loss of life, on Christmas night 1811, the later play (*The Patriot Cool'd*) exists only in rough draft. It is interesting in the present context, however, because it has a character who appears in the dénouement as "the Hermit of the Mountain."[12]

Wirt concludes this August 7th letter by asking Tucker's aid in perusing a file he has recently acquired of the *Enquirer* printings of the *Old Bachelor* series to date and to "drop me any hints for correction that may occur to you" so that Wirt could prepare them for book publication, adding that he was "not unlike other men in being one of the worst judges as to what may be obscure, false, harsh, low, trivial, extravagant or otherwise [worthless] in what I write."

The day before this letter was written (i.e., on August 6th) the *Enquirer* had printed the twenty-third number of *The Old Bachelor.* From December 22, 1810 until April 5, 1811, the first twenty-one numbers of the series had appeared almost weekly in the newspaper. There followed an hiatus of three months, with the twenty-second number appearing on July 5, 1811, and another hiatus of four weeks before the twenty-third was published. It was probably during this lull that Tucker felt constrained to add his bit, but since only five more *Old Bachelor* essays were to appear in the *Enquirer* (four of them identifiably by Wirt, Watson and Parker) it is easy to see why nothing of Tucker's, with the possible exception of the twenty-seventh number noted above, could possibly have been printed in the newspaper series which ended with essay twenty-eight on December 24, 1811.

Whatever his reasons, Thomas Ritchie did not immediately carry out his presumed intention of publishing a volume containing even thirty numbers (as Wirt had indicated) and when, three years later, he finally published a collection of thirty-three, all but three of these had been in hand at the time of Wirt's first extant acknowledgment of Tucker's "elegant communications for The O.B." The second volume, for which Wirt was "bespeaking materials" in August 1811, never materialized, but there seems no reason to believe that Wirt did not then think it would nor that his encouragement of Tucker's efforts was in any way insincere. A possible clue to Ritchie's motives in retarding publication of the first volume and in breaking off the series prematurely may be seen from Tucker's reply to Wirt (on August 8, 1811), as follows:

> I am truly thankful for your friendly letter of last Evening, although it contains many things that make me shrink within myself, ashamed of being so far over-rated in your partial Estimation. I was apprehensive that *Mitis* contained too much severe Truth. I therefore beg that you will carefully obliterate every word in his Letter, in the 4th no: and substitute that which I now enclose. The Vanity and Impetuosity of *Zelotes*, may either precede, or accompany it, as you think proper. I am gratified that you approve of the Allegory on *Memory*, and now enclose you another on *Contentment*, which I dare not hope you will be equally pleased with. . . .
>
> The Epithet *Squaretoes* was the most unusual one which occurred to me as proper to put into the mouth of Diogenes. I am at a loss what to substitute for it that would be in character. What think of *Goosequill?* [13]

Tucker then adds that he knows too little of Walter Scott to do the suggested character or critique and that he does not feel himself sufficiently qualified as a literary critic to "correct" or "improve" in any way the previously published numbers of the series that Wirt had asked him to peruse for this purpose. Then he penned the following cryptic postscript: "NB: Do not let Ritchie know whom the numbers sent you were written by." From this and similar, but less explicit, remarks about Ritchie in later correspondence with Wirt, one surmises that Ritchie and Tucker were at odds for some now obscure reason and that the publisher, recognizing Tucker's hand or style, may have vetoed the Tucker contributions that Wirt passed to him.

In any case, Tucker was not discouraged by the lack of any immediate prospect of publication. On August 12, 1811 (with a postscript added the next evening), he wrote to Wirt, enclosing at least three additional "old Batchellor" items, among them "another allegory, on Liberty & Faction," a letter on an unspecified subject "I feel much at heart," and still another containing "a discovery" that he had just made. In a postscript to this he observed: "I am afraid you will be sick of Allegories, and of Liberty and Faction too. Reject what you disapprove, without Ceremony. I write *currente Calamo,* & keep no copy. You must therefore be guarded against Repetition, for I know not what I have written."[14] This may well serve to explain why some of Tucker's "old Batchellor" essays—such as "the letter from Mitis the Federalist," the "allegory on memory," the "Allegory on Liberty & Faction," and the essay on "The Vanity and Impetuosity of *Zelotes,*" all of which are mentioned in the letters quoted above—are not to be found among his extant manuscripts. In subsequent letters to Wirt, Tucker requested the return of his unpublished essays and, although Wirt made efforts to accede to Tucker's wishes in this, some of the essays (among them, presumably, those submitted to Ritchie) proved irretrievable.

The essay Tucker mentioned on August 12 as being on a subject he felt "much at heart" was quite probably one "On Patriotism," signed by "Benevolus" and bearing the arabic numeral "9" in Tucker's "old Batchellor" manuscripts. A major portion of this essay is lifted verbatim and without ascription of source (except for the bald admission that he had transcribed "the observations and opinions of a great and enlightened author") from Henry St. John, Viscount Bolingbroke's "A Letter on the Spirit of Patriotism" (1736).[15] In acknowledging receipt of this, on August 18, 1811, Wirt was mildly reproving of Tucker's tactics:

> I thank you for your communications of today: I must set you right, tho', in one respect. Bolingbroke is much more read than you are aware of—especially his letters on the spirit [of Patriotism]. The passage which you have interwoven in the first letter has been rendered the more familiar by having been quoted and criticized in Blair's lectures: and it is not long since another very beautiful passage from his letters on party spirit was quoted in the [Richmond] Argus. . . . Under these circumstances would it not be better to avow the quotation by inverted *commas,* and super-add your own remarks: as it is, I am afraid the reviewers will crack their whips at us, and accuse us, *in this way,* of being guilty of high treason, in debasing the current coin of the kingdom, or some such impertinence. You have put the subject in a strong light & we must not lose sight of it.[16]

But, reconsidering his admonition, he posted this brief letter to Tucker the following day (August 19):

> On reflection I incline to think that it will be as well to acknowledge in a note the *excerpta* from Bolingbroke as to recast the piece—I like the strong light in which the subject is now presented and fear that it may suffer by an attempt to alter it.
>
> On the comparison I prefer the allegory on contentment, first sent. Your first draught has some points of superiority, I think—but the toute ensemble of the second is preferable.
>
> I am delighted to hear you speak of continuing your contributions— they will be salt to my dough—but like salt I must scatter them thinly among my own flat, unleavened mass—I pray you to amuse yourself in this way often. Without an accident, I shall go on through the next winter at least—and will endeavor to profit by your hint of advising Ritchie to enlarge the first volume.[17]

To his credit, Tucker did attempt to recast "On Patriotism," retaining the salient ideas in it—these being a discussion of the differences between the "real patriot" as opposed to "the demagogue," or false patriot—and omitting altogether the unacknowledged quotations from Bolingbroke. This second, unnumbered and unsigned version of the essay survives in the Tucker-Coleman Collection. It is much shorter than the original draft but lacking the rhetorical power of the original—the "strong light" which Wirt mentioned so admiringly twice in the letters quoted above. Nevertheless, one may discern in Wirt's statement, in the second of these letters, that "I must scatter [Tucker's contributions] thinly among my own . . ." a hint that he was beginning to demure on Tucker's literary efforts, possibly from some latent doubts about Tucker's employment of his literary sources and influences. If so, this might also serve to explain why the growing bulk of Tucker's submissions were not being printed and why, despite his announced intention, Wirt did not really want to extend the series "through the next winter at least."

Howsoever that may be, there was once again a three-month hiatus in the *Enquirer* between the twenty-fourth and twenty-fifth *Old Bachelor* essays (published August 13 and 20, 1811, respectively) and the remaining three numbers in the newspaper series, which were printed December 12, 17 and 24, 1811. Concerning the twenty-fourth number, written by Wirt, Tucker showed signs of a growing critical attitude toward "Dr. Cecil's" sallies. He wrote to the author on August 23, 1811, that "although taken litterally [sic] and alltogether [sic], it ought not to wound a friend, but had I seen it in manuscript I might possibly have advised some changes and omissions. . . ." In the same communication, he sent Wirt "an allegorical account of avarice," adding curtly and perhaps a bit querulously, "If you approve, run it. If not reject it."[18] It is difficult not to interpret this as indicating that the Tucker-Wirt "collaboration" in *The Old Bachelor* was beginning to show signs of strain.

There remains one more extant letter in their correspondence concerning the series before a silence on the matter for nearly a year during which both occupied themselves with other things. On September 4, 1811, Tucker wrote to Wirt that

> I have as you requested continued occasionally my attentions to the *blue* packet business & have got as far as no. 18—I know not whether I shall get much further. I am highly gratified that you approve of what I gave you at Major Yanceys. My subsequent essays have, like the former, been an *unornamented* Series on such subjects as happened to strike my mind at the moment. In spite of all that you could persuade me to

think to the contrary, I am equal to nothing more—To a Man whose acquaintance with the principles of Science is very limited (for I was but one year at College, & began Euclid, & was cutting capers all the time) it is too late at my time of life to hope he can ever shed any light, that is not *borrowed*, & borrowed light, even that of the Moon, we know loses infinitely of that lustre which may aid us in the use of the Miscroscope [sic].—As long as you continue to pursue the desire of improving our young folks by your Essays, I shall think myself happy indeed if I can so far assist you as to furnish one, when you have not the leisure to write a better.[19]

There is, it seems to me, more than a slight hint of defensiveness in Tucker's adversions on "borrowed light" (perhaps a reference to Wirt's *caveat* on his "borrowings" from Bolingbroke) and of petulance in his offer to "assist" in the series only "when you have not the leisure to write a better." By his own admission, Tucker had composed at least eighteen essays (some of them in more than one version) within a period of little more than a month. It would seem from subsequent correspondence that, while he occupied himself in the autumn of 1811 with the writing of his play (*The Times: or, The Patriot Rous'd*), Tucker wrote no more "old Batchellor" essays. Indeed, effectively discouraged by the failure of all but (perhaps) one of those already written to get into print, he seems to have delayed almost two years before again taking up his pen in this genre.

It was apparently only after a year of their seeming neglect that Tucker first asked Wirt to return his unpublished "old Batchellor" manuscripts. On August 22, 1812, Wirt wrote Tucker from Warm Springs (Virginia), where he was vacationing, that he had "received your favor relative to the return of the manuscripts prepared for the O.B. at this place." The request was impossible to fulfill immediately, he explained, because the manuscripts were in Richmond, "nor indeed should I do it were I in Richmond, as your request is predicated on the idea of my having dropped the thought of continuing the essays under the title." Wirt excused himself on the ground that the press of judicial business had kept him too occupied during recent months to permit him to resume the series but that he intended, if possible, to do so forthwith, concluding:

Should I be disappointed in this, as it will be uncertain when I may have it in my power to continue the work, if you insist on it, the manuscripts shall then be returned; although I should part from them with reluctance, as I should still entertain the hope of being able at some time, thereafter, to profit by them.[20]

To this, Tucker replied (September 11, 1812) that he had, indeed, assumed it to be Wirt's intention to cease *The Old Bachelor* series altogether and "upon that presumption *alone* my request was made. He observed however, that

If it be your intention to favor your Country with a continuation of those essays from your pen, which have given so much pleasure, I shall deem it an honour to march under your Banners as a volunteer. But whenever you come to a contrary resolution, I must request the return of the essays in question, as I have no copy of any of them.[21]

Whatever the reason, Wirt was unsuccessful in any conjectural efforts he may have made to resume publication of the *Enquirer* series and, in fact, he had to wait another two years more before Ritchie would bring out the first and only volume of the collected edition.

The final chapter in the abortive Tucker-Wirt collaboration on this project may be read from the only two surviving letters from them about this matter. On September 12, 1813 (a year after he had first asked for the return of his manuscripts), Tucker again requested Wirt to send back his "old Batchellor" numbers two through eleven, adding

I have a very particular reason for this request. The O.B. has been silent for more than eighteen months. I have serious thoughts of proposing to you to let me *kill* him, with a paralitic [sic] stroke next Winter, and to revive and continue the publication under the title of the *Hermit of the Mountain*, whom I propose to make his Legatee, as far as his papers go. If you would join me in this project, in the mind I am in at present, we might carry it on in concert under this new title, until we should furnish at least a couple of volumes. All the numbers which you contribute, and all that I have written with a view to the old Batchellor, might be offer'd as papers found in his Escritoire, etc. etc. When we meet again we will talk over this subject more at large.[22]

Wirt's response to this, from "Montevideo" (his country place) on October 10, 1813, was as follows:

> As to the O.B., I will, with pleasure, contribute what I can to the scheme, tho' I fear that will be but little—When I go down [to Richmond], I will make a thorough search from Dan to Beersheba, for our stray flocks—and hope to be able to drive them to their stalls before hard weather sets in.[23]

Nothwithstanding this offer of assistance, couched in a clever Biblical metaphor, in rounding up Tucker's "stray" manuscripts and qualifiedly to "contribute what I can," Wirt does not seem to have written anything at all for what Tucker was now calling his "Hermit of the Mountain" series and, of the numbers that Tucker asked Wirt to return, only the fifth, entitled "The History of Contentment: An Allegory," the manuscript of which bears a notation, "Written over again & altered—Aug. 9th (1811)," and the ninth, the essay "On Patriotism" which Wirt presumably returned as early as August 1811 for recasting, are extant in the Tucker-Coleman Collection.

Tucker did not wait, however, until "next Winter" to report the demise of the "old Batchellor." On the very day that he proposed the idea to Wirt he started a notebook, the first page of which bears the inscription: NUGA: THE HERMIT OF THE MOUNTAIN.This is followed immediately by "No. 1" and an epigraph in both Latin and English: "*Nunquam minus solus, quam cum solus*/I am never less alone than when alone" (the original from Cicero, but the translation obviously from Samuel Rogers' *Human Life,* 1801). Tucker's new *persona* then begins to introduce and characterize himself and to give his life history in the manner of "Dr. Cecil" nearly three years earlier in the first number of *The Old Bachelor.* A note at the bottom of this first page reads:

> Being very unwell this summer, both at home and at Warminster, & not a little unhappy about my beloved Fanny, I have endeavoured to beguile my feelings, & dissipate melancholy, by several trifles, some of which I may possibly copy in this little book. Sept. 12, 1813.[24]

According to the account the "Hermit" provides of himself in the first two numbers (each of which fills eight notebook pages and is dated "Sept. 13, 1813"), he is a man just over sixty—i.e., the same age as Tucker—who has retired to a simple farmhouse west of the Blue Ridge Mountains to reflect upon a life which, although outwardly successful enough, has been in recent years beset by personal misfortunes, including the loss of most of his family. Yet more melancholy than even "Dr. Cecil," he has preferred Romantic solitude in the mountains to an urban society where ill-mannered boors now abound. Although he has not been much in the habit of committing his observations and reflections to writing, a peculiar series of developments has recently forced him to make the effort to produce a series of "moral essays written in an entertaining manner, after the example of the Spectator, Tatler, & Guardian [which] have been generally supposed to produce excellent effects upon Society. . . ." These developments, he explains, are related to "my excellent and much regretted friend, DOCTOR ROBERT CECIL [who] commenced the publication of his OLD BATCHELLOR [sic] about three years ago," and who departed on a business trip to the "western Country" shortly after the publication of his last number, requesting the "Hermit" to "take charge of some numbers which he had partly prepared" and promising to confer about their publication upon his return. Alas, "Dr. Cecil" did not return from his long western journey and, after many months, his death at a remote country inn where he was an unidentified guest, was confirmed by the good doctor's nephew, "Alfred." In his will, "Dr. Cecil" has bequeathed the "Hermit" the papers he had left with him, adjuring him to continue their publication. So goes the imaginary account.

There is a fragment, covering little more than half a notebook page, of a third number in which the "Hermit" sets out to accomplish "the request of my much valued, & regretted friend." He breaks off, however, in mid-page and, on the verso (dated "Sept. 27th, 1813"), Tucker records receiving the long-expected news of the death at the age of thirty-four of his daughter, Anne Frances ("Fanny") Coalter, whose final illness had caused her family—and her father, in particular—great anxiety. This entry mixes expressions of relief that his daughter's long suffering has ended with intense parental bereavement and it ends with a short, pious poem in his "Fanny's" memory. There are no further entries in the

"Hermit of the Mountain" notebook for more than a year after this and, even then, the remainder of this manuscript is filled with published poems of Tucker's, a prose eulogy by him of Mrs. Anne Banister (widow of Col. John Banister and daughter of the illustrious John Blair), and a series of quaint scientific treatises with drawings of theoretical "models" of the universe, all of the entries bearing dates between 1814 and 1818. In the two months following his breaking off his "Hermit" writings, Tucker was evidently too enervated and too dispirited by his favorite daughter's death to be able to resume it. In November 1813, his entry into the Federal judiciary deprived him of that leisure in which he might have been able to carry his project to fruition.

To pick up the existing pieces of this project where St. George Tucker left them and to try to carry out what can be ascertained of his intentions to publish his essays seems now an altogether defensible and, indeed, long overdue undertaking. The completed two and the fragmentary third "Hermit" numbers, in themselves, provide a *raison d'être* and narrative framework for a collected edition of the twenty-odd "old Batchellor" essays. The problem of establishing a logical order to these is not great. On seven of the extant essays there are roman numerals written in lead pencil in the upper right corners, probably by Tucker himself in an unfinished re-ordering of the compositions to fit them into a scheme for *Nuga: The Hermit of the Mountain.* So far as possible, these numbers can now be followed. For the remaining essays, the available evidence on probable dates of composition—both from internal evidence and from references in Tucker's correspondence—can be utilized to advantage.

Quite naturally, the collection is uneven and of unequal merit. At their best, Tucker's essays compare very favorably with the finest of those published in *The Old Bachelor* but, in the aggregate and the total comparison, it is easy to see how his compositions might have been improved (as the "O.B." numbers of the Carrs, et al., undoubtedly were) by the sure editorial hand of a William Wirt. For instance, Tucker's bent ran heavily to allegory, no less than four of his pieces (one of them in two distinct versions) being cast in this mold. Although he improved in his ability to handle allegorical techniques as he went along—the obviously later allegories are markedly better than the earlier ones—he was not always capable of sustaining the kinds of narratives that his allegorical essays required, the dénouements of his tales often being too abrupt and too pat. Nevertheless, this frequent preference for the allegorical mode and his attraction to exoticism of various kinds are, in themselves, interesting phenomena in a writer who is otherwise so characteristically Augustan in his predilections. Nor are these the only peculiarities in the "Hermit" essays that show us a Virginian writer in a period of transition in American letters, standing with one foot firmly planted in the eighteenth century and the other poised towards an era that would ere long produce a writer than toddling in Richmond—Edgar Allan Poe. For these and many other reasons, *Nuga: The Hermit of the Mountain* at last claims attention in our literary history.

NOTES

1. (William Wirt, et al.), *The Old Bachelor,* "Second" Edition (Richmond, 1814). A "Third" Edition was published in Baltimore (1818) by Fielding Lucas, Jr. (Presumably, the newspaper printing was the "first" edition, as there was no previous book publication of these essays.) The additional five essays included in the collection were not, in fact, first published in the *Enquirer* in 1813, as has been asserted by Jay B. Hubbell, "William Wirt and the Familiar Essay in Virginia," *The William and Mary Quarterly,* 2d Ser., XXIII (March 1943), 145; and by Richard Beale Davis, *Intellectual Life in Jefferson's Virginia, 1790-1830* (Chapel Hill: University of North Carolina Press, 1964), 283.

2. Cf., John Pendleton Kennedy, *Memoirs of the Life of William Wirt,* Revised Edition (Philadelphia, 1851), I, 262-69; Jay B. Hubbell, *The South in American Literature, 1607-1900* (Durham, N.C.: Duke University Press, 1954), 151, 238; and Davis, 283-85.

3. Cf., Davis, 284, and Hubbell, *WMQ,* 136-52.

4. Wirt to Dabney Carr, December 24, 1810, quoted in Kennedy, *Wirt,* I, 263. Kennedy seems to have falsely concluded that a *Sylph* series was published in *The Enquirer* in November 1811.

5. Richmond *Enquirer,* February 2, 1811.

6. Richmond *Enquirer,* December 22, 1810.

7. Cf., Kennedy, *Wirt,* I, 262; Hubbell, *WMQ,* 147-50; and Davis, *Intellectual Life,* 283-84. Davis believes that Francis Walker Gilmer (1790-1826), a brilliant young man who read law with Wirt and became his brother-in-law, may well have been one of the unidentified contributors and, in Tucker's personal copy of the collected edition (1814) the name "Senator R. B. Taylor" appears in a pencilled list of some of the contributors in the end papers, probably written in Tucker's own hand.

8. *Enquirer,* March 8, 1811. In the *Enquirer* on January 26, 1811, "Dr. Cecil" acknowledged: "Theodore Hopewell's letter has been thankfully received." The following week (February 2, 1811) he acknowledged "receipt of several communications from youthful writers."

9. Wirt to Dabney Carr, April 30, 1813, quoted in Kennedy, *Wirt,* I, 313.

10. Quoted in Mary Haldane Coleman, *St. George Tucker: Citizen of No Mean City* (Richmond, Va.: Dietz Press, 1938), 148.

11. William Wirt to St. George Tucker, August 7, 1811, in The Tucker-Coleman Collection, Swem Library, The College of William and Mary, Williamsburg, Virginia.

12. The manuscripts of these two plays are in the Tucker-Coleman Collection, Swem Library.

13. St. George Tucker to William Wirt, August 8, 1811, in Wirt papers, The Maryland Historical Society, Baltimore, Maryland.

14. Tucker to Wirt, August 12, 1811, Wirt papers, Maryland Historical Society.

15. Daniel Gaver Harvey, unpublished M.A. Thesis ("St. George Tucker's 'Old Batchellor' Essay 'On Patriotism': A Critical Edition"), The College of William and Mary, May 1972.

16. Wirt to Tucker, August 18, 1811, Tucker-Coleman Collection, Swem Library.

17. Wirt to Tucker, August 19, 1811, Tucker-Coleman Collection, Swem Library.

18. Tucker to Wirt, August 23, 1811, Wirt Papers, Maryland Historical Society.

19. Tucker to Wirt, September 4, 1811, Wirt Papers, Maryland Historical Society.

20. Wirt to Tucker, August 12, 1812, Tucker-Coleman Collection, Swem Library.

21. Tucker to Wirt, September 11, 1812, Tucker-Coleman Collection, Swem Library. This remained in Tucker's papers because it was never sent. The letter breaks off after two paragraphs with the notation: "Mr. Wirt arriving at this moment, I showed him the above."

22. Tucker to Wirt, September 12, 1813, Wirt Papers, Maryland Historical Society.

23. Wirt to Tucker, October 10, 1813, Tucker-Coleman Collection, Swem Library.

24. This manuscript is in the Tucker-Coleman Collection, Swem Library. *Nuga,* in the title of this notebook, is Latin for "something trifling or trivial" (according to the Oxford English Dictionary, it is more generally used in the plural, *Nugae,* in English). On the back of the notebook itself, Tucker has written "Trivia" in pencil.

INDEX

CONTRIBUTORS

Robert D. Arner, Professor of English at the University of Cincinnati, has written widely on early American authors and is preparing a book on comic literature in colonial America and the early Republic.

Philip L. Barbour is the author of *The Three Worlds of Captain John Smith* and editor of *The Jamestown Voyages Under the First Charter 1606-1609.*

Stephen D. Cox is a graduate student at UCLA specializing in eighteenth-century and romantic literature.

Carl Dolmetsch, Chairman of the Department of English at The College of William and Mary in Virginia, is the author of *The Smart Set: A History and Anthology* and co-editor of *The Poems of Charles Hansford.* He is now preparing collected editions of the unpublished essays and plays of St. George Tucker.

Everett Emerson, Professor of English at the University of Massachusetts at Amherst, is the author of *John Cotton, English Puritanism from John Hooper to John Milton* and *Captain John Smith.* He is editor of *Major Writers of Early American Literature* and the journal *Early American Literature.*

Jack P. Greene, Professor of History at Johns Hopkins University, is the editor of *The Diary of Colonel Landon Carter of Sabine Hall, 1752-1778.*

Leota Harris Hirsch, Professor of English at Rosary College, River Forest, Illinois, is the author of *Pre-Novelistic Traits in Seventeenth-Century Writing* and "Seventeenth Century Stirrings in Native American Humor."

Wilbur R. Jacobs, Professor of History at the University of California, Santa Barbara, is author of *Dispossessing the American Indian, Wilderness Politics and Indian Gifts*, and *The Historical World of Frederick Jackson Turner*.

Homer D. Kemp, Assistant Professor of English at Tennessee Technological University, is presently working on an annotated edition of the American correspondence of the Rev. Jonathan Boucher.

Lewis Leary, William Rand Kenan, Jr., Professor of English at the University of North Carolina at Chapel Hill, is the author, among others, of *That Rascal Freneau: A Study in Literary Failure, Southern Excursions: Mark Twain and Others*, and *Soundings: Some Early American Writers*.

J. A. Leo Lemay, Professor of English at UCLA, is the author of *Men of Letters in Colonial Maryland* and *A Calendar of American Poetry in the Colonial Newspapers and Magazines*.

A. R. Riggs, Associate Professor of History at McGill University, Montreal, is the author of a short biography for the Colonial Williamsburg Foundation entitled *The Nine Lives of Arthur Lee: Virginia Patriot*.

William J. Scheick, Associate Professor of English at the University of Texas at Austin, is the author of *The Will and the Word: The Poetry of Edward Taylor* and *The Writings of Jonathan Edwards: Theme, Motif, and Style*.

Wilber Henry Ward is Assistant Professor of English at Appalachian State University. The author of articles on St. George Tucker's *Hansford* and folksinger Doc Watson, he is at work on a book dealing with the literary treatments of Bacon's Rebellion.